W.E.B. DU BOIS

AND RACE

Voices of the African Diaspora

This series presents the development of the intellectual tradition of the African diaspora. The series will bring together a variety of disciplines, including literary and social/cultural criticism, anthropology, sociology, religion/philosophy, education, political science, psychology, and history—by publishing original critical studies and reprints of classic texts. The reprints will include both nineteenth- and twentieth-century works. The goal is to make important texts accessible and readily available both to the general reader and to the academic.

Chester J. Fontenot, Jr.
Series Editor

W.E.B.
DU BOIS AND RACE

edited by
Chester J. Fontenot, Jr. *and* Mary Alice Morgan
with Sarah Gardner

MERCER UNIVERSITY PRESS, 2001

Essays Celebrating the Centennial Publication of The Souls of Black Folk

ISBN 0-86554-727-0
MUP/545

© 2001 Mercer University Press
6316 Peake Road
Macon, Georgia 31210-3960

First Edition.

∞The paper used in this publication meets the minimum requirements of American National Standard for Information Sciences—Permanence of Paper for Printed Library Materials, ANSI Z39.48-1992.

Library of Congress Cataloging-in-Publication Data

W.E.B. Du Bois and race : essays celebrating the centennial publication of The Souls of Black Folk / edited by Chester J. Fontenot, Jr. and Mary Alice Morgan.—1st ed.
p. cm.—(Voices of the African diaspora)
Collection of essays from a symposium held at Mercer University in March 2000.
Includes bibliographical references and index.
ISBN 0-86554-727-0
1.Du Bois, W. E. B. (William Edward Burghardt), 1868-1963—Views on race—Congresses. 2. Du Bois, W. E. B. (William Edward Burghardt), 1868-1963 Souls of Black Folk—Congresses. 3. African Americans—Race identity—Congresses. 4. United States—Race Relations—Congresses. I. Fontenot, Chester J. II Morgan, Mary Alice. III. Du Bois, W. E. B. (William Edward Burghardt), 1868-1963. IV. Series.

E185.97.D73.W1645 2001
305.896'073'0092—dc21   2001032639

CONTENTS

Foreword to the Series

It gives us great pleasure to introduce this book series, "Voices of the African Diaspora," with this volume of proceedings from the W.E.B. Du Bois Symposium held at Mercer University, March 2000. Conceived as an interdisciplinary publishing venue that continues Du Bois's vision of Pan Africanist scholarship, we have organized this series with two purposes: (1) To present the development of the African American intellectual tradition from the vantage point of a number of disciplines—including literary and social/cultural criticism, anthropology, sociology, religion/ philosophy, education, political science, and history—by publishing reprints of classic texts, beginning in the nineteenth century, in each discipline, that are currently out-of-print, but are useful for teaching and research purposes. (2) To publish original critical studies written or edited by scholars in African, African Caribbean, African Latino, and African American studies in the disciplines and fields mentioned above.

This book, as well as the Du Bois Symposium would not have been possible without the support of the following: The Georgia Humanities Council who awarded us a grant to help underwrite the costs of the symposium; President R. Kirby Godsey, Provost Russell G. Warren and Dean (now Emeritus) Douglas Steeples of the College of Liberal Arts at Mercer University for providing funding for the symposium and publication subvention for this book; Cecil Staton, Marc Jolley, and the Mercer University Press staff for their steadfast devotion to bring this project into fruition; Sarah Gardner for her timely help in managing the details for the meeting; the Mercer University Office of University Advancement for their help in planning this event; Bonnie Meyers, former English Department Senior Secretary, Carmen Hicks, present English Department Senior Secretary, and student workers, Shervette Miller and Israel Rowe, for their untiring efforts to attend to administrative chores; the departments and programs of Mercer University who helped co-sponsor the Symposium with financial contributions and attendance; and the scholars and participants in the Du Bois Symposium who contributed significantly to the high quality of presentations and academic exchanges during the gathering.

In this series, we will publish significant texts within the field of African Diasporic Studies biannually. We hope that our efforts will contribute significantly to the teaching and scholarly materials available to a general literate audience. For this reason, we encourage manuscripts devoid of scholarly jargon, but rather intended for an audience that is at once interdisciplinary and educated.

CHESTER J. FONTENOT, JR.
MARY ALICE MORGAN

CONTRIBUTORS

MARK BRALEY teaches English at the United States Air Force Academy.

RUFUS BURROW, JR. is professor of theological social ethics at Christian Theological Seminary. He is author of *James H. Cone & Black Liberation Theology* (1994) and *Personalism: A Critical Introduction* (1999).

CHESTER J. FONTENOT, JR. is Baptist Professor of English and Chair, English Department at Mercer University. Fontenot served as the director of the symposium on which this book is based. He is the author or editor of four books, including two books in the influential series *Studies in Black American Literature* and the first book-length treatment of Frantz Fanon. He works extensively with gangs and is currently writing two books on his experiences. He is a founding member and was first chair of the Modern Language Association African-American Literature Section and editor of the Black American Literature Forum.

LEE W. FORMWALT, Executive Director of the Organization of American Historians, was professor of history (1977-1999) and Dean of the Graduate School (1997-1999) at Albany State University in southwest Georgia. An earlier version of his essay appeared in the *Georgia Historical Quarterly* 71(1987): 693-700.

BILL HARDWIG received his Ph.D. in English from the University of Florida in December 2000. His dissertation is titled, "A Rule of Thumb: Objectivity, Racial Classification and the Politics of Genre." He is currently working as a lecturer in the English Department at the University of Florida.

DOLAN HUBBARD is professor and chair of the Department of English and Language Arts at Morgan State University, Baltimore, Maryland. He previously served as an associate professor of at the University of Georgia (1994-98) where he held a joint appointment in English and African American Studies. A graduate of Catawba College in Salisbury, North Carolina, he earned his M.A. degree at the University of Denver and his Ph.D. degree at the University of Illinois at Urbana-Champaign. He is a member of the Catawba College Board of Trustees. He is the author *The Sermon and the African American Literary Imagination* (University of Missouri Press, 1994), selected by *Choice* as an Outstanding Academic Book for 1995, and is Editor of *The Langston Hughes Review*. He served as Chair, Executive Committee, MLA Division on Black American Literature and Culture, 1996. He is editor of *Recovered Writers/Recovered Texts: Race, Class, and Gender in Black Women's Literature* (University of Tennessee Press, 1997) and "Critical Essays on W.E.B. Du Bois' *The Souls of Black Folk*" (University of Missouri Press, forthcoming). He is a past president of the College Language Association (1994-96).

KWAKU LARBI KORANG is an assistant professor of English and African Studies at the University of Illinois. He is a citizen of Ghana.

KALAMU YA SALAAM is founder of Nommo Literary Society, a Black writers workshop; co-founder of Runagate Multimedia; leader of the WordBand, a poetry performance ensemble; and moderator of e-Drum, a listserv of over 600 Black writers and ethnically diverse supporters of literature. His latest book is *The Magic of Juju: An Appreciation of the Black Arts Movement* (Third World Press). Salaam's latest spoken word cd is *My Story, My Song*. Salaam can be reached at kalamu@aol.com.

WILFRED D. SAMUELS (Ph.D., University of Iowa) is an associate professor of English and Ethnic Studies at the University of Utah and Director of the African American Studies Program. With his published essays, literary reviews, and interviews he has published works on Caribbean writers of the Harlem Renaissance, an edition of Equiano's original 1789 narrative, and a book with Clenora Hudson Weems on Toni Morrison.

JULIET E. K. WALKER (Ph.D., University of Chicago) is an award-winning historian who specializes in Black Business History, Antebellum African American history, and African Diaspora studies in black business. She is the author of several books and is the editor of the *Encyclopedia of African American Business History* (1999). She teaches African American History at the University of Illinois.

ON BEING A PROBLEM IN AMERICA

CHESTER J. FONTENOT, JR.

A few years ago, I was in Cologne, Germany, relaxing for the weekend with a group of Americans. We had come to this historic city from the University of Duisburg, where we had each presented papers at an international symposium on women and religious discourses. We arrived in Cologne by train, and were immediately impressed with a seventeen-story Gothic cathedral, one of the few in this part of the country that had not been significantly damaged during World War II. After taking pictures of this grotesque, albeit beautiful structure, we wandered through the outdoor mall that proceeded from the cathedral's entrance. One of my new found friends queried, "Do you folks want to find a good restaurant and eat some German food?" Neither of us had eaten since breakfast, and time had passed seemingly unnoticed by any of us. Since none of us spoke German well enough to ask any of the hundreds of people who were walking in concert through this outdoor mall to point us in the direction of good, edible German food, we resorted to wandering aimlessly in hopes that we would stumble, almost by divine guidance, into a good restaurant could both report and, more importantly, take credit for discovering. Our sojourn took us by a sidewalk café, where a considerable number of people were relaxing, talking, and eating. One of my colleagues exclaimed, "Look! I think I see what looks like a good German restaurant." Heartened by our American comrade's discovery, we quickened our step toward the café, when our pursuit was interrupted by a German man who was sitting with his group at the sidewalk café. For when we increased our pace and literally began to run toward the restaurant, this fellow shouted out, "Look! Americans!"

Since our group of Americans was composed of both African Americans and whites, we responded to this man's words in two ways: My white friends felt culturally undressed, so to speak, because they had been trying their best to blend into German society by not giving any obvious signifiers of American identity—cultural arrogance, insisting that Germans speak English, and so forth. This man's words imposed the cultural marker of difference on them, a feeling that, as European Americans, they are unaccustomed to experiencing. On the other hand, I and my African American colleagues were taken back by this man's words, not because we were attempting to blend in and pass as Germans, but simply because he had identified us as Americans. As we strode towards the restaurant, our group that had previously been homogeneous became divided in our discourse by this man's exclamation that homogenized all of us into the Hegelian self/other binary represented by the word "Americans."

During our meal, both subgroups discussed among themselves the impact that this man's words had on us. The African Americans agreed in unison that being called an American had shaken our consciousness because, in America, we are almost never identified in language that suggests that we are significant citizens. For many of us, this experience was, in fact, the first time that any one had ever called us an American. We discussed the irony we felt at having to travel nearly six thousand miles to another country to feel that we are, indeed, Americans.

After returning to the states, I continued to ponder this experience. I recalled the writings of W. E. B. Du Bois, specifically *The Souls of Black Folk*, in which after studying at the University of Berlin, this great African American intellectual wrote about the duality of black identity. Since I had already been discussing with some of my colleagues at other universities the possibility of organizing an international symposium to commemorate the centennial publication of *The Souls of Black Folk*, my experience in Cologne during which this man unconsciously uttered a word that had racialized my group of Americans helped me to provide some focus to this future gathering of Du Bois scholars. When I accepted an offer from Mercer University in 1999 to join the faculty, I immediately enlisted the aid of Mary Alice Morgan and Sarah Gardner, two professors on Mercer's faculty, who instantly shared my vision and passion for this assembly.

The focus of this symposium, "W. E. B. Du Bois, Race, and the New Millennium," then, was conceived in Cologne, Germany, within shouting distance, so to speak, of Berlin, from the perspective of an American, yet a world removed from the Germany that Du Bois experienced while studying abroad. After more than a year of planning, this symposium occurred in March 2000 at Mercer University. Nearly fifty scholars representing thirty four states, two foreign countries, and over forty eight academic and cultural institutions spent three days discussing the centrality of Du Bois seminal text in the construction of racial discourse in America during the twentieth century. The essays in this volume represent a selection of these presentations.

While the presentations herewith, and during the symposium differ by disciplinary focus, methodological emphasis, and textual explications, they share in common one of the most basic problems of black identity that I and my African American colleagues had experience years before in Cologne. In a sense, the German man's innocent acknowledgment of the cultural differences the members of my group exhibited reminded us that, in Germany, we were not the formless black bodies we have become accustomed to being in America. W. E. B. Du Bois, writing in *Dusk of Dawn*, expresses his conundrum about being homogenized as the black other. Even though Du Bois embraced the small black student body at Harvard and attempted to "forget as far as was possible that outer, whiter world," he found that

> naturally it could not be entirely forgotten, so that now and then I plunged into it, joined its currents and rose or fell with it. The joining was sometimes a matter of social contact. I escorted colored girls, and as pretty ones as I could find, to the vesper exercises and the class day and commencement social functions. Naturally we attracted attention and sometimes the shadow of insult as when in one case a lady seemed determined to mistake me for a waiter...[1]

---

[1] W. E. B. Du Bois, *Dusk of Dawn: An Essay Toward an Autobiography of a Race Concept* ([1940] New Brunswick: Transaction, 1984) 35.

Ralph Ellison, writing nearly fifty years later, expresses this same crisis in black identity in the prologue to *Invisible Man:* the nameless narrator says,

> I am invisible, understand, simply because people refuse to see me. Like the bodiless heads you see sometimes in circus sideshows, it is as though I have been surrounded by mirrors of hard, distorting glass. When they approach me they see only my surroundings, themselves, or figments of their imagination— indeed, everything and anything except me.[2]

⌠During the symposium, we were aware that the problem with black identity that both Du Bois and Ellison identify is grounded in the experience of chattel slavery. The culture of dominance that initially produced slavery, and later, a racial hierarchy, constructed black people as a race of bodies valued only for its market value as a commodified physical subject. These tropes of the body substantially influenced the ability of African Americans to represent themselves from the point of view of their own culture that sought to assert the primacy of the totality of subjecthood. It restricted their representation to tropes that corresponded with the dominant hegemony. These fragmented tropes both fixed within the cultural texts of the Western world, and divided the black subject into two separate selves: Mind and body. Racist discourse emphasized the representation of African Americans as material bodies, and delimited the mind as a signifier of black identity.

This mind/body binary is grounded in Christianity, since it evolves, first, from the Apostle Paul's assertion that Christians must mortify the flesh in order to achieve spiritual purity, and later, refined by St. Augustine who, in his *Confessions,* argues that the body is sinful and must be negated in order to reach spiritual communion with God. This body/spirit binary gives rise to the body/mind one here, since the Enlightenment, heavily influenced by Christianity, held that the intellect was, in fact, the ability to deny the body, resist its natural carnal nature, and impose the order of human agency on an object that resists such restrictions. Conversely, the balance of mind and body indicated the

---

[2] Ralph Ellison, *Invisible Man* ([1952] New York: Vintage, 1982) 7.

inability to control the body as material subject; it was perceived as a sign of intellectual weaknesses, cultural backwardness, and savagery.

When Du Bois wrote that the cultural identity of African Americans during the nineteenth century restricts their representation to that of a problem in American society, he must have been aware that the inability to see people of African descent as anything other than a problem can be traced to the selling of Sara Baartman, a twenty year old woman from the Khoi Khoi tribe in South Africa, in 1810. When her owner sold her to an Englishman, and she got on a boat heading for London, she could not have known that she would become the icon of racial inferiority and black female sexuality for the next one hundred years. Exhibited as a freak across Britain because of her steatopygia, a scientific term coined to represent the "overdeveloped buttocks," and her "Hottentot apron," a popular euphemism that signified the over development of the skin covering her genitals, she earned a meager salary as the subject of British curiosity. Known throughout Britain as the "Hottentot Venus," Sara Baartman became famous as an aberrant creature that represented the racial differences between Europeans and Africans. In the British press, she was regularly referred to as "savage," "primitive," "monkeyish," and "hideous."

In 1814, Sara Baartman was taken to France, and became the object of scientific and medical research that formed the basis of European ideas about people of African descent. A famous anatomist, Cuvier, used this African woman's body to prove that people of African descent were not only different in appearance, but also anatomically. In 1815, Baartman became ill; she was mistakenly treated for catarrh, a pleurisy and dropsy of the breast. She died later that year of smallpox and alcohol poisoning. In the name of science, Cuvier led a team of well-known scientists who dissected Baartman's body. They removed her brain and sexual organs; they placed them in anatomical jars for further study and display. Until 1985, her body parts were still on display in the Musee de l'homme in Paris.

When W. E. B. Du Bois organized his Negro Exhibit in Paris in 1900, consisting of photographs of "real" African Americans, and published three years later his groundbreaking text, *The Souls of Black Folk*, he must have been aware that the body parts of Sara Baartman, the "Hottentot Venus," were still on display in Paris. This led him to utilize double-voiced discourse that signifies on the submerged mind/body binary in nineteenth century American life as he expresses the dilemma of self representation for African Americans. In *The Souls of Black Folk*, he writes,

> Between me and the other world there is ever an unasked question: unasked by some through feelings of delicacy; by others through the difficulty of rightly framing it. All, nevertheless, flutter round it. They approach me in a half-hesitant sort of way, eye me curiously or compassionately, and then, instead of saying directly, How does it feel to be a problem? they say, I know an excellent colored man in my town; or I fought at Mechanicsville; or, Do not these Southern outrages make your blood boil?[3]

Similarly, the great African American writer, Jean Toomer, writes

> Generally, it may be said that the Negro is emergent from a crust, a false personality, a compound of beliefs, habits, attitudes, and emotional reactions superimposed upon him by external circumstance.... First, there are those factors which arise from the condition of being a black man in a white world. Second, there are those forms and forces which spring from the nature of our civilization, and are common to Americans...[4]

The common thread that runs through my experience in Cologne, Du Bois mention of the "unasked question" by those of the "other world," Ellison's nameless protagonist's experience of being "bumped against" by "people of poor vision," and Jean Toomer's analysis that "blackness" is the social construct of "whiteness," is the inability of African Americans to represent themselves from the perspective of their own cultural traditions, or in other words, in other than mind/body binaries that depicts them as a problem in American society. Surely Du Bois and Toomer were aware that this was not a new predicament. In

---

[3] W. E. B. Du Bois, *The Souls of Black Folk* (New York: Penguin, 1989 [1903]) 3-4.

[4] Frederick L. Rusch, *A Jean Toomer Reader: Selected Unpublished Writings* (New York: Oxford University Press, 1993) 87.

1841, the abolitionist movement published *The New England Anti-Slavery Almanac for 1841*, a "how to" book which directed abolitionist editors of slave narratives to "speak for the slave," and "write for the slave," since "they [the slaves] can't take care of themselves."[5] This perspective toward slaves as subjects and abolitionist narrators as their authenticating narrative voice both belies the implicit goal of eighteenth century slave narratives—to justify slavery—and expresses a hegemonic relationship between the silenced slave and empowered narrator. It begins, within American cultural texts, a tradition which is a trope against the self representation of the African American personality. The inability of African Americans to represent themselves publicly, however, can be traced back as early as the late eighteenth century, with the controversy surrounding the authenticity of Phyllis Wheatley's poems, and throughout the nineteenth century in its emphasis on the minstrel tradition as an authentic representation of black life. Indeed, Eric Lott, in *Love and Theft*,[6] demonstrates admirably both the construction of "blackness" through the minstrels and the tendency of white working class males to insist that the white minstrels accurately represented African Americans. The performance language created for minstrel characters, dialect, was in fact a way of representing the belief of many whites that African Americans were less intelligent, barely human, and incapable of grasping even the most basic concepts of the English language. Later in the nineteenth century, the plantation era attempted to justify slavery through revising tropes of the mind/body binary in which black subjects were represented as black bodies deprived of minds, rational intellects, who actually enjoyed their experience of slavery.

While this cultural assault on the African American personality rendered impotent their attempts to represent themselves from the point of view of their own cultural traditions, political legislation insured that they would not gain control of their own social narratives by insisting that the African American was a fractured, incomplete, inauthentic person, less valuable than his/her white counterparts, and suitable only to be hewers of wood and drawers of water. The underpinnings of both

---

[5] *The New England Anti-Slavery Almanac for 1841* (Boston: 1841).

[6] Eric Lott, *Love and Theft: Blackface Minstrelsy and the American Working Class* (New York: Oxford University Press, 1993).

processes were centered in the beliefs, first, that African Americans were not citizens, but property, and thus enjoyed only the advantages guaranteed to them which governed property rights, and second, that if African Americans were to exist as free men and women, they could not share the same social, political and economic space as whites, but instead had to be relegated to that space ascribed to them by those who had initially constructed "blackness" to represent the racialized other.

In *The Souls of Black Folk*, Du Bois attempts to represent what he calls "the world within the veil," the spiritual world of African Americans by articulating, from the perspective of African Americans, an identity that is fixed rather than permeable. His often quoted statement on "double-consciousness," expresses for Du Bois the otherness that lies at the core of black identity. Although Du Bois's statement has been criticized for its over-simplistic nature in that it is primarily a male construct that fails to acknowledge class and gender, this double identity is central to twentieth-century racial discourse. Du Bois deconstructs the trope of bodies, derived from the mind/body binary, by fixing black identity in the mind/spirit binary and privileging the spirit. Du Bois locates the problem of self representation in the African American's struggle to merge his/her "two-ness,"—American and Negro.

This dual cultural identity continues, even to this day, to create a problem for African Americans who are seeking to bring together this duality without sacrificing their distinctiveness. This is an arduous task, indeed, that is made more difficult by the reluctance of many white Americans to share public space with African Americans. When African Americans move from the private space of blackness in which they have been circumscribed, they become a problem that must somehow be managed, controlled, contained, and made impotent. So the experience my African American colleagues and I had in Cologne is a common occurrence that threatens the attempts of African Americans to resolve the tension between the history of racism in the Western world, and their desires to enjoy the benefits of full membership in American society.

I must say here that knowing the foundations of racist thought that has made me and other African Americans a problem in American life has not done much to resolve what Du Bois calls the "warring selves" within the person. In an attempt to deconstruct the false representations of African Americans that produce this spiritual struggle, Du Bois found, much like Jean Toomer, that in the South, he could at least locate what literary critic Donald Gibson calls black "bodies,"[8] their social essence. But these black bodies are not the same as those created for the purpose of advancing theories of racial inferiority by Western imperialists masquerading as Enlightenment philosophers and scientists. Rather, these black bodies are the actual physical existence of African Americans within their own culture. In other words, Du Bois tried to locate the "Black essence" through what British cultural critic Paul Gilroy calls "routes," not "roots."[9] That is to say, he found that geographical routes, the black South, allow him to represent African Americans accurately. Reflecting about his experience in Georgia, Toomer wrote,

> There, for the first time, I really saw the Negro, not as a pseudo-urbanized and vulgarized, a semi-Americanized product, but the Negro peasant, strong with the tang of fields and the soil. It was there that I first heard folk-songs rolling up the valley at twilight, heard them as spontaneous with gold, and tints of an eternal purple. Love? They gave birth to a whole new life.[10]

Du Bois's attempt to combat racialized images of African Americans led him, like Toomer, to the Georgia Black Belt where, he felt, the true African American was best represented in an area Du Bois identified as "below Macon." In a photo essay, "W. E. B. Du Bois's View of the Southwest Georgia Black Belt Illustrated with Photographs by A. Radclyffe Dugmore," Lee W. Formwalt discusses the importance of Du Bois's field work in Georgia. Dolan Hubbard's contribution, "Riddle Me This: Du Bois, the Sphinx, and the Crisis of Identity," investigates Du Bois's attempt in *The Souls of Black Folk* to correct the history of African Americans that both separated them from West African civilizations and posited a corrupt history that decentered West Africa in the development of western cultures. In "Confluence, Confirmation, and Conservation at the Crossroads: Intersecting Junctures in *The Interesting*

---

[8] See Gibson's introduction to the Penguin edition of *The Souls of Black Folk.*

[9] Paul Gilroy, *The Black Atlantic: Modernity and Double Consciousness* (New York: Oxford University Press, 1993).

[10] Jean Toomer, "Outline of Autobiography." [1934] Nashville: Toomer Papers, Fisk University Library, 2.

Narrative of the Life and *The Souls of Black Folk*," Wilfred D. Samuels establishes an intertextual relationship between Olaudah Equiano's narrative and Du Bois seminal text. Juliet Walker presents in "Racial Capitalism in a Global Economy: The Double Consciousness of Black Business in the Economic Philosophy of W. E. B. Du Bois," a groundbreaking study in Du Bois's racialized economic thought. Recognizing the complexity of Du Bois's scholarship and activism, Mark Braley discusses, in "The Sweetness of His Strength: Du Bois, Teddy Roosevelt, and the Black Soldier," Du Bois's mixed feelings toward racial progress in the American military. Although many contemporary scholars have taken Du Bois to task for what they believe was his neglect of the conditions African American women faced in the early twentieth century, Rufus Burrow argues, in "W. E. B. Du Bois and the Intersection of Race and Sex in the Twenty-First Century," that, although Du Bois was trapped within the conventions of Victorian sexism, he nonetheless argued for the humanity and rights of women. In his essay, "The Sentimental Du Bois: Genre, Race, and the Reading Public," Bill Hardwig argues that, in *The Quest of the Silver Fleece*, Du Bois abandons masculinized rhetoric and opts for the sentimental discourse characterized by African American women writers. Kwaku Korang argues in "As I Face America: Race and Africanity in Du Bois's The Souls of Black Folk" against contemporary Du Boisian critics who attack him for attempting to claim a romanticized Africa that never existed. Kalamu ya Salaam offers a poetic tribute to Du Bois that attempts to de-romanticize him as a Victorian intellectual.

By making available this selection of essays that were presented during the Du Bois Symposium we hope to make a significant contribution both to the constant reconsiderations of Du Bois writings and career, and to the centennial celebration of the publication of *The Souls of Black Folk.* Du Bois's seminal text is still, arguably, the one that stands at the center of racial discourse in American life.

W. E. B. Du Bois's View of the Southwest Georgia Black Belt

By Lee W. Formwalt

Illustrated with Photographs by A. Radclyffe Dugmore

"Out of the North the train thundered, and we woke to see the crimson soil of Georgia stretching away bare and monotonous right and left." Thus W. E. B. Du Bois began the description of his research trip to southwest Georgia in the summer of 1898 to study life in Albany and Dougherty County, "the heart of the Black Belt," the "centre of those nine million men who are America's dark heritage from slavery and the slave-trade."[1] The celebrated African American historian, on the threshold of a long and influential career, had received his Ph.D. in history from Harvard University only three years earlier and was then teaching at Atlanta University. When he decided to study the Black Belt, he chose Dougherty County because it had "about as large [a] majority of negroes as any county in Georgia" and it was small enough to cover in the two or three months of summer vacation. Accompanied by two or three research assistants, Du Bois boarded the Jim Crow car at the Atlanta

---

[1] W. E. B. Du Bois, *The Souls of Black Folk* ([1903] reprint, Boston, 1997) 103, 105, 103–4.

depot and headed south to begin collecting data on Dougherty County's African American population.[2]

"Below Macon," Du Bois noticed, "the world grows darker; for now we approach the Black Belt,—that strange land of shadows, at which even slaves paled in the past, and whence come now only faint and half-intelligible murmurs to the world beyond." They finally arrived at Albany, "a wide-streeted, placid, Southern town, with a broad sweep of stores and saloons, and flanking rows of' homes,—whites usually to the north, and blacks to the south....For a radius of a hundred miles about Albany, stretched a great fertile land, luxuriant with forests of pine, oak, ash, hickory, and poplar; hot with the sun and damp with the rich black swamp-land; and here the corner-stone of the Cotton Kingdom was laid."[3]

With rich imagery, Du Bois recreated on his verbal canvas the texture of life and work in the Georgia black belt. When first published in the magazine *World's Work* in June 1901, Du Bois's observations on southwest Georgia were illustrated with nineteen photographs taken in and near Albany by A. Radclyffe Dugmore. A thirty-year-old Englishman on the verge of a well-known career as a natural history artist, photographer, author, and filmmaker, Dugmore had been doing some photographic work for several New York publishers when *World's Work* hired him to do the photography for Du Bois's article.[4]

The world that Du Bois described and Dugmore illustrated was a depressing one characterized by poverty, work, and lack of leisure. The image was based on more than just a few days' observation. With his assistants, the Atlanta professor "visited nearly every colored family in the county," collecting data on the 6,093 blacks who lived in the country

---

[2] "Testimony of Prof. W. E. Burghardt Du Bois," 13 February 1901, in *Reports of the Industrial Commission on Immigration, Including Testimony, with Review and Digest, and Special Reports* (Washington DC: 1901) 15:160, 159; *Souls of Black Folk*, 104. The best biography of Du Bois, David Levering Lewis, *W. E. B. Du Bois: Biography of a Race, 1868–1919* (New York, 1993), does not mention Du Bois's summer research trip to Dougherty County in 1898.

[3] *Souls of Black Folk*, 105.

[4] Du Bois, "The Negro As He Really Is," *World's Work* 2 (June 1901):848-66; A. Radclyffe Dugmore, *The Autobiography of a Wanderer* (London, 1930), 9, 79-116, 250, 266, 281.

district as well as the 2,500 blacks in Albany.[5] In March 1901, when
Dugmore went to Albany to shoot the pictures for the article, Du Bois
returned to guide him around the county. Although the Albany
assignment was a small commission in his long career, it left a lasting
impression on the photographer. Three decades later, Dugmore recalled,
"my wife and I stayed at a hotel which was so dirty that it was a disgrace
to the white race, and yet Du Bois was not allowed even to come on the
verandah to talk to me because he was 'coloured.'"[6]

Du Bois used his Dougherty County data in a variety of ways beyond
the *World's Work* article. In 1900, he compiled and prepared a map of
Albany showing the geographical distribution of the city's African
Americans by social class which appeared in the Negro Exhibit of the
American Section of the Exposition Universelle in Paris.[7] The following
year he testified at length on conditions in Dougherty County before the
Industrial Commission established by Congress in 1898.[8] And in 1906, he
discussed Dougherty County in an article published in a German journal
edited by his former teacher, Max Weber.[9] Du Bois also revised and
expanded his magazine article into two chapters of his famous *Souls of
Black Folk* which appeared in 1903.

While Du Bois's thoughts about the Black Belt have been read by tens
of thousands of readers in numerous editions of *Souls*, the Dugmore
photographs that accompanied the original version of the historian's
published remarks lay hidden away in a few surviving copies of the June
1901 issue of *World's Work*. Rediscovered a few years ago, a selection of
the Dugmore photographs are presented here. The italicized phrase at the
beginning of each photograph is Du Bois's original caption from his
World's Work article. Additional descriptive passages from Du Bois's
writings expand on the original magazine caption. The statistical data and
skillful prose Du Bois developed from his visit to Dougherty County,

---

[5] "Testimony," 13 February 1901, 15:159-60.

[6] Dugmore, *Autobiography*, 115.

[7] "Albany, Dougherty County, Ga. Distribution of 2,500 Negro Inhabitants," Division
of Prints and Photographs, Library of Congress, Washington, D.C. See Du Bois, "The
American Negro at Paris," *American Monthly Review of Reviews* 22 (Nov. 1900): 575-77.

[8] "Testimony," 13 Feb. 1901, 15:159-75.

[9] Du Bois, "Die Negerfrage in den Vereinigten Staaten" ["The Negro Question in the
United States"] *Archiv für Sozialwissenschaft und Sozialpolitik*, Tubingen, Germany, 22
(Jan. 1906): 31-79.

however, cannot fully convey the feeling and atmosphere in the Dugmore photographs. Our understanding of life in the Black Belt at the turn of the century is all the richer because of them.

Log Cabin Home. "All over the face of the land is the one-room Cabin,—now standing in the shadow of the Big House, now staring at the dusty road, now rising dark and sombre amid the green of the cotton-fields. It is nearly always old and bare, built of rough boards, and neither plastered nor ceiled. Light and ventilation are supplied by the single door and by the square hole in the wall with its wooden shutter." *Souls,* 119.

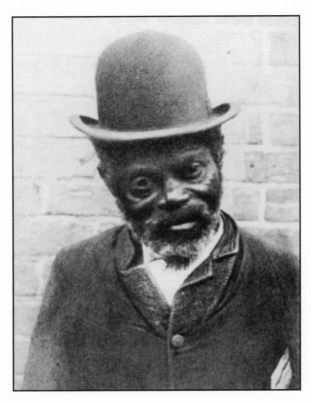

A Friend of George Washington. This "old ragged black man" stated "he was with Washington when the cherry tree was cut down," a claim that reflects the pervasiveness of Parson Weems's myth in American culture. *Souls,* 109; "The Negro As He Really Is," 860.

Learning to Shuffle Early. "Most of the children get their schooling after the 'crops are laid by,' and very few there are that stay in school after the spring work has begun....The degree of ignorance cannot easily be expressed. We may say, for instance, that nearly two-thirds of them cannot read or write. This but partially expresses the fact. They are ignorant of the world about them, of modern economic organization, of the function of government, of individual worth and possibilities, of nearly all those things which slavery in self-defence had to keep them from learning. Much that the white boy imbibes from his earliest social atmosphere forms the puzzling problems of the black boy's mature years. America is not another world for Opportunity to *all* her sons." *Souls,* 121–22.

Women "Sowing" Guano. "Among this people there is no leisure class....Here ninety-six per cent [sic] are toiling; no one with leisure to turn the bare and cheerless cabin into a home....The toil, like all farm toil, is monotonous, and here there are little machinery and few tools to relieve its burdensome drudgery. But with all this, it is work in the pure open air, and this is something in a day when fresh air is scarce." *Souls*, 122–23.

Women from the Country and *A Parson and Part of His Flock.* "Six days in the week [Albany] looks decidedly too small for itself, and takes frequent and prolonged naps. But on Saturday suddenly the whole county disgorges itself upon the place, and a perfect flood of black peasantry pours through the streets, fills the stores, blocks the sidewalks, chokes the thoroughfares, and takes full possession of the town. They are black, sturdy, uncouth country folk, good-natured and simple, talkative to a degree....They walk up and down the streets, meet and gossip with friends, stare at the shop windows, buy coffee, cheap candy, and clothes, and at dusk drive home." *Souls*, 105–6.

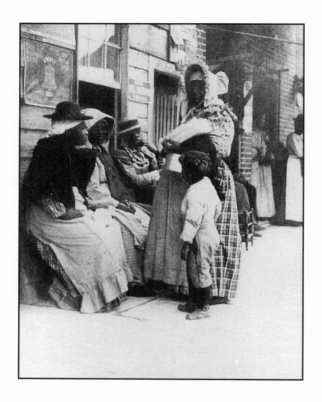

Her Week's Marketing. "Albany is a real capital,—a typical Southern county town, the centre of the life of ten thousand souls; their point of contact with the outer world, their centre of news and gossip, their market for buying and selling, borrowing and lending, their fountain of justice and law." The crowds on Saturday "drink considerable quantities of whiskey, but do not get very drunk; they talk and laugh loudly at times, but seldom quarrel or fight." *Souls*, 105–6.

In the Cobbler's Shop and *At Work Making Brooms*. While most Dougherty County blacks were farmers, there were a few artisans, carpenters, shoemakers, blacksmiths, and machinists. "All of the carpenter work is done by colored men," wrote Du Bois, who stayed in a house built by an Albany carpenter and described it as "a very good house indeed, very well built, and unusually good for the town." "Testimony," 170.

"Big House" and Negro Quarters. "The plantations of Dougherty County in slavery days were not as imposing and aristocratic as those of Virginia. The Big House was smaller and usually one-storied, and sat very near the slave cabins....The form and disposition of the laborers' cabins throughout the Black Belt is to-day the same as in slavery days." *Souls,* 119.

Working by the day in the Cotton Field. "The land on the whole is still fertile, despite long abuse. For nine or ten months in succession the crops will come if asked: garden vegetables in April, grain in May, melons in June and July, hay in August, sweet potatoes in September, and cotton from then to Christmas. And yet on two-thirds of the land there is but one crop [cotton], and that leaves the toilers in debt." *Souls,* 123.

A Negro School Near Albany, Georgia. "The schools in Dougherty County are very poor. I saw only one schoolhouse there that would compare in any way with the worst schoolhouses I ever saw in New England. That was a board house equipped with rude benches, without desks, no glass in the windows, with no sort of furniture except a blackboard and three boards put together for a teacher's desk. Most of the schoolhouses were either old log huts or were churches—colored churches—used as schoolhouses." "Testimony," 161.

A Typical Negro Store and *Negro Cottages.* "There are some colored men who live in town and own plantations in the country. Some of them are wealthy men. There is, for instance, a man named....Billingslea, who usually owns anywhere from one to two thousand acres of land which he cultivates. He must be worth at least $20,000....He runs a store, a blacksmith shop, and things of that sort." The proprietor of this "typical Negro store" owned the "Negro cottages," which he rented to tenants in town. "Testimony," 170.

RIDDLE ME THIS:
DU BOIS, THE SPHINX, AND THE CRISIS OF IDENTITY

The riddle of existence is the college curriculum that was laid before the Pharaohs, that was taught in the groves by Plato....(69).

No secure civilization can be built in the South with the Negro as an ignorant, turbulent proletariat...they will not cease to think, will not cease attempting to read the riddle of the world. (87)[1]

DOLAN HUBBARD

W. E. B. Du Bois draws on the rich lexicographical history of "riddle" in *The Souls of Black Folk* (1903), especially as it pertains to the culture of black folks from Ethiopia and Egypt to here "in America, in the few days since Emancipation," where blacks are caught in a "double-aimed struggle" (6). This ancient word, which is related to the interpretation of texts, signified on one's ability at problem solving. It presents an implicit compliment to the intelligence of the listener, who is associated with a silent majority that cannot penetrate its invincible simplicity or unravel its cultural code. In its etymology, the network of definitions is "a kind of small thesaurus,"[2] indicative of its wide geographical distribution, but the effect of the whole provides insight into the human condition. "Riddle" covers a considerable range of activity from sorting (to separate or shift, as grain from the chaff), perforating (to make many little holes in; as, a

---

[1] W. E. B. Du Bois, *The Souls of Black Folk.* ([1903] New York: Penguin, 1989). All citations from the text refer to this edition and are marked parenthetically in the text.

[2] Robert Alter and Frank Kermode, ed., *The Literary Guide to the Bible* (Cambridge: Harvard University Press, 1987) 253.

house *riddled* with shot), to interrogating (a problem or puzzle in the form of a question, a conundrum).[3]

"Riddle" in Greek is *enigma*, which comes via Latin from the Greek *ainigma*, "obscure or dark statement." This term is a derivative from the verb *ainissesthai* "to talk in riddles," which in turn came from the noun *ainos*, "tale, story."[4] A riddle or enigma carries the implication that stories are always darkly told, which has a particular resonance for the African in the modern Western world whose life is an exercise in refuting interpretations of self and history based solely on the color of the skin. In his customary way, Du Bois starts with the Anglo-Saxon definition of "riddle" (as a coarse-meshed sieve, particularly that used in foundry work or in mines for the sifting of coal) and makes it his own (the issue of identity)—in his life-long project on the re-valorization of the African in the modern Western world. His goal is to reconnect people of African descent culturally by centering Africa as the source of black discourse. Through *The Souls of Black Folks*, Du Bois decodes the hieroglyphs of modernity. He makes it possible for black people to comprehend the meaning of "race" in the Atlantic formation. It is the central construct that prevents blacks in the New World from knowing themselves and the role they have played in world history.[5]

---

[3] Archer Taylor (*The Literary Riddle Before 1600* [Berkeley: University of California Press, 1948] 1n1) observes that "many varieties of puzzling questions are loosely called riddles. Arithmetical problems, conundrums, questions requiring for the answer a shrewd wit, questions demanding a knowledge of the Bible, and many other kinds of puzzles are sometimes called riddles....These puzzles appear in popular and literary versions." Though Taylor notes the use of riddle in Sanskrit, Arabic, and Hebrew, standard definitions contain almost no references to its tradition in Asia or Africa. For example, see Lesley Brown, ed., *The New Shorter Oxford English Dictionary* (Oxford: Clarendon Press, 1973) or *Webster's New Twentieth Century Dictionary of the English Language Unabridged.* Second edition (1968): 1559.

[4] John Ayto, ed., *Dictionary of Word Origins* (New York: Arcade Publishing, 1990) 202.

[5] For discussion of this recentering of Africa in world thought, see Melville Herskovits, Chancellor Williams, Roger Bastide, Ali A. Mazuri, and Martin Bernal. In *Afrotopia: The Roots of African American Popular History* (New York: Cambridge University Press, 1998), Wilson Jeremiah Moses offers an unsentimental critique of Afrocentrism and Egyptocentrism. "Egyptocentrism is the sometimes sentimental, at other times cynical, attempt to claim ancient Egyptian ancestry for black Americans. It involves the attempt to reconstruct the peoples of ancient Egypt in terms of traditional American racial perceptions. Afrocentrism, on the other hand, is simply the belief that the

This essay will examine Du Bois's use of "riddle" to interrogate the distortions of history and call attention to the crisis of identity that confront blacks in a world in which they need not exist except as beasts of burden ("hewers of wood and drawers of water" [6]). They live in a world in which history has been emptied of its significance as an empowering narrative. Consequently, as Du Bois reminds us, "the shadow of a deep disappointment rests upon the Negro people...."(7) who confront daily the unending reality that blacks live in a world that "[inculcates] disdain for everything black" (15). Adopting the posture of the wisdom teacher, Du Bois hammers away at the twin problems of black suffering and America's inability to see that in degrading the African, it degrades itself. For the sage of Atlanta, the solution, in large part, lies in the recovery of the African's discredited historical patrimony.

Du Bois saw history as a sieve; black people are the ones who have fallen through and been left out of it. The ritual action in sifting involves judging and separating what is important from what is not. The modern Western world has judged the African as unimportant to world history. Through his act of sifting, Du Bois shifts the perspective from Africa as essence and therefore commodity to Africa as central to human history. The static reading of history holds blacks in a fixed position and renders Africa invisible as a meaningful contributor to world history. Du Bois wants to transform conventional thinking on how to approach Africa in world history, as is evident in his passage on "double-consciousness" that captures the African predicament in America:

> After the Egyptian and Indian, the Greek and Roman, the Teuton and Mongolian, the Negro is a sort of seventh son, born with a veil, and gifted with second-sight in this American world,—a world which yields him no true self-consciousness, but only lets him see himself through the revelation of the other world. It is a peculiar sensation, this double-consciousness, this sense of always looking at one's self through the eyes of others, of

---

African ancestry of black peoples, regardless of where they live, is an inescapable element of their various identities—imposed both from within and from without their own communities" (6). Even as they strive to "redeem a message of hope from Africa's image of relative blackness" (16), Moses reminds us that many African Americans remain ambivalent in their feelings toward Africa.

measuring one's soul by the tape of a world that looks on in amused contempt and pity. One ever feels his two-ness,—an American, a Negro; two souls, two thoughts, two unreconciled strivings; two warring ideals in one dark body, whose dogged strength alone keeps it from being torn asunder. (5)

While it can be argued that Du Bois reads "race" according to the nineteenth-century script of biology with its preoccupation for classification or sorting, Du Bois breaks with the biological reflex crowd and asserts that what the modern world classifies as "race" was always a part of (instead of apart from) human history. The modern construct of "race" is a riddle for it seduces people to mistake surfaces (skin color) for essences. The European "discoverers" of ancient Egypt dwelled on the surfaces of what they encountered and failed to inquire about the contexts and depths of what they saw. Du Bois's radical reading of history lies hidden before the eyes of his readers conditioned to accept the biological hypothesis as fact. (Elsewhere he asserts that "race" is no crime.) They leave this passage on "double-consciousness" with the awareness that blacks are caught on the horns of a dilemma—faced with a choice between alternatives that are equally undesirable or dangerous. By the time Du Bois's readers reach his penultimate chapter "The Sorrow Songs," he shows them the folly of mistaking the shadow for the substance.

The riddle of the Sphinx from the Oedipus story, the classic interpretation of interpretation, shadows *The Souls of Black Folks.* Du Bois, however, is not particularly interested in the actual riddle: "What creature goes on four feet in the morning, on two at noonday, and three in the evening" and speaks with one voice.[6] The answer is man as a baby, an adult, and as an elder with a cane. As stated above, Du Bois is neither interested in the idea of the riddle nor in the answer to the riddle, nor in the Sphinx, "a creature shaped like a winged lion, but with the

---

[6] I am indebted to Carrie Cowherd's "The Wings of Atalanta: Classical Influences in *The Souls of Black Folk*" (Dolan Hubbard, ed. *Critical Essays on W. E. B. Du Bois's The Souls of Black Folk* (Columbia University of Missouri Press, forthcoming), for its insights on Du Bois's use of riddle.

breast and face of a woman."[7] Du Bois draws a correlation between the first stage of man in the Oedipus story and the newly emancipated blacks taking their first tentative steps in freedom as they deal with the one hundred-headed hydra known as the Freedman's Bureau and its ensuing collapse. Unlike the infant in the Oedipus story, black America lacked the resources to stop crawling politically, economically, and culturally because white America lacked the political will to establish genuine democracy in America. Therefore, for Du Bois, the Sphinx is a moveable metaphor. Sometimes, the Sphinx is the Greek monster; sometimes it is the monumental sculpture at Giza; sometimes it is neither, as in the Du Bois poem cited by Arnold Rampersad, "The Riddle of the Sphinx," originally titled "The Burden of Black Women," a work unrivaled in the Du Bois *oeuvre* for its "intense bitterness toward the white world."[8]

Du Bois's goal in mentioning the Sphinx and Africa in the same breath is more concrete. He wants to re-connect black people to their distinguished Ancient-World history that has now grown dim: "The shadow of a mighty Negro past flits through the tale of Ethiopia the Shadowy and of Egypt the Sphinx. Throughout history, the powers of single black men flash here and there like falling stars, and die sometimes before the world has rightly gauged their brightness" (6). Du Bois opens up this conceptual possibility, a window on what is unrecovered, and the call is being answered. The power of this passage is to see with a sweep of

---

[7] In Edith Hamilton, *A Dictionary of Symbols* (New York: Norton, 1996) 257, Juan Chevalier and Alain Gheerbrant give an overview of the power of the Sphinx on the modern imagination. The most famous Sphinx stands on the edge of the desert, below the pyramid of Chefren among the pyramids and tombs at Giza.

The Sphinx still watches over these gigantic cemeteries, its red-painted face staring at the sole point on the horizon from which the Sun will rise. It is the warden of these forbidden thresholds and royal mummies. It listens to the song of the planets; it watches on the brink of eternity over all that has been and all that is to come; it gazes at distant Niles flowing across the Heavens and the Sunboats floating on their waters (Cham 10).

In fact, these divine lions bore the heads of Pharaohs and, according to Jean Yoyotte, stood for a royal power, merciless towards rebels but protecting the good....(Posd. 267).

In the course of its evolution in the imagination, the Sphinx has come to symbolize, too, something from which there is no escape. The very word 'Sphinx' conjures up the idea of riddles, the Oedipan Sphinx, the riddle which overpowers and contradicts. In fact, the Sphinx stands on the brink of a fate which is both necessity and mystery. (267)

[8] Arnold Rampersad, *The Art and Imagination of W. E. B. Du Bois* ([1976] New York: Schocken, 1990) 106.

the pen the beginnings of a discipline or quest for knowledge—the germinating idea the consequences of which are manifold. What are the consequences for sense of self of this newly fostered historical agency? He gives new historians an angle and calls for them to read from that lens, with that question in mind. History itself presents as a riddle that must be interpreted. Note the double riddle behind the riddle: What is Africa? What is man? The answer to both of these questions lies obscured by the prevailing notion of race—a most difficult act of interpretation for it keeps the sovereign human soul enveloped in darkness.

Africa was the invisible leg in what Du Bois in *The World and Africa* (1946) called the "crisis of civilization" (vii). He reminds readers of the critical role Africa "has played in human history, past and present, and how impossible it is to forget this role and rightly explain the present plight of mankind" (vii). His impact can be seen in cultural and historical terms. Engaged in a trans-Atlantic conversation, Du Bois seeks to change the exegesis or practice of interpretation, based on a Eurocentric model (or a model of the universe with Europe at the center). Du Bois, thereby, changes the understanding not only of *Africa* but also of *Europe* as text. He refutes the prevailing orthodoxy that Africans were on the bottom rung of the great chain of being and that black skin was a sign of inferiority and therefore a badge of shame. Du Bois illuminates the trinity of aesthetics, color, and economics in the global economy. Along with a few others, he advanced the radical notion that the world would not be free until Africa was free.

The phrase "Ethiopia the Shadowy and of Egypt the Sphinx" to a large extent functions as an imaginary signifier, a practice of language, a network of negative images designed to keep blacks in a fixed position, prisoners of the text, captive. In the discursive space of Africa, as in the construction of the black in the modern Western world as a beast of burden, black people are both absent and captive: absent as a theoretical subject, captive as a historical object. Du Bois as participant-narrator in *The Souls of Black Folks* demonstrates to others in the African Diaspora that they, too, can mount an assault on the closed economy of discourse that defines them as commodities ("hewers of wood and drawers of water" [6]).

Much of what the world knows as Ancient Egypt (which, according to David Roberts in *Encarta 2000* "seemed to rise out of nothing") was shaped by black people whose contributions seemed to have disappeared into the sands of the Sahara, or into history's dark hole. The Sphinx and the great pyramids stand as the apex of this civilization that influenced the culture of Greece and Rome, and was ultimately passed down through Western civilization. Blacks in the west are caught up in the destructive gaze of those who wrote history. To take but one example, I cite the opening paragraph of a popular history on Egypt from the Time-Warner Library written by Lionnel Casson, a former professor of classics at New York University:

> Egypt was ancient even to the ancients. It was a great nation a thousand years before the Minoans of Crete built their palaces at Knossos, about 900 years before the Israelites followed Moses out of bondage. It flourished when tribesman still dwelt in huts above the Tiber. It was viewed by Greeks and Romans of 2,000 years ago in somewhat the same way the ruins of Greece and Rome are viewed by modern man.
>
> The great Greek historian Herodotus made a grand tour of ancient Egypt in the Fifth Century B.C. and wrote of "wonder more in number than those of any other land and works it has to show beyond expression great." Later writers bore him out. Journeying the Nile, they passed the imposing mounds of the pyramids, avenues of sphinxes, slender obelisks. They were dwarfed by towering images in stone and intrigued by enigmatic hieroglyphics covering the wall of temples.
>
> For one thing, Egypt was one of the earliest of the ancient lands to weave the threads of civilization into a truly impressive culture. More to the point, it sustained its achievements unabated for more than two and a half-millennia—a span of accomplishment with few equals in the saga of humanity.[9]

We can deduce four central points from this discourse on Egypt. First, the great Greek historian Herodotus stands unchallenged as a disinterested observer who blithely recounts the history of Egypt, bringing it into the discursive universe of the Western world. Second,

---

[9] Lionel Casson, etal., *Ancient Egypt* (New York: Time, 1965) 11.

Casson represents Egypt's greatness as an enigma or dark story of history. Casson's sweeping history glosses over education, systematic study of nature and complex systems, hard work, and discipline, all the while discounting individual achievement. His history is transparent in regard to the color of those who produced this towering culture that held the ancient world in awe. Third, "the imposing mounds of the pyramids, avenues of sphinxes, slender obelisks" come to stand as a barrier between blacks in the Diaspora and Africa, an *a*historical, eternal Egyptian essence, so the modern Western world thinks. Behind this line of thought lies Art as universal, divested of the concrete specificity of the black hands who built a world-class culture. Finally, Casson presents an Egyptian history without footnotes that is largely replicated in the founding fathers of the Western philosophical tradition, Plato and Aristotle, as though they sprang forth *sui generis*, with no acknowledgment of the intellectual bridge that spanned the Mediterranean Sea. As a result of this discourse of invisibility, history itself is mute, sphinx-like, when blacks in the New World stand before it. They do not see their reflection in the Sphinx, this guardian of their history. They no longer participate in the socio-symbolic exchange of a discursive universe that is recognizable to them. For these New World blacks, who have been displaced as subjects, history holds more questions than answers. Consequently, they encounter one riddle after another; for precisely conversation, speech and language now stand as the terrain from which they have been exorcised. They have been reduced to speaking a language that Fanon in *Black Skin, White Masks* calls "the divine gurgling" (20) or mumbo jumbo.[10]

Ultimately, Du Bois's project of re-centering Africa and re-connecting New World blacks to their ancestral roots in the book's silent refrain ("Ethiopia the Shadowy and of Egypt the Sphinx") is about beginnings. The observations of Cain Hope Felder in his introduction to *The Original African Heritage Bible* (1993) are applicable in this discussion. He

---

[10] Basil Davidson, etal., (*African Kingdoms* [New York: Time 1966] 17-22) offer a corrective to Casson's Eurocentric reading of Egypt largely bereft of the contributions and intellectual traditions of its African neighbors in his. That Egypt is not depicted in engaging in a dynamic exchange of ideas with its Saharan neighbors continues the West's projection of Africa as "the dark continent," a land inhabited by people "believed to be monsters, with souls as black as their skin" (18) in contrast to an enlightened, civilized Europe. Sadly this historical binary still informs too many histories of Africa.

describes a distorted history that prevents blacks from connecting to the beginning of their history:

> The origin of [a particular people and a "particular God"] has been shrouded in the mysteries of the various versions and translations of the Bible (especially the King James Version) for many years...due, in part, to the misinterpretations of those who rendered the original translations from Hebrew and Greek into Latin, English, and other languages....In the period between the fourth century and the Enlightenment of the seventeenth and eighteenth centuries, Europe recast the entire Bible into a saga of European people. And their interpretation has been accepted as fact by the Western world. [Felder stresses that] readers today must understand that in biblical times "Africa" included much of what European maps have come to call the "Middle East." Remember, the name *Africa* is actually of Latin origin and was imposed on that great continent by European explorers. (vii-ix)

The black in the West is an invention, a purposeful misreading of history. The West invests much intellectual capital in keeping New World Africans from seeing themselves as agents in history. Du Bois plunges into the abyss to reclaim a discredited history and make it visible to a people trapped inside of a horological hula hoop in which they only see a dim reflection of themselves: "The shadow of a mighty Negro past flits through the tale of Ethiopia the Shadowy and of Egypt the Sphinx" (6). Ethiopia and Egypt are metonymns for a displaced African history. Riddles and how they are answered, and stories and how they are told, map out structures of thought, how a people deal with the concrete and abstract, how they view the elements of the world, what they are comfortable taking for granted and what they must inquire about—in short their philosophy. Why is history largely silent on the philosophy of Africans? Why, when given religious and architectural texts to read, do we value what Herodotus says versus what the evidence itself reveals? The end point of this displacement, or theft of history, is to define blacks as Caliban, the antithesis of Ariel, the Divine, in Shakespeare's *The Tempest.* Blacks, on the other hand, refuse this definition of themselves as deformed and strive mightily to be "a co-worker in the kingdom of culture, to escape both death and isolation, to husband and use [their] best powers and [their] latent genius" (5).[11] For Du Bois, an accomplished "co-worker in the kingdom of culture" (5), this reversed status meant both exploring the ideas of the West through his perspective as an African American as well as pointing the way toward reclamation of a history of Africa which is un-contingent on the accomplishments, borrowings, etc. of other cultures and the psychological need to find a guarantor of one's history as though legitimization comes from without rather than from within. Thus, we call the aesthetic paradox that confront blacks in the Western World (and is experienced most acutely by the artist) "Caliban's dilemma":

> The would-be black *savant* was confronted by the paradox that the knowledge his people needed was a twice-told tale to his white neighbors, while the knowledge which would teach the white world was Greek to his own flesh and blood. The innate love of harmony and beauty that set the ruder souls of his people a-dancing and a-singing raised but confusion and doubt in the soul of the black artist [preacher, singer, musician, painter, intellectual]; for the beauty revealed to him was the soul-beauty of a race which his larger audience despised, and he could not articulate the message of another people. (6)

Caliban hates the culture that refuses to see him as a caring human being but must curse it in the language of that culture, and that is a fundamental arm of his oppression—the structures of his thoughts are in some regard determined by the oppressor's language, so he is forced into the stance of subversion. The bounty and the beauty of his former dominion are determined by the philosopher to be not for him. In short,

---

[11] Houston A. Baker ("Caliban's Triple Play," in Henry Louis Gates, ed., *"Race,"
Writing and Difference* [Chicago: University of Chicago Press, 1985]) offers an instructive reading on "the framing of Otherness'" (382) in his discussion of Shakespeare's *The Tempest* where Prospero and Caliban are portrayed in terms of self and other or the West and the Rest of Us, respectively (389). Also see Roberto Fernández Retamar's "Caliban: Notes Toward a Discussion of Culture in Our America" in *Caliban and Other Essays,* trans. Edward Baker (Minneapolis: University of Minnesota Press, 1989) 3-45.

Du Bois is talking about the disappearance of the black subject from history and the discourse of trauma that shapes the character of black life.

THE CRISIS OF IDENTITY AND THE DISCOURSE OF TRAUMA

In *Go Tell It on the Mountain* (1953), James Baldwin provides us with a useful gloss on Du Bois's project on reversing the disappearance of the black subject from history. Set in Harlem, this novel of the Great Migration is told largely in a series of flashbacks from the perspective of three supplicants in a storefront church. They come to grips with their shortcomings as human beings (the eternal issue of spiritual dilemma) and they also pray fervently that the storm they and by extension the community has been in (the veil of race) will soon be over. The fourteen year-old John Grimes is the symbol of their hope. During her prayer, Elizabeth recalls the simultaneous fear and wonderment that carried her from her home in the deep South to her search for a better life in the North. Love stricken, she follows Richard, twenty-two, whom she first met in Maryland, to New York, where he worked as an elevator boy and she found a job as a chambermaid in the same hotel (162). Their Saturday rituals included tours of the Museum of Natural History, or the Metropolitan Museum of Art, where they were almost certain to be the only black folk, with Richard as her guide. While the exhibits "never ceased in her imagination to be as cold as tombstones," they fired his imagination. "It was then that she saw another life in him. It never ceased to frighten her, this passion he brought to something she could not understand" (165–66).

> For she never grasped—not at any rate with her mind—what, with such incandescence, he tried to tell her on these Saturday afternoons. She could not find, between herself and the African statuette, or totem pole, on which he gazed with such melancholy wonder, any point of contact. She was only glad that she did not look that way....She did not know why he so adored things that were so long dead *and not a part of her history* [my emphasis]; what sustenance they gave him, what secrets he hoped to wrest from them *and make history talk* [my emphasis]. But she understood, at least, that they *did* give him a kind of bitter

nourishment, and that the secrets they held for him were a matter of his life and death. It frightened her because she felt that he was reaching for the moon and that he would, therefore, be dashed down against the rocks; but she did not say any of this. She only listened, and in her heart she prayed for him. (166)

Elizabeth finds herself on an aesthetic archipelago that produces the cognitive dissonance Du Bois calls "double-consciousness" (5). History has lost its symbolic authority; it does not speak to her in any meaningful way as a narrative of power. For example, the negation of the self in a claustrophobic South means that she does not see herself reflected in "the African statuette, or totem pole." She does not see them as fully referential forms of communication of the self located in a vibrant discourse originating at home in the Old World. In this context, "Ethiopia the Shadowy" and "Egypt the Sphinx" represent the rhetorical incompatibility between blacks in America and Africa. This rhetorical incompatibility manifests itself as the blues aesthetic that colors black thought in the New World.[12]

Elizabeth and Richard stand before the African artifacts, whose discursive universe is alien to them, as racially marked subjects. The artifacts are also isolated from their original context; the riddle is to reconstruct their meaning. Elizabeth and Richard represent the (in)articulate part that stands for the whole, for the collective black community, right down to the divided self.[13] Elizabeth represents the

---

[12] In "'In the Kingdom of Culture': Black Women and the Intersection of Race, Gender, and Class," *Lure and Loathing: Essays on Race, Identity, and the Ambivalence of Assimilation*, ed. Gerald Early (New York: Allen Lane/Penguin Press, 1993) 337–51. Darlene Clark Hine notes the shortcomings of Du Bois's use of race as "the master key to understanding American reality and the most potent factor shaping identity....The history of the American Negro is more than a history of efforts as Du Bois puts it to 'attain self-conscious manhood,' it is simultaneously a story of the development and preservation of a dynamic, multiconscious black womanhood" (338). For recent discussions of Du Bois on race and culture, see Bernard W. Bell, Emily R. Grosholz, and James B. Stewart, ed., *W. E. B. Du Bois: On Race and Culture* (New York: Routledge, 1996) and Shamoon Zamir, *Dark Voices: W. E. B. Du Bois and American Thought, 1888-1903* (Chicago: University of Chicago Press, 1995).

[13] Gates, ed., *The Classic Slave Narratives*, xiii. In "Hunting is Not Those Heads on the Wall," LeRoi Jones offers a trenchant critique on the West's penchant for separating art from the site of production—the establishment of Art as a separate category apart from its

majority view in the black community; she sees very little that connects her to the material culture of the ancient world. Richard represents the minority view in the black community; he sees much in the New World that connects him to the material culture of the ancient world. However, they share one thing in common: they have difficulty in making history speak in a way that is relevant to them.

When blacks look at the sphinx and the pyramid or other African artifacts, they see themselves (a la Elizabeth) inside the jaws of history, in the order of nature rather than in the flux of civilization. This is what Du Bois alludes to in his reference to "the Negro as a sort of seventh son." Thus, we can see the visit of Richard and Elizabeth to the museum as an act of "reading" that functions for the black subject as the apotheosis of double-consciousness; it is simultaneously emancipatory (Richard) and debilitating (Elizabeth). In Richard Wright's words, it simultaneously "buoys up" the black reading subject while "casting him [or her] down." The jarring confrontation with history offers the racially marked subject what Du Bois calls "the gift of second sight"; that is, if we read with Jacques Derrida, the term "gift" etymologically as both gift and poison. For this reason, the artistically inclined Richard must die (and the aesthetically challenged Elizabeth must pray). A cursory reading of his death suggests that the society allows no social space in which he can claim his subjectivity or give expression to his deep-seated anger, what Baldwin in "Stranger in the Village" calls "the rage of the disesteemed" (165). It is displaced into sites of the spirituals, now converted into the gospel sound by the new arrivals in the city. One recalls Elizabeth's prayer as one way of articulating the self as a cultural agent. Through the spirituals, the community in unison brings the disparate strands together and comes to grips with the riddle of the self, if only momentarily. The ritual action—preaching, praying, and singing—liberates the self from a preoccupation with essentialism and the aesthetics of trauma. Concomitantly, it helps one move toward understanding itself as a critical operation of the mind, as is evident in James Weldon Johnson's magisterial poem "O Black and Unknown Bards." He sings the praises of those anonymous black people who created a body of music "which stirs

---

everyday use in a culture ("Hunting is Not Those Heads on the Wall," *Home: Social Essays* [New York: William Morrow, 1966] 176–77).

the soul or melts the heart to tears."[14] Given no other outlet, the multivalent spirituals function as social history and poetry as well. They are, among other things, a social text of oppression. As Baldwin reminds us in "The Discovery of What It Means to Be an American," those black and unknown bards helped translate "the rich confusion" (22) of our traumatic history into a language understood by all. This subliminal knowledge enables the members of the Temple of the Fire Baptized to achieve a peace that surpasses understanding and steels them to endure the indignities hurled at them by white people.

Du Bois and Baldwin call into question the relationship between history and aesthetics. What happens to a people when history has lost its "incandescence,"[15] when history itself has become a negation of the self? The philosophical ethic is centered on beauty and knowledge, and in their conjunction. Image creation drives aesthetics. To say what is beautiful is in some sense to say what is of value, what is an act of godhood. At the meta– or supra-philosophical level, beauty and knowledge are more equivocally combined in that they are knotted together by a representation of the Divine that is congruent with one's image of the self. The cost of trying to satisfy two unreconciled ideals is high for black people and it has, Du Bois reminds us, "sent them often wooing false gods and invoking false means of salvation" (6) due their deformed image of self.

Du Bois resolutely stands before the Sphinx with the knowledge that there is no avenue of escape from her gaze or the burden of history. Though Du Bois knew that blacks would not be going back to Africa, he also knew that in order for them to get beyond the "double-consciousness," they must be connected to Africa in a meaningful way. The Fisk-Harvard-Berlin riddle-master, recognizing Sphinx as the site of the self that is beyond race, knows that the Sphinx is "the term that designates at once the vanishing point of our culture's fictions of itself and the condition of the discourses in which the fictions are

---

[14] James Weldon Johnson, "O Black and Unknown Bards," *The Black Poets*, ed. Dudley Randall (New York: Bantam, 1971) 43.

[15] James Baldwin, "Stranger in the Village," *Notes of a Native Son* (Boston: Beacon Press, 1955) 166.

represented."[16] For, as Teresa De Lauretis notes in another context, "there would be no [Sphinx or Pyramid] without the attraction of the image to be looked at, no desire without an object... (5)."[17]

In terms of semiotic productivity, the black African is both telos and origin. Yet blacks of the African Diaspora, whose ancestors contributed to the design and building of the Sphinx, pyramids, and obelisks, that are the foundation and the very condition of representation are no where to be found in affirmative representation in modern history books, nevertheless stand as a brooding presence around the margins, as is evident in the fables of modernity of Joseph Conrad. As text, Africa is the ultimate paradox. While civilization originates in Africa, Africans are all but absent from history and cultural process. The cleavage that exists between subject and object, thereby producing "the rage of the disesteemed," is rooted in history as a dull cultural mirror: black people look into it and do not see a positive image of self. This in large part explains those ruptured moments in black American cultural productions—the moan of the spirituals or the howl of the blues—that defy the logic of origins as a result of the absence of black people as historical subjects. Africans not only occupy a critical space within a historical materialist theory of the Atlantic formation, but they directly concern its basic premises.[18]

---

[16] Teresa De Lauretis, *Alice Doesn't: Feminism, Semiotics, Cinema* (Bloomington: Indiana University Press, 1984) 5.

[17] In this section I draw upon the work of De Lauretis, *Alice Doesn't: Feminism, Semiotics, Cinema.*

[18] Through an examination of modernists such as Joseph Conrad, T.S. Eliot, Ezra Pound, and William Carlos Williams, Michael North (*The Dialect of Modernism: Race, Languages and Twentieth-Century Literature* [New York: Oxford University Press, 1994]) uncovers the crucial role the black world played in the emergence of literary modernism. For commentators on the Atlantic formation, see Charles H. Long's *Significations: Signs, Symbols, and Images in the Interpretation of Religion* (Philadelphia: Fortress, 1986), especially "Primitive/Civilized: The Locus of a Problem" (165–71); Paul Gilroy, *The Black Atlantic: Modernity and Double Consciousness* (Cambridge: Harvard University Press, 1994); and Maria Diedrich, Henry Louis Gates, Jr., and Carl Pedersen, eds., *Black Imagianton and the Middle Passage* (New York: Oxford University Press, 1999). In "Of the Training of Black Men," Du Bois illuminates the position of black people as trapped in history's dark reflection buttressed by the belief that "somewhere between [white] men and cattle, God created a *tertium quid,* and called it a Negro...." (75). Also see Jonathan

The cultural equivalent of John the Baptist, Du Bois prepares the way for the re-appearance of the black subject in history. He closes the distance of space and time by unlocking the riddle of blackness in the modern world. When others follow after him—writers, artists, critics, filmmakers—turn the question on itself (What is Africa? What is man?) and remake the story of Egypt, Ethiopia, Timbuktu, Sundiata, or even Oedipus, opening up a space of contradiction in which to demonstrate the centrality of Africa and black people to world thought, they also destablize and finally alter the meaning of representation. In short, *The Souls of Black Folk* is the Rosetta Stone of New World letters. It gave First World writers and artists a language in which to articulate their "Otherness" and make the world recognize the full weight of the black subject in history.

Culler's discussion of "The Mirror Stage" (*The Pursuit of Signs: Semiotics, Literature, Deconstruction* [Ithaca: Cornell University Press, 1981] 155–56.

SPHINX SELECTED BIBLIOGRAPHY

Abrams, M.H. *A Glossary of Literary Terms.* New York: Holt, Rinehart, and Winston, 1971.

Alter, Robert and Kermode, eds. *The Literary Guide to the Bible.* Cambridge: Harvard UP, 1987.

Asante, Molefi Kete. *The Afrocentric Idea.* Philadelphia: Temple University Press, 1987.

Asante, Molefi Kete. *Kemet, Afrocentricity, and Knowledge.* Trenton, NJ: Africa World Press, 1990.

Baker, Houston A., Jr. "Caliban's Triple Play." *"Race," Writing and Difference.* Ed. Henry Louis Gates, Jr. Chicago: University of Chicago Press, 1985. 381-95.

Baldwin, James. "The Discovery of What It Means to Be an American." *Nobody Knows My Name: More Notes of a Native Son.* New York: Dell, 1961. 17-23.

Baldwin, James. "Stranger in the Village." *Notes of a Native Son.* Boston: Beacon Press, 1955. 159-75.

Bastide, Roger. *African Civilizations in the New World.* New York: Harper Torchbooks, 1971.

Bell, Bernard W., Emily R. Grosholz, and James B. Stewart, eds. *W.E.B. Du Bois: On Race and Culture.* New York: Routledge, 1996.

Bernal, Martin. *Black Athena: The Afroasiatic Roots of Classical Civilization.* New Brunswick, NJ: Rutgers University Press, 1987.

Casson, Lionnel and the Editors of Time-Life Books. *Ancient Egypt.* New York: Time, 1965.

Chevalier, Juan and Alain Gheerbrant. *Dictionary of Symbols.* New York: Norton, 1996.

Cowherd, Carrie. "Classical Allusions in *The Souls of Black Folk.*" *Critical Essays on W.E.B. Du Bois's The Souls of Black Folk.* Ed. Dolan Hubbard. Columbia: University of Missouri Press, forthcoming.

Culler, Jonathan. *The Pursuit of Signs: Semiotics, Literature, Deconstruction.* Ithaca, NY: Cornell University Press, 1981.

Davidson, Basil and the Editors of Time-Life Books. *African Kingdoms.* New York: Time, 1966.

De Lauretis, Teresa. *Alice Doesn't: Feminism, Semiotics, Cinema.* Bloomington: Indiana University Press, 1984.

Dictionary of Word Origins. Ed. John Ayto. New York: Arcade Publishing, 1990.

Diedrich, Maria, Henry Louis Gates, Jr., and Carl Pedersen, eds., *Black Imagination and the Middle Passage*. New York: Oxford University Press, 1999.

Diop, Cheikh Anta Diop. *Civilization or Barbarism: An Authentic Anthropology*. Trans. Yaa-Lengi Meema Ngemi. 1981. Brooklyn, NY: Lawrence Hill, 1991.

Drake, Sinclair. *Black Folk Here and There: An Essay in History and Anthropology*. Los Angeles: Center for Afro American Studies, University of California, 1987: Vol.; 1990: vol. 2.

Du Bois, W.E.B. "The Burden of Black Women." *Darkwater: Voices from Within the* Veil. 1920. New York: Schocken, 1969. 53-54.

Du Bois, W.E.B. *The Souls of Black Folk*. 1903. New York: Penguin, 1989.

Du Bois, W.E.B. *The World and Africa: An Inquiry into the Part Which Africa Has Played in World History*. New York: Viking, 1946.

Ellis, Joseph. *American Sphinx: The Character of Thomas Jefferson*. New York: Vintage, 1998.

Fanon, Frantz. *Black Skin, White Masks*. Trans. Chartles Lam Markmann. 1952. New York: Grove Press, 1967.

Gilroy, Paul. *The Black Atlantic: Modernity and Double Consciousness*. Cambridge: Harvard UP, 1993.

Felder, Cain Hope. *The Original African Heritage Study Bible*. Nashville: James C. Winston Publishing Co., 1993.

Gates, Henry Louis, Jr. Introduction. *The Classic Slave Narratives*. Henry Louis Gates, Jr. Ed. New York: Mentor/Penguin, 1987. ix-xviii.

Herskovits, Melville J. *The Myth of the Negro Past*. New York: Harper, 1941.

Hine, Darlene Clark. "'In the Kingdom of Culture': Black Women and the Intersection of Race, Gender, and Class." *Lure and Loathing: Essays on Race, Identity, and the Ambivalence of Assimilation*. Ed. Gerald Early. New York: Allen Lane/Penguin Press, 1993. 337-51.

Johnson, James Weldon. "O Black and Unknown Bards." *The Black Poets*. Ed. Dudley Randall. New York: Bantam, 1971. 42-43.

Jones, LeRoi. "Huntng is Not Those Heads on the Wall." *Home: Social Essays*. New York: William Morrow, 1966. 173-78.

Lewis, David Levering. *W.E.B. Du Bois: Biography of a Race: 1868-1919*. New York: Henry Holt, 1993.

Long, Charles H. *Significations: Signs, Symbols, and Images in the Interpretation of Religion*. Philadelphia: Fortress, 1986.

Mazuri, Ali A. *The Africans: A Triple Heritage.* Boston: Little, Brown and Company, 1986.

Moses, Wilson Jeremiah. *Afrotopia: The Roots of African American Popular History.* New York: Cambridge University Press, 1998.

The New Shorter Oxford English Dictionary. Ed. Lesley Brown. Oxford: Clarendon Press, 1973, 1993.

North, Michael. *The Dialect of Modernism: Race, Languages and Twentieth-Century Literature.* New York: Oxford University Press, 1994.

Rampersad, Arnold. *The Art and Imagination of W.E.B. Du Bois.* 1976. New York: Schocken, 1990. 68-90.

Retmar, Roberto Fernández. "Caliban: Notes Toward a Discussion of Culture in Our America." 1971. *Caliban and Other Essays.* Trans. Edward Baker. Minneapolis: University of Minnesota Press, 1989. 3-45.

Roberts, David. "Age of Pyramids: Egypt's Old Kingdom." *Encarta 2000.* Redmond, WA: Microsoft Corp., 1999.

Segal, Charles. "The Music of the Sphinx: The Problem of Language. *Modern Critical Interpretations: Sophocles Oedipus Rex.* Ed. Harold Bloom. New York: Chelsea House, 1988. 127-42.

Snowden, Frank. *Blacks in Antiquity: Ethiopians in the Greco-Roman Experience.* Cambridge, MA: Harvard University Press, 1979. 188-95.

Taylor, Archer. *The Literary Riddle Before 1600.* Berkeley: University of California Press, 1948.

Webster's New Twentieth Century Dictionary of the English Language Unabridged. 2nd ed. Newly Revised. Gen. Editor, Jean L. McKechnie. Cleveland: World Publishing Co., 1968.

Williams, Chancellor. *The Destruction of Black Civilization.* Chicago: Third World Press, 1987.

Williams, Vernon, Jr. *Rethinking Race: Franz Boas and His Contemporaries.* Lexington: University Press of Kentucky, 1996.

Zamir, Shamoon. *Dark Voices: W.E.B. Du Bois and American Thought, 1888-1903.* Chicago: University of Chicago Press, 1995.

Confluence, Confirmation, and Conservation at the Crossroads

Intersecting Junctures in *The Interesting Narrative of the Life* and the *Souls of Black Folks*

Wilfred D. Samuels

We are almost a nation of dancers, musicians, and poets.[1]

And so by fateful chance the Negro folk-song—the rhythmic cry of the slave—stands to-day not simply as the sole American music, but as the most beautiful expression of human experience born this side of the seas.[2]

---

[1]Olaudah Equiano, *The Interesting Narrative of the Life of Olaudah Equiano, Or Gustavus Vassa, The African, Written by Himself* 2 vols [1789] (Coral Gables FL: Mnemosyne Publishing Co, Inc.: 1989). I: 10. All references are to this edition and will appear within the text.

[2] W. E. B. Du Bois, *The Souls of Black Folks.* Edited by David W. Blight and Robert Gooding-Williams ([1903] Boston: Bedford Books, 1997) 186. All references are to this edition and will appear in text.

...before he can look forward in any meaningful sense, [the writer] must first be allowed to take a long look back....I think that the past is all that makes the present coherent...[3]

I've known Rivers ancient as the world and older than
the flow of human blood in human veins.
My soul has grown deep like the rivers.[4]

It seems fitting to begin this medley of voices in celebration and praise for the Harvard scholar, gentleman, and author of the now classic *The Souls of Black Folk* (1903): Dr. William Edward Burghardt Du Bois, with "The Negro Speaks of Rivers," the signature poem of Langston Hughes. Hughes is the poet laureate of the Harlem Renaissance, or more appropriately "The New Negro Manhood Movement," of the 1920's, whose impetus was, in many ways, provided by this author and work. The refrain: "My soul has grown deep like the rivers" is clearly antiphonal. Indeed, it is a celebration and response to Du Bois's call/ claim in *Souls* that the African American's "gift of Spirit" to humanity has been fathomless.[5]

---

[3]James Baldwin, *Notes of a Native Son*, 6.

[4]Langston Hughes, "The Negro Speaks of Rivers," found in *Selected Poems*. My presentation begins with a reading of this poem in its entirety.

I've known rivers:
I've known Rivers ancient as the world and older than
the flow of human blood in human veins.
My soul has grown deep like the rivers
I bathed in the Euphrates when dawns were young.
I built my hut near the Congo and it lulled me to sleep.
I looked up the Nile and raised the pyramids above it.
I heard the singing of the Mississippi when Abe Lincoln
went down to New Orleans, and I've have seen its muddy
bosom turn all golden in the sunset.
I've known rivers:
Ancient, dusky rivers.
My soul has grown deep like the rivers.

[5]Needless to say, Hughes's poem is also a response to County Cullen's "Heritage," in which the refrain: "What is Africa to me" resounds with the speaker's ambivalence towards the notion that Africa is the motherland of as African Americans.

As spokespersons for everyday black folk, men and women whose arbitrary conversion to chattel with the "3/5th clause" of the Constitution of the United States legally denied their humanity, whose continued dehumanization was underwritten by its "separate but equal" affirmation in its 1896 *Plessy v. Ferguson*[6] neo-slavery endorsing decision, and whose ultimate marginalization was justified at the end of the nineteenth century by the pseudo scientific works of a world dominated by notions of "race," Du Bois and Hughes sought to identify, re/claim, and celebrate the deep and complex humanity and spirituality (notice Du Bois pluralized the word "soul") they were firmly convinced were embodied in the very Being—indeed, the very Essence—of "the Negro."[7]

Both Du Bois and Hughes gazed in the direction of Africa to reclaim the Negro's—African's and African American's—primordial place on the human family tree, as well as to describe and inscribe the African's role in human civilization. Describing Africa as "the most marvelous of continents," Du Bois wrote:

---

[6] For an extensive discussion of this Supreme Court decision see *Plessy v. Ferguson, A Brief History with Documents*, ed. Brook Thomas (Boston: Bedford Books, 1997).

[7] David L. Lewis (*W. E. B. Du Bois: Biography of a Race* [New York: Henry Holt and Co., 1993] 276) provides the following succinct picture of this historical juncture:

With rare exception, noted anthropologists located Negroes somewhere on the frontier between the great apes and hominids. Biologists found their average brain weight less than Caucasians'—considerably less than English-speaking Protestants. Psychologists identified a primal sexuality and irrationality in Negroes that were invariably supposed to erupt in situations of intimacy or stress. Physicians predicted their extinction from disease and depravity, while criminologists and eugenicists warned of the menace of Negro brutality and fecundity. The national white consensus emerging at the turn of the century was that African-Americans were inferior human beings whose predicament was three parts their own making and two parts the consequence of misguided white philanthropy. Not long before serving Booker Washington dinner in the White House, a characteristically blunt Theodore Roosevelt had given a nutshell opinion: "A perfectly stupid race can never rise to a very high plane; the negro[sic], for instance, has been kept down as much by lack of intellectual development as by anything else."

The Mystery Solved: The Negro a Beast was one of the notable book titles of 1900, followed two years later by Thomas Dixon's bestseller, *The Leopard's Spots*, a building block for D. W. Griffith's film *The Birth of a Nation*.

On its black bosom arose one of the earliest, if not the earliest, of self protecting civilizations, which grew so mightily that it still furnished superlatives to thinking and speaking men. Out of its darker and more remote forest fastnesses came, if we may credit many recent scientists, the first welding of iron, and we know that agriculture and trade flourished there when Europe was a wilderness ("The Hand of Ethiopia," 939).

Hughes echoes this refrain when his speaker assumes the collective voice of the Negro and unabashedly places himself not only at the site on the continent of Africa associated with the birth of civilization, the Nile River, but also the Euphrates, at the site considered by Western, Christian thought to be the very genesis of humankind, the site of the biblical Garden of Eden, "when dawn was young."

Significantly, in each account, the African (Negro) lacks neither agency nor subjectivity. As the action verbs in Hughes's poem denote, the Negro is no mere sideline observer: he bathes, builds, looks, and hears. In fact, Hughes's signifying game of braggadocio clearly broadens Du Bois's spectrum, for he looks beyond the boundaries of the United States to encompass the totality of humanity. Whereas Du Bois asks: "Your country? How came it yours? Before the Pilgrims landed we were here. Here we have brought our three gifts and mingled them with yours..." ("The Sorrow Songs" 192–193), Hughes's speaker chauvinistically declares that without the Negro there would be no humanity—no civilization. In what is clearly an antiphonal moment with the speaker in James Weldon Johnson's "The Creation," Hughes's speaker rejoins that when the "Unmoved Mover," the "Great I am," stepped out on space to create a world: "clapping his hands to create thunder, lightening, [*sic*] and rain- bringing forth "lakes [that] cuddled down in the hollows of the ground,/*And. . . rivers that ran down to the sea*," the Negro was there; his soul growing deep like the rivers.

Support for their contention comes form Genesis, in which we read that when the Gihon River flowed out of the Garden of Eden, it "compassesth the whole land of Ethiopia," the land of Cush, where the Negro's soul ran deep like the river (Genesis 2:13). Understand immediately, however, that these river beds are not mere valleys of dried bones; for it is here, along the banks of these deep rivers, that one finds what Quincy Troupe calls "sweet memory" in his poems "Skulls Along the River." Ebullient with memory, these "skulls," as Troupe's speaker tells us, carry "memories from the heart [that] are secret arpeggios of spirit / flying toward the light."[8]

Fundamentally, in this essay I wish to propose that *The Souls of Black Folk*, which David Levering Lewis describes as "light enlivening the inert and the despairing," totally embodies Troupe's trope of a "secret arpeggios of spirit / flying toward the light," for in it Du Bois sets out to re/discover, describe, and inscribe that place where he—the son of historic "seventh sons born with a veil"—could not only listen to the bitter-sweet memories echoed in the "strivings in the souls of black folk," but also find within it his *axis mundi*: that is, the nucleus in which the early stages of his historical self was firmly grounded. Aware that, more than three decades after their emancipation, and standing on the threshold of a new millennium, African Americans continued to face perpetual liminality, through the "color line," socio-political oppression and domination, Du Bois sets out to confront the premise and mandate that those who had been made to walk "in darkness" "in the olden days" must continue to do so at the dusk of a new dawn.

Du Bois's dual purpose is visible. First, he sets out to indict the hypocrisy of American democracy—in sum to "show the strange meaning of being black here in the dawning of the Twentieth Century" ("The Forethought" 34); next, and perhaps more important, he sets out to celebrate the unparalleled cultural contributions of Africans / African Americans which, despite their marginalization, made them gift bearers for all humanity—perhaps even the bearers of the "keys to the kingdom" of human salvation—an objective which in its signification, paradoxically and ironically, also reveal "the strange meaning of being black here in the dawning of the Twentieth Century."

In his effort to celebrate the unparalleled cultural contributions of African Americans through song—their "sorrow songs"—Du Bois confirms and, for me most important, conserves Olaudah Equiano's objective of preserving the properties of traditional African life and culture in his eighteenth century autobiography, *The Interesting Narrative of Olaudah Equiano, Or Gustavus Vassa, The African Written by Himself*

---

[8]Found in *Weather Reports: New and Selected Poems* 65–74.

(1789). Conceptually and metaphorically, *The Souls of Black Folk* is Du Bois's vicarious crossing of rivers—his journey from the Housatonic River of Great Barrington, Massachusetts, where he was born: "behind the shadow of the *veil*"—"an outcast and a stranger" ("Of Our Spiritual Strivings" 38)—on 23 February 1868; to the Niger and Cross Rivers, of West Africa's Nigeria, where, in 1745, Olaudah Equiano, the African (Ethiopian), was born in Essaka, "a charming fruitful *vale*," in the Kingdom of Benin. Left with only the "tale of Ethiopia," the "shadow of a mighty Negro past" ("Of Our Spiritual Strivings" 39), and perpetual liminality within the "shadow of the veil," Du Bois descends into Atlantis, the world of "America's dark heritage," to find Equiano's well preserved "nation of dancers, musicians and poets," a world of renewal where songs represent some interesting "scenes of real life" and are "ever new" and renewing.

Thus, my central concern in this essay is with this site of "memories from the heart," or more relevantly stated, memories from the *souls* /spirit of black folk that seduced these men over a century apart. I want to focus briefly on what Du Bois called the "sorrow songs" and the possible connection between them and Africa by exploring moments of confluence and convergence in Du Bois's *The Souls of Black Folks* and Olaudah Equiano's *The Interesting Narrative of the Life of Olaudah Equiano,* a text Du Bois identified as "the beginning of that long series of personal appeals,"[9] the black autobiography. He includes in this series *Up From Slavery,* the life story of his adversary, Booker T. Washington. Other scholars have added *The Souls of Black Folk* to this series of personal appeals, implying, if not directly declaring, the continuing and intertextual relationship between Equiano's text and Du Bois's.[10]

One way to conceive of these songs—to perceive them—is to view them—as the venue through which African slaves and their descendants "escaped" or transcended slavery. Unlike the Africans or their

---

[9]See "The Negro In Literature and Art," 863. Du Bois incorrectly claims Equiano's work was first published in 1787; the correct date is 1789. He identifies Equiano as a literary pioneer, along with poet Phillis Wheatley and engineer Benjamin Banneker.

[10]See for example, Stephen Butterfield, *Black Autobiography in America* (Amherst: University of Massachusetts Press, 1974); William L. Andrews, ed., *African American Autobiography* (Englewood Cliff: Prentice Hall, 1993); Robert Stepto, *From Behind the Veil: A Study of Afro- American Narrative* (Urbana: University of Illinois Press, 1979).

descendants, such as the "flying Africans" in the folk myth, or versions of it found in Morrison's *Song of Solomon*, Paule Marshall's *Praisesong for the Widow*, or Charles Johnson's *Middle Passage*, who take physical flight from slavery; the enslaved black masses and their descendants that wander, like ghosts, in the background of these texts, take metaphoric spiritual flights. An excellent example is offered by Morrison's "uncalled, unrobed, unanointed" Baby Suggs Holy in *Beloved*. Entering "the Clearing," a sacred space of cleansing and rejuvenation, she calls upon the entire "company" (i.e. the community) to laugh, cry, dance, and above all, to love themselves—their heart. At the end, Baby Suggs, Holy "stood up then and danced with her twisted hip the rest of what her heart had to say while the others opened their mouths and gave her the music. Long notes held until the four part harmony was perfect enough for their deeply loved flesh." (*Beloved* 87–89)

"[G]roundlife shuddered under [the] feet" of Morrison's Bluestone Road community of fugitive and former slaves. Central to their existential (re)creation in a slave economy that converted them to chattel are the "sacred words" locked in the "long notes" of their songs—not just the lyrics (the words) but their sound/s, the perfect "four part harmony" they created. Together the words and the sounds create an arpeggio which, like the sounds of the rapidly beating wings of Dunbar's caged bird,[11] become daily metaphoric "spirit / flight toward" the light, i.e.

---

[11]My reference here is to Paul L. Dunbar's masterpiece "Sympathy," which includes the powerful trope of the singing caged bird. Although most are familiar with the beginning of the last stanza: "I know why the caged bird sings," the third stanza has a different image:

I know why the caged bird beats his wing
Till its blood is red on the cruel bar;
For he must fly back to his perch and cling
When he fain would be on the bough a-swing;
And a pain still throbs in the old, old scars
And they pulse again with a keener sting—
I know why he beats his wing!

freedom, although the slaves, like the bird, remain locked "in grey chains in a place / full of winters."[12]

At the end of "Of Our Spiritual Strivings," the first chapter of *The Souls of Black Folk*, Du Bois invites us to pause and "listen to the strivings in the souls of black folk (44), that is, to contemplate, if we could in our wildest imagination, the significance not only of their lost communal life and debasement, but more importantly their quest, despite their negative experiences, for spiritual wholeness. For me, this exercise would provide insight into the genesis of their composite "spirit / flying toward the light" and our own personal renewal and rejuvenation.

Du Bois's invitation (invocation?) provides the moment of confluence between the disparate texts of my focus: *The Souls of Black Folk* and *The Interesting Narrative of Olaudah Equiano*. In recalling the traditional African home from which he was kidnaped at age eleven Equiano provides insights into the truncation that would lead to the genesis of the strivings Du Bois wishes us to meditate over. Equiano writes:

---

[12]See Baraka's "Ka Ba":

We are beautiful people
with african imaginations
full of masks and dances and swelling chants
· ·
Though we sprawl in grey chains in a place
full of winters, when what we want is sun.

We have been captured
Brothers. And we labor
to make our getaway, into
the ancient image, into a new

Correspondence with ourselves
and our black family. We need magic
now we need the spells, to raise up
return, destroy and create. What will be

The sacred words?

We are almost a nation of dancers, musicians, and poets. Thus every great event, such as a triumphant return from battle or other cause of public rejoicing, is celebrated in public dances, which are accompanied with songs and music suited to the occasion....Each represents some interested scene of real life, such as a great achievement, domestic employment, a pathetic story, or some rural sport; and as the subject is generally found on some recent event, it is therefore ever new. (1:10)

In Equiano's re-remembered world, great events are celebrated in dances which are accompanied with the appropriate songs and music. He describes a pastoral world characterized by the harmonious existence of the whole and its parts that stands in stark contrast to the world of slavery Du Bois chronicles both in *Suppression of the African Slave Trade to the United States of America, 1638–1870* (1896)[13] and in *Souls of Black Folk.*

In *The Interesting Narrative of the Life,* Equiano provides an apt description of the functional nature of folk art and oral culture, the heartbeat of traditional societies, a task Du Bois takes on in *Souls.* Through songs and dances, Equiano tells us, his clansmen entertain themselves, instruct the young, and pass on traditions, celebrating in the process group solidarity, achievements, and values. Equiano returns time and again to what we can designate as the most important idyllic image and sustained note of his song: an unspoiled African traditional communal life, which remains the controlling force, he wishes us to believe, in his own life. Africa and Benin-ruled Essaka, his birthplace, remain his *axis mundi,* the nucleus that nurtured the early stages of his life and also around which his adult life vicariously continued to orbit in the face of his sense of perpetual liminality.

Equiano's trope of "a nation of dancers, musicians, and poets" is of singular importance because it establishes the conflict and contradiction that remain the pervasive discordant notes he sounds throughout his narrative: the loss of communal life, initiated with his captivity, removal

---

[13]This document was Du Bois's dissertation. It later became the first published text in Harvard's Department of History's Historical Series, which was first published by Longman, Green & Co., in New York City, not Harvard University Press as it is often claimed. According to Herbert Aptheker, *Suppression* is "the first full length product of Afro-American scientific scholarship" (11).

from his village, placement on the slave ship, journey through the Middle Passage, and ultimate sale on the slave auction block. Unlike the Edenic world of his Ethiopian past, the world of slavery is, like his often referenced movements in Milton's *Paradise Lost*, a plunge into darkness—into hell. Darkness and nocturnal images, representing his "fall" from his luminous world, amplify this theme. Equiano's movement as human cargo on to the slave ship's deck continues this journey into darkness. He experiences the ultimate debasement of this journey downward when he encounters the stench of decay, decomposition, and catabolism in the hold/hole of this floating tomb.

Unlike the spiraling paths of his Ethiopian world that during rituals of rejuvenation lead towards communal renewal and rebirth, the angular roads of economic slavery lead downward to waste tubs into which captured children—symbols of rebirth, rejuvenation and preservation in his beloved Essaka—reduced to human feces, would sometimes fall. In contrast to the choreographed communal movements Essakans take during important communal rituals and ceremonies, one sees Equiano's individual death dance and through his eyes the death dance of now "othered" deracinated Africans. His new song is a dirge, one that is amplified by the piercing sounds of cultural and spiritual death, heard as he crosses what Douglass called "the blood-stained gate, the entrance to the hell of slavery."[14] Unlike his father's "charming fruitful vale," where festive drums and rhythmic music and dance assemble the community together, Equiano becomes a witness to and participant in a world of alienation and decay. He is overcomed by the paralyzing sounds of galling chains, the ear-piercing shrieks of women, and the mournful groans of the dying as his flesh meshes with his new community of commodities. As trope the ship's hold stands at the opposite end of the spectrum from his "charming fruitful vale."

The excruciating separation of family members becomes the most mournful note in Equiano's threnody of his fall. Recalling his own separation and that of others, he indicts and demands: "Is it not enough that we are torn from our country and friends to toil for your luxury and lust of gain?....Surely this [separation of families] is a new refinement in cruelty" (1:88). A final and most discordant note of his elegy is the

---

[14] Douglass, *Narrative of the Life of Frederick Douglass, An American Slave*, 18.

degradation and pollution of his name which, once "mentioned with the greatest of reverence" (1:31), was ruthlessly changed by each successive slave master to names which initially have no cultural significance for Olaudah Equiano, the African (Ethiopian) warrior. Equiano is left only with "memories from the heart" (Essaka and Africa) as he continuously takes flight towards freedom in perpetual land/sea travels.

That Du Bois is concerned with repositories of "memories from the heart [that] are secret arpeggios of spirit/flying toward the light " is concisely inscribed at the beginning of "The Sorrow Songs," Chapter 14 of *The Souls of Black Folk*, where he writes: "They that walked in darkness sang songs in the olden days—Sorrow Songs—for they were weary at *heart*." (185; emphasis added). Here, images of death abound in Du Bois's trope of weary travelers trapped behind the shadow of the veil. Sorrow and darkness, clear signifiers of the shackles of chattel slavery and its impact on black spirituality and literacy, denote the weight of their oppression. Significantly, however, the intended nihilism and erasure are circumvented, though not totally escaped. The venue of their ephemeral wholeness is their empowering songs.

Frederick Douglass gives deft insight into the katharsis provided by these earth shattering sounds, when he describes the slaves' movements through the woods, a movement that resonates with Morrison's "groundlife shudder[ing] under [the] feet" trope in *Beloved*. According to him, the slaves

> [W]ould make the dense old woods, for miles around, reverberate with their wild songs, revealing at once the highest joy and the deepest sadness.
>
> They would compose and sing as they went along, consulting neither time nor tune. The thought that came up, came out—if not in word, in the sound—and as frequently in the one as in the other. They would sometimes sing the most pathetic sentiment in the most rapturous tone, and the most rapturous sentiment in the most pathetic tone.[15]

---

[15] Ibid.

Although created within the confines of Western tradition and its bent towards the written text and literacy, the rhythm and timber of the slaves' songs are unbound; they float in a black (w)hole of timelessness. Their ancient properties: spontaneity and improvisation, become incantations of re/creative power-energy grounded in orality; "every thought" could be represented not only "in the word" (logos) but also in the sound. In noting the spontaneity and improvisational quality of the "sorrow songs," Douglass resonates with Equiano, calling attention to a legacy bequeathed by Africans who, like him, were extirpated from "a nation of dancers, musicians, and poets."

To indicate the significance of these sorrow songs and their role as venues to spiritual flight, healing, and rejuvenation, Du Bois begins the fourteen chapters of his masterpiece with bars of music taken from the master songs of the former slaves as epigrams. Ultimately, each song confirms that African slaves were not consumed by the inferno they entered in the slave ship's hold/hole Equiano described. Stated differently, the sorrow songs clearly indicate that, despite the fact that African slaves sang about their alienation in such songs as "Nobody Knows the Trouble I've Seen" and "Motherless Child," they, like Douglass, also declared through their songs: "You have seen how man was made a slave; you shall see how a slave was made a man"(47). Songs, such as "My Lord what a mourning when the stars begin to fall," which Du Bois intentionally places at the beginning of Chapter II: "Of the Dawn of Freedom," which focus on emancipation and reconstruction, were not merely "songs of the End, but also of the Beginning." ("The Sorrow Songs" 188). They are sounds of hopeful, not hopeless, strife, a fact that gives this particular song "militant overtones."[16]

Thus, in the end, Du Bois would have us to believe that, paradoxically, out of Equiano's inconceivable slave ship hold's "scene of horror," the Africans, who for him were "primarily...artist[s]," rose to give the world their greatest gift: their song. He chauvinistically declares: "And so by fateful chance the Negro folk-song—the rhythmic cry of the

---

[16]I am borrowing here from Eric Sundquist who argues in his *To Wake The Nations: Race in the Making of American Literature* (Cambridge: Harvard University Press, 1994), a title he takes from the title of this spiritual, that Du Bois's use of "mourning" rather than "mourning" "has militant overtones of [Du Bois's] own sometimes strident rhetoric and polemical use of literature" (2).

slave—stands today not simply as the sole American music, but as the most beautiful expression of human experience born this side of the seas" ("The Sorrow Songs" 186); and he argues for the inevitability of this specific offering: "To America, the Negro could bring only his music, but that was quite enough. The only real American music is that of the Negro American."[17]

To reiterate, in his effort to celebrate what he saw as the the unparalleled cultural contributions of African Americans through their songs, Du Bois confirms and conserves the continuity of the "nation of dancers, musicians, and poets" Equiano vociferously celebrates in his *Interesting Narrative of the Life* more than a hundred years before he published *The Souls of Black Folk*. Unlike the Calvinist settlers of New England whose "errand into the wilderness" led them to envision a providentially designed and clearly stratified "city upon a hill," and western Europeans settlers whose amalgamation resulted in an American "melting pot" which, according to J. Hector St. John de Crevecouer, created "a new [white] race," Africans, reluctant voyagers and perpetual strangers in a strange land, conserved semblances of their *gemeinshaft*: their "nation of dancers musicians, and poets," from their assigned place in the margin, "six rods distance."[18]

Du Bois comes face to face with this restored "nation" when he enters a "village" in the rustic South, while working as a country school teacher. Traveling one evening up a dry river bed: "up the stony bed of a creek, past wheat and corn"—a setting that mirrors the one traveled by Troupe's speaker in "Skulls Along the River," one that clearly stands at the opposite spectrum of the "fertile soil" and "charming fruitful vale" of Equiano's Essaka—Du Bois witnesses for the first time ever a Southern Negro revival. He is drawn to it by "rhythmic cadence of song—soft, thrilling, powerful that swelled and died sorrowfully in our ears" ("Of the Faith of the Fathers" 148). Du Bois recalls:

And so most striking to me, as I approached the *village* and the little plain church perched aloft, was the air of intense excitement

---

[17] "The Negro in Literature and Art," 862.

[18] See Crevecour's "Letter III" in *Letters From An American Farmer* and John Winthrop's *A Model of Christian Charity*.

that possessed that *mass of black folk.* A sort of suppressed terror hung in the air and seemed to seize us,—a pythian madness, a demoniac possession, that lent *terrible reality to song and word....* *The people moaned and fluttered, and then the gaunt-cheeked brown skinned woman beside me suddenly leaped straight into the air and shrieked* like a lost soul, while round about came wail and groan and outcry, and a scene of human passion such as I had never conceived before. (148-149; emphasis added)

Indeed, Du Bois journeys back to a familiar site. Ultimately, in this new world "village," this "mass of black folk" form a "nation" whose metaphoric dance lend "terrible reality to song and word." Indeed, Du Bois recalls Douglass's singing slaves whose "thought...came up, came out—if not in word, in sound"; and resonates with Morrison's clearing where "Long notes held until the four part harmony was perfect enough for [the dancers] deeply loved flesh."

Perhaps more important, however, Du Bois recalls Equiano's communal rituals and rites that represented some "interesting scene of real life." To circumvent any confusion about what he had witnessed, Du Bois explains that the revival scene he had witnessed had, "Sprung from the African forests, where its counterpart can still be heard, it was adapted, changed, and intensified by the tragic soul-life of the slave, until under the stress of law and whip, it became the one true expression of a people's sorrow, despair, and hope." ("Of the Faith of the Fathers" 149) However, Du Bois's New England eyes prevent him from conceiving this scene from any other perspective than that of a witness; a stranger to physical slavery, he can not be a participant in the way that Douglass, Stamp Paid, or Baby Suggs Holy were "witness[es] and participant[s],"or as Equiano was a witness and a participant in Essaka's communal dance.[19]

---

[19]In reporting Captain Anthony's brutal beating of his Aunt Hester, Douglass wrote: "I remember the first time I ever witnessed this horrible exhibition. I was quite a child, but I will remember it. I never shall forget it whilst I remember any thing [sic]. It was the first of a long series of such outrages, of which I was doomed to be a *witness and a participant.* It struck me with awful force. It was the blood-stained gate, the entrance to the gate, the entrance to the hell of slavery, through which I was about to pass. It was a most terrible spectacle. I wish I could commit to paper the feelings with which I beheld it." (18–19; emphasis added) Douglass adamantly distinguishes the two perspectives. One may know vicariously about slavery by looking from a distance—from the outside in

Nevertheless, this is a significant juncture of intertextualization between *The Souls of Black Folk* and the *Interesting Narrative of the Life*, for here Du Bois metaphorically descent from his Berkshire home, a space within distance from Winthrop's "city upon a hill," into the backwoods of Georgia resonates with Equiano's journey from Essaka down into the slave ship's hold, where he (Equiano) becomes both witness and participant. The church *revival* (a word whose importance lies its signification of restoration) signifies in many ways on the scene in the slave ship hold/hole, where Equiano encountered the "shrieks of the women and the groans of the dying, [which] rendered the whole scene of horror almost inconceivable" (159). The differences are significant, however; for whereas Equiano's scene of horror is "inconceivable" because of the sheer physical violence and brutality against humanity it represents, Du Bois's revival scene of "suppressed terror" is "most striking" because it literally boggles the mind that those who had witnessed and participated, like Equiano, in the experience of the Middle Passage, had retained not only the will to live but had done so with fiendish passion—"pythian madness"—a transformative death-dance and transcendence to a higher, spiritual level. Theirs is the power of self resurrection, restoration, and transcendence from physical and meta-phoric death; and music—the "rhythmic cadence of song—soft, thrilling, powerful" is their vehicle. In his "long look back"—his assessment of the past—Du Bois succeeds in making, as Baldwin suggests, "the present more coherent."

Ultimately, the intertextual junctures I have focused on thus far suggest that the similarities and differences in Equiano's and Du Bois's lives are bracketed by the similarities and differences between "veil" and "vale," for whereas Equiano's "charming fruitful vale" signifies a nurturing space, a womb, the vast veil young William encountered in his "wee wooden schoolhouse" when his classmate refused his card—"refused it—peremptorily with a glance"—shut him out, demanding that he, like other blacks, shrink "into tasteless sycophancy, or into silent hatred of the pale white world around them" ("Of Our Spiritual Strivings" 38). Young William resolved to not make his a "tragic

---

(witness), but this is not the same as knowing from first-hand experience, i.e., as a participant, or from the inside out.

soul life of the slave," to not act in bad faith and falsehood, but instead to set in motion what Troupe calls "spirit / flying towards the light," even if it meant reconfiguring the meaning of metaphoric physical death, as the adult Du Bois does upon the passing of his first born son. Reflecting, Du Bois poignantly wrote: "All that day and all that night there sat an awful gladness in my heart / nay blame me not if I see the world thus darkly through the Veil, / and my soul whispers ever to me, saying, 'Not dead, not dead but escaped; not bond but free'" ("Of the Passing of the First Born" 162).

Despite the obvious distance from the slave ship's hold to the wee school house, however, Du Bois's and Equiano's personal histories also converge on the continent of Africa, in the germinal soul sound he comes to value and celebrate as a child in the shadows of the Housatonic. He confirms as much when he recalls the legacy he inherited from his maternal great grandmother, an African who had "been seized by an evil Dutch trader" (187) and made a slave during the eighteenth century.[20] He records: "[C]oming to the valleys of the Hudson and Housatonic, black, little, and lithe, she shivered and shrank in the harsh winds, looked longingly at the hills and often crooned a heathen melody to the child between her knees, thus: "Do ba-na co-ba me, ge-ne me! Do ba-na co-ba me, ge-ne me! Ben d' nu-li, nu-li, nu-li, ben d' le." (187)

Du Bois's recollection of his African grandmother's (his surrogate mother) prescriptive role echoes Equiano's recollection of his relationship with his African mother. "As I was the youngest of the sons, I became, of course, the greatest favourite [sic] with my mother, and was always with her; and she used to take particular pains to form my mind" (1:47). More importantly, Du Bois's recollection of his African grandmother's song validates David Roediger's contention that "African imports sustained—on a conscious level—a love for Africa and even a desire to return there"; and that "subsequent generations of slaves...often cherished a positive image of Africa. In fact, Du Bois seems to also endorse Roediger's conclusion that the enslaved's pride in Africa "constituted one source of psychological strength which enabled the slaves to preserve their humanity and powers of resistance in the face of

---

[20]Du Bois's maternal grandfather was Othelo Burghardt, whose grandfather was Tom Burghardt. Little is known of Tom's wife, who taught the young William this song.

severe oppression."[21] Young William's place between his grandmother's knees positions him in the role of novice; for, like Equiano, he, too, was being "trained up from [his] early years" (Equiano 1:47) about tradition African culture. The degree to which Equiano learned well his lesson is found in his declaration over forty years later that: "whether the love of one's country be real or imaginary, or a lesson of reason, or an instinct of nature, I still look back with pleasure on the first scenes of my life, though that pleasure has been for the most part mingled with sorrow" (1:46)—perhaps the sorrow Du Bois heard recorded in the sorrow songs.

Similarly Du Bois testifies to the merit of the lessons his grandmother passed on orally from generation to generation. He tells us that "the children sang it to his children and they to their children's children and so two hundred years it has traveled down to us and we sing it to our children, knowing as little as our fathers what its words may mean, but knowing well the meaning of its music" ("The Sorrow Songs" 188).

Rhetorically, Du Bois's construction or words and sounds that "travel down to us" and "we sing it to our children" resonates loudly with the function of folk art and oral culture, the heartbeat of traditional societies, which Equiano claimed as his legacy. This is a legacy that has not been lost or destroyed, not even with more than two centuries of slavery. In fact, Equiano's record of a sense of a communal essence and being ("we are") in his declaration that his cultural legacy was provided by his well stratified "nation of dancers, musicians, and poets" is indirectly echoed by Du Bois. The language of the community might have been lost, but not "the meaning of the music."

Ultimately, the sounds and lessons Du Bois heard and learned while sitting between his grandmother's knees—ones produced by former bondsmen and women-embody the "articulate message for the world" ("The Sorrow Songs" 187) they provided as legacy. The multifaceted significance of Du Bois's premise clearly includes the way he confronts prevailing notions that African Americans were the source of every ill in America at the turn of the twentieth century, when the real question confronting African Americans was: "How does it feel to be a problem?" ("Of Our Spiritual Strivings 37"). However, most important is his use of the word "articulate," for with it Du Bois revisits and revises the very way

---

[21]Roediger, "The Meaning of Africa for the American Slave," 9.

African slaves and their descendants were written into the American canon, not merely in the Constitution, in which, as noted earlier, their status as chattel was denoted by the 3/5 clauses, but also by such writers as Jefferson and, above all, Crévecouer best known for his America-is-a-melting pot trope in "Letter III" of his *Letter From An American Farmer.*

Crévecouer is less well known for the "inarticulate monosyllables" he puts into the mouth of the "Negro," although the now classic scene in "Letter IX" in which he does so is as disturbing today as it must have been when he first created it in the mid-eighteenth century. On his way to dinner with the landed gentry of Charleston's plantocracy, Crévecouer's gentleman farmer protagonist, while traveling through "the pleasant woods," became, in his words, "a witness" to a most horrific scene. Interestingly enough, he is first drawn to the scene by "a sound resembling a deep rough voice" that "uttered...a few *inarticulate monosyllables*" (emphasis added). He names the source *before* he sees it. Finally, at "six rods distance" he "perceives" the source of the sound: a bird covered "cage, suspended in the limbs of a tree"; and, as he later confesses, "horrid to think and painful to repeat...a Negro, suspended in the cage and left there to expire." The birds had picked out the victim's eyes, his cheekbones were bare, his body covered with "a multitude of wounds," and "from the laceration from which he was disfigured, the blood slowly-dropped and tinged the ground beneath."[22] Crévecouer describes his Black Christ-figure as a "living spectre" still capable of speech, though only in an "uncouth dialect." (178)

Although Crevecouer's Gentleman Farmer walks away from this horrific scene to dine with friends and contemplate the "fate of this Negro," and despite his sympathetic tone throughout his letter, it is clear that, as a member of the gentry class and himself a slave owner, Crévecouer (and his gentleman farmer) did much to seal the "fate of the Negro" and insure the marginalization of his well-marked, commodified, and totally liminal black body, denying him the right to his own empowering gaze, and "othering" his voice with the label of inarticulateness—of barbarity. Thus, whether by design or accident, this literary "founding father" contributed to the "caricature and defilement" (if I may borrow Du Bois's description of how the sorrow songs had been

---

[22]Crevecour, *Letter From an American Farmer,* "Letter IX," 177–78.

mistreated) of the black speaking voice which he places "six rods distance" from the privilege path of the mainstream.[23]

Significantly, in inscribing and celebrating, like Equiano, the trope of Africa and the African past Du Bois casts his hat into the ring of prevailing debates about "race"—traceable to the eighteenth-century notion of a "Great Chain of Being." In fact, Du Bois redefines (if not supercedes) Crévecouer's premise of a western European melting pot of a "new race of men" from which black Africans and their descendants were excluded. Acknowledging that African Americans have been impacted by the arbitrary action of "a world which yields him no true self consciousness, but only lets him see himself through the revelations of the other world," and confessing: "It is a peculiar sensation, this double consciousness, this sense of always looking at one's self through the eyes of others, a measuring of one's soul by the tape of a world that looks on in amused contempt and pity," Du Bois boldly argues that the African American "would not bleach his Negro soul in a flood of white Americanism." Is this another way of saying the Negro would not care to enter the "melting pot?" In fact, for Du Bois, the African American wished "to merge his double self into a better and truer self, " though not at the expense of his older (African) self, nor would he "Africanize America, for America has too much to teach the world and Africa." Ultimately important, Du Bois chauvinistically advocates: "the Negro blood has a message for the world"(38).

Du Bois's emphasis continues to be on the spiritual, for it is his "Negro soul" not his Negro skin, that the Negro, in Du Bois's word, would not whiten or make devoid of color, i.e. bleach. Whereas the latter would be no less than a re/shackling of the already liminal and oppressed black body, the former continues their loftier spiritual quest for liberation and freedom, body and spirit, their "flight / towards light," begun at the moment of their extirpation from Africa. In the face of a rush towards whiteness at the turn of the twentieth century, African Americans held firm, wishing only to merge into a "better and truer self." Unlike the KKK whose rampant lynchings were unprecedented,[24] and

---

[23] See particularly "Letter IX" of *Letters from an American Farmer.*

[24] According to Lewis there were ninety-nine lynchings in 1901, a period that historian Rayford Logan called the nadir in the African American experience. See *W. E. B. Du Bois,* 275.

whose white sheet was meant to signify the whiteness and purity of their very soul, black Africans and their African American descendants had a more creative and salubrious message for the world, one that required the conservation of their spirit/their soul, an entity that even in its abstractness was not a biological misnomer like "race."

Thus, with his use of the word "blood" Du Bois not only signifies on Crévecouer's trope of a "new *race* of men" (the "biological" creation of amalgamating western Europeans-a transformation from nationality to racial identity), but with it he correctly identifies "race" as the critical variable in the African American's *ad infinitum* striving, even on the threshold of a new century. As Henry L. Gates tells us in "Writing 'Race' and the Difference It Makes," during the eighteenth century, more than a century before the publication of *Souls of Black Folk*, "race" had crystalized into a trope of "irreducible difference between cultures, linguistic groups or adherents of specific belief systems...."[25] However, decades before Gates, while arguing about the arbitrariness or "race" wrote, "The biological criteria used to determine 'difference' in sex simply do not hold when applied to 'race,'" Du Bois, writing in "The conservation of Races," advanced a similar thesis, although he warned that "in our calmer moments, we must acknowledge that human beings are divided into races" (229).

Identifying what he considered to be eight "distinctly differentiated races" in the world, Du Bois argued that "while race differences have followed mainly physical race lines, yet no mere physical distinctions would really define or explain the deeper differences—the cohesiveness and continuity of these groups. The deeper differences are spiritual, psychical, differences...a common history, common law and religion, similar habits of thought and a consciousness striving together for certain ideals of life." Du Bois concluded that "The full, complete Negro message of the whole Negro race has not yet been given to the world." (231–32)

In the end, on the one hand, as Anthony Appiah correctly points out, Du Bois's did no more than offer a "sociohistorical conception of race" that transcended prevailing "scientific—that is biological and anthropological conceptions of race," which he (Appiah) equates with a "classical dialectic" that Sartre once called "antiracist racism." Du Bois's

---

[25] Henry Louis Gates, 5.

premise on the sociohistorical concept of race, Appiah maintains, is no more than the antithesis to a prevailing thesis that denies difference.[26]

Appiah asks: "If he has fully transcended the scientific notion of race, what is the role of this talk of "blood?" Be that as it may, on the other hand, one thing is clear, Du Bois was convinced that biological "race" differences were not to be prioritized over the cultural uniqueness of any one group, and certainly not above what for him was "the solidarity of human progress." Each group had specific roles to play—specific gifts to give humanity. Du Bois maintained that "The solidarity of human interests in a world which is daily becoming physically smaller, cannot afford to grope in darkness as to the causes and incentives to human advances when the *advance of all depends increasingly on the advance of each*" ("The Development of a People" 239; emphasis added).

That African Americans had much to offer the world, and, indeed, contributing "to the advance of all," culturally and even scientifically, is the message that undergirds the Negro Exhibit which Du Bois took to Paris, France, during l'Eposition Universelle de 1900—still considered the greatest of all French exhibitions. The exhibition's motto: *Le bilan du siècle* (the summation of the century), concisely stated its pivotal objective, while indirectly naming the Negro, with his inclusion, as a meaningful player in human progress. Designed in part for an international intellectual elite to display its scholarly and technical knowledge and progress, the exposition of 1900 was, according to Richard D. Mandell, "the last time anyone tried to include all of man's activity in one display."[27]

In response to the French's specific request for a "Negro Section" Du Bois compiled, with the assistance of Daniel A. P. Murray of the Library of Congress, Thomas Calloway, and feminist photographer Francis Benjamin Johnston, "The Negro Exhibit," a "panorama of progress" that, housed in the Palace of Social Science, became an award-winning display of musical compositions, books by African American authors (for example the poetry of Paul Laurence Dunbar and fiction of Charles Chesnutt), photographs, models, maps, patents, and plans from

---

[26]See "Illusions of Race," *In My Father's House, Africa in the Philosophy of Culture,* 28–46.

[27]See Richard D. Mandell, *Paris, 1900* (Toronto: University of Toronto Press, 1967) xi.

several black universities, including Atlanta, Fisk, Howard, Hampton, and Tuskegee. The exhibit showed the world African Americans "studying, examining, and thinking of their own progress, and prospect."[28]

To no small degree, through "The Negro Exhibit" DuBois (who would soon embark on a major leadership role in the Pan African Movement) set out to refocus the French's obsession with African culture and the black (Nubian) body which was most evident in the financially successful ethnographic exhibitions (human zoos) staged in public parks and fairgrounds, sponsored at first by the Jardin D'Acclimatation and later by a government with dreams of a colonial empire in Africa. Through these venues the French gazed at the bodies of black African "subjects" in their natural habitat, "going about their daily routine displaying what life was like in distant lands."[29] Members of the French Anthropological Society, particularly those interested in craniometry, reaped tremendous benefits, as they were able to have, through these exhibitions, a conveniently available laboratory in which to measure not only skull shape and volume that is, the brain size and intelligence of their black "subjects," but also all aspects of human anatomy, though not without some limitations, as a society member reveals in his lament that "The only thing we could not do was to examine and measure genital organs. It was not possible to see any lower than the upper part of pubic areas."[30]

By assuming an active, leadership role in re/presenting Africans and African Americans in the Negro Exhibit, literally by including his own series of photographs, Du Bois engages, in words and action, in a signifying act of deformation; he refuses, as Houston Baker asserts, the "master's nonsense"—slave and colonial—to transcend "the veil" or the "barrier of American [and global]racial segregation that keeps Afro-Americans always behind the color line."[31] He celebrates a cultural triumph and spirituality that moves beyond the physicality and

---

[28]Du Bois, "The American Negro in Paris," 577.
[29]See William H. Schneider, *An Empire for the Masses: the French Popular Image of Africa, 1870–1900* (Westport CT: Greenwood, 1982) 124–201.
[30]Schneider 131.
[31] Turner, "W. E. B. Du Bois and the Theory of a Black Aesthetic," 74.

materiality of class and race to a level where the "most beautiful expression of human experience" is found.

In the end, in *The Souls of Black Folk* and other works, Du Bois did not set out to lament but to record and celebrate a personal and communal praise song and journey that had moved generations of African slaves and their descendants from sites of negation and erasure where they were perceived, described and defined on a spectrum that ran from "property" to "problem," to a sacred space of ritual celebration where, as gift bearers, they bring their songs to humanity. Du Bois wrote, "Little beauty has America given the world save the rude grandeur God himself stamped on her bosom, the human spirit in this new world has expressed itself in vigor and ingenuity rather than in beauty" ("The Sorrow Songs" 185–86).

Here, Du Bois, like Johnson's god, steps out on space-beyond the midnight blackness of racial debates prevalent at the turn of the twentieth-century to create light. With his pronouncements of black existential self-creation in the face of nihilism, he makes the invisible visible and chivalrously—even chauvinistically—carves in the heart of American culture, indeed human culture, an indelible place for the "Negro spirituals," the religious music of former slaves *and* for their creators: Africans and African Americans.

Significantly, by pairing these songs with European verses as epigraphs at the beginning of each chapter in *The Souls of Black Folk*, Du Bois, as Lewis correctly notes, "advance[d] the then—unprecedented notion of the creative parity and complementarity of white and black folk alike"; and, in doing so, he acted in a "profoundly subversive" manner towards the hierarchy of his time (278). Du Bois's action makes him, as Darwin T. Turner maintains, a forerunner to the black aesthetic in literature movement, which "even before the Harlem 'Renaissance'...was articulated distinctively by W. E. B.DuBois."[32]

[B]efore the New Negro movement had been labeled, years before Langston Hughes insisted upon the right of new artists to express their individual dark-skinned selves without caring whether they pleased white or black audiences, W. E. B. Du Bois proposed a Black Aesthetics or—as I prefer to designate it in

---

[32] Baker, *Modernism and the Harlem Renaissance*, 53–69

relation to Du Bois—a theory of art from the perspective of black Americans.[33]

In the end it must be said that perhaps Du Bois's action was not totally unprecedented, for Equiano's behavior can also be described as "profoundly subversive." Equiano's *The Interesting Narrative of the Life*, his "readerly," eighteenth-century auto/biography, is simultaneously a "speakerly" praise song, a regenerative communal celebration and performance for Essaka and its great warrior, Olaudah Equiano, one that confirms the African proverb: *"I am because we are!"* Stated differently, with a single stroke of his pen, Equiano writes and sings himself into being, moving the black literary tradition closer to western culture, while simultaneously anchoring it to the foundation of his own traditional African culture: African oral lore and praise song.

Herein lies the ultimate significance of the confluence between the Harvard scholar, Dr. W. E. B. Du Bois, and the former Ibo slave, Olaudah Equiano, whose eighteenth-century narrative, *The Interesting Narrative of the Life of Olaudah Equiano*, like the *Souls of Black Folk*, called into question prevailing myths about Africans in the Old and New Worlds, subversively challenged the hierarchy of their time. To a world that sought to shackle Africans and their descendants to the bottom wrung of a sub/human ladder, to a world whose cultural bearers claimed "there never was a civilized nation of any other complexion other than white, nor even any individual eminent either in action or speculation. No ingenious manufacturers amongst them, no arts no sciences," as does Hume in "Of National Characters" (1748), Equiano and Du Bois thunderously replied: *"We are almost a nation of dancers, musicians, and poets."*[34] Indeed, Du Bois claims that from the rhythmic cries of this nation comes *"the most beautiful expression of human experience."* Indeed Sundquist is correct in identifying *The Souls of Black Folk* as Du Bois's resurrecting trumpet call to awaken the "nations": "at once the spirits (souls) of the ancestors, on American soil and in the homeland of Africa; the many nations of Africa historically represented in the diaspora; and

---

[33]Recorded in Gates, "Writing 'Race' and the Difference it Makes," 10.

[34]This is not the same concept as "Ethiopianism" which, as Wilson Moses tells us, includes the argument "that Africans are a special people with special gifts and that blacks are in some ways superior to whites." See "The Poetics of Ethiopianism," 95.

those present generations who still lead an underground existence, subjugated by the neo-slavery of segregation but nevertheless drawing sustaining spiritual power from the heritage of slave culture"(2), from Equiano's "nation of dancers, musician, and poets."

Racial Capitalism in a Global Economy:

The "Double-Consciousness" of Black Business in the Economic Philosophy of W. E. B. Du Bois

Juliet E. K. Walker

Introduction

W. E. B. Du Bois stands as an intellectual force in American and international world thought. As Adolph Reed said in his book, *W. E. B. Du Bois and American Political Thought*, "'Du Bois is generally recognized as a central figure in the history of Afro-American politics, a major contributor to more than a half-century's debate over the condition of and proper goals and strategies for blacks in the United States, and more broadly, peoples of African descent worldwide."[1] Yet, while Du Bois's work is consulted, essentialized, referenced, and reassessed for virtually every aspect of African-American life, culture, thought, and history, scholars and intellectuals, paradoxically, have peripheralized their assessments of Du Bois's pronouncements on black business.[2] It is not

---

[1] Adolph L. Reed, Jr., *W. E. B. Du Bois and American Political Thought: Fabianism and the Color Line* (New York: Oxford University, 1997) 3.

[2] Also Joseph P. DeMarco, *The Social Thought of W. E. B. Du Bois* (Lanham MD: University Press of America, 1983); Thomas E. Harris, *Analysis of the Clash Over the Issues Between Booker T. Washington and W. E. B. Du Bois* (New York: Garland Publishers,

that these commentaries have ignored his economic thought, analysis, and pronouncements on capitalism, race, class, colonialism, imperialism, Marxism, socialism, pan-Africanism, decolonization, communism, the Cold War, and world peace. It is just that those discussions have not been framed within the context of Du Bois's economic thought regarding African American business for the up-lift of the race.[3]

Rather, intellectual discourse in its emphasis on Du Bois's economic thought continues to focus on his bitter, scathing, and sharp-edged critiques of the reality of capitalism as well as his theoretical assessments of its demise. Yet, despite Du Bois's pronouncements on the death of capitalism, his predilection for Marxism, and his commentaries on the economic potential of communism, African Americans have not embraced socialism, except for those who profess an ideological and intellectual affinity to Marxism. Even Du Bois had problems with the limitations of Marxism in that racism precluded any hope of the unity of black and white workers.[4] Moreover, with the exception of Cuba, communism is dead, while capitalism at the dawn of the new millennium propels the global economy.

Still, in his economic thought on the place of black business activity in American life, Du Bois moved beyond theory and intellectual discourse.

1993) and David L. Lewis, *W. E. B. Du Bois: Biography of a Race, 1868-1919* (New York: Henry Holt, 1993), both considered the definitive studies for their respective time periods. Also, Rayford Whittingham Logan, ed., *W. E. B. Du Bois: A Profile* (New York: Hill and Wang, 1971), Elliott Rudwick, *W. E. B. Du Bois, Propagandist of the Negro Protest* (New York: Atheneum, 1968; originally published as *W. E. B. Du Bois: A Study in Minority Group Leadership* [Philadelphia: University of Pennsylvania Press, 1960]).

[3] Juliet E. K. Walker, *The History of Black Business in America: Capitalism, Race, Entrepreneurship* (New York/London: Macmillan/Prentice Hall International, 1998). Historically, black business activities have been suppressed in the nation's economic life since the colonial era. Indeed, there were more laws suppressing the economic activities of both slave and freedmen than there were laws suppressing both the militant and day-to-day resistance of slaves. Yet, even Du Bois just a generation away from the institution had underestimated the extent to which there was an antebellum black economy and businesspeople, when he made the comment in that the post-Civil War business class emerged from the house servant class. To the contrary—the post-Civil War business class for the fifteen years or so after the Civil War represented a continuation of the self-employed activities of blacks that had existed before the Civil War.

[4] W. E. B. Du Bois, "Social Planning for the Negro past and Present," *Journal of Negro Education* 5 (January 1936): 110-25.

His proposals on the economic survival of blacks, first, through black capitalism operating in a separate economy and, then, through the development of cooperative enterprise were formulated pragmatically, based on the reality that, while free enterprise propelled business in America and was the basis of wealth accumulation, racial capitalism limited black economic equality. As he said, and quite bluntly at that: "the chief and only obstacle to the coming of that kingdom of economic equality which is the only logical end of work, is the determination of the white world to keep the black worker poor and make themselves rich."[5] Du Bois's formulations on racial capitalism were reinforced by the rising tide of segregation, discrimination, and the oppressive labor exploitation not only of blacks in America, but also of people of color throughout the world. Consequently, within the context of Pan-Africanism and the economic iniquities inherent in colonialism and imperialism, Du Bois advanced black economic thought in his formulation of racial capitalism.

The focus of this essay, then, is to broaden analysis of Du Bois's economic thought within the context of the dichotomy inherent in his intellectual discourse on black business activity. Included in this discussion are assessments on Du Bois's promotion of black capitalism in a separate economy. Also, his views on black business education are considered, particularly within the context of his "Talented Tenth." In addition, Du Bois's activities to encourage black economic cooperatives are assessed. The economic position of African Americans at the end of the twentieth century is assessed. Despite Du Bois's scathing criticism on capitalism and his concern for people of color worldwide, he recognized the reality of black Americans living in a capitalist society in which wealth was derived from business activity. And, just as Du Bois denounced the economic and labor exploitation of blacks by whites, he also expressed apprehension for what he viewed as the potential exploitative power of black capitalists: "If this capital is going to be controlled by a few [black] men for their own benefit, then we are destined to suffer from our own capitalists exactly what we are suffering from white capitalists." On the other hand, he added, that, "while this is not a pleasant prospect, it is

---

[5] W. E. B. Du Bois, "The Negro College," *The Crisis* (1933) in David Levering Lewis, ed., *W. E. B. Du Bois: A Reader* (New York: Henry Holt and Company, 1995).

certainly no worse than the present actuality."[6] Within the conceptual frame of Du Bois's construct of racial capitalism, black business participation in a global economy is problematized within the construct of American neocolonialism.

Before proceeding with my assessments of Du Bois's economic thought, I would first like to establish my construct of his "double consciousness." Invariably, traditional intellectual discourse of Du Bois's "double consciousness," is distinguished by critical, but theoretical, philosophical, social, political, literary, theological, and psychological analyses. As a historian, however, my formulation of Du Bois's double consciousness proceeds from the construct inherent in the work of Shamoon Zamir who said that: "The frequency with which Du Bois's description [of the double consciousness] is used suggests that it is commonly accepted as a universally and transhistorically true analysis of a tragic aspect of an African-American self-consciousness." However, he said, "Du Bois's dramatization of 'double-consciousness' is [instead] a historically specific and class-specific psychology." Within this context of historical reality and class-specific psychology, Zamir contends that: "The account of 'double-consciousness' in the first chapter of *Souls* represents the black middle-class elite facing the failure of its own progressive ideal in the late nineteenth century, in the aftermath of failed Reconstruction and under the gaze of a white America."[7]

Certainly Du Bois was a representative member of the black middle class and, within the context of Zamir's construct of Du Bois's "double consciousness," Harvard University's first black Ph.D. was confronted with the failure of what he considered were progressive ideas in the economic programs he formulated for black America. While Du Bois

---

[6] W. E. B. Du Bois, "The Class Struggle," *The Crisis* 22 (June 1921): 55-56.

[7] Shamoon Zamir, *Dark Voices: W. E. B. Du Bois and American Thought, 1888-1903* (Chicago: University of Chicago Press, 1995) 116, considered the most critical and thorough examination of *The Souls of Black Folk*. Also, Reed, W. E. B. *Du Bois and American Political Thought,* 92-99 for brief but thoughtful assessments of Du Bois's "double consciousness" in the works of some thirty-four scholars in several fields from the 1920s to the early 1990s. Only seven are historians, while others are sociologists, political scientists, sociologists, philosophers, and literary critics. Reed states that he "argues that Du Bois's double consciousness was embedded most significantly in the new-Lamarckian thinking about race, evolution, and social hierarchy that prevailed in a strain of reform-oriented, fin-de-siecle American social science."

recognized that men with business acumen were needed to ensure the economic uplift of the black community, the development of a black capitalist class, however, stood in contradistinction to the egalitarian basis of the cooperative enterprises he envisioned. Inherent in Du Bois's economic philosophy on black business activity, as it developed, was that the primary motivating force should be the pursuit of profits for the purpose of investment in the economic uplift of the black community as opposed to the pursuit of profits for individual gain and wealth accumulation.

Unable to persuade black businessmen to eschew profits for personal gain Du Bois, whose whole life was devoted to the achievement of racial equality and the integration of blacks in American life, found himself not only promoting black capitalism in a separate economy but also a socialist-based black economic cooperative movement. Consequently, perhaps in no way more than in his economic philosophy do we see the conflict inherent in Du Bois's "double consciousness," when problematized pragmatically within the context of his failure to find resolution not only to his "two-ness,—[as] an American [and as] a Negro," but also his failure to find resolution to his "two thoughts, two unreconciled strivings; two warring ideals," as he grapple with whether capitalism or socialism could provide the answer to his goal of finding economic justice for African Americans. My focus on Du Bois's "double-consciousness" proceeds, then, by way of illuminating the two "warring ideals" inherent in his economic thought on black business, with the focus on his pragmatic responses to black economic injustices that were formulated from a strong sense of historical consciousness that throughout his life were at "war" with his theoretical constructs on race and culture.

BLACK BUSINESS

In assessing Du Bois's economic philosophy regarding black business, one can begin in 1898, with the Fourth Atlanta University Conference, which that year had as its theme, "The Negro in Business." It was not the first African-American conference that gave consideration to the state of black business in America. Before the Civil War the promotion of black business was very much a part of the agenda of the conferences held by the National Negro Convention movement, including proposals in which concerns were expressed for the promotion of international trade in the African Diaspora. Also, the establishment of a national black bank that would provide capital for black business expansion was proposed as well as recommendations for the boycott of slave produced goods. At these conferences proposals were also presented on the need to provide formal training for blacks in business.[8] In addition, information on the business activities of antebellum America's leading black entrepreneurs was provided in by Martin Delany in his 1850 book on the condition and elevation of the "Colored" race.[9]

By the late nineteenth century, confronted with industrialization, black business people who had participated in the mainstream of America's preindustrial economy found it increasingly difficult to establish viable enterprises. The implications for the economic future of black Americans in an industrial-based economy embarked on imperialism precipitated the fourth Atlanta University Conference convened by Du Bois with the theme "The Negro in Business." In an address that set the tone for the conference as well as the future direction for blacks in business, Professor John Hope, as he acknowledged America's embarkation on imperialism, said:

We are living among the so-called Anglo-Saxons and dealing with them. They are a conquering people who turn their conquests into their pockets....Living among such people, is it not obvious that we cannot escape its most powerful motive and survive?....To say the least, the policy of avoiding entrance in the world's business would be suicide to the Negro...As a matter of account, we ought to note that as good a showing as we made, that showing is but as pebbles on the shore of business enterprise.

---

[8] Juliet E. K. Walker, "Promoting Black Entrepreneurship and Business Enterprise in Antebellum America: The National Negro Convention, 1830-1855," in Thomas D. Boston, ed., *A Different Vision: Race and Public Policy* (London: Routledge Press, 1997) 280-318.

[9] Martin R. Delany, *The Condition...of the Colored People of the United States* ([1852] New York: Arno Press, 1968).

At the conference several resolutions written by Du Bois incorporated the first of many business plans formulated by him for black America. Foremost, these resolutions that called for both the expansion and support of black business. The first resolution was that: "Negroes ought to enter into business life in increasing numbers." Also it was emphasized that "the growth of a class of merchants among us would be a far-sighted measure of self-defense, and would make for wealth and mutual cooperation." A second resolution stated that "We need as merchants the best trained young men we can find. A college training ought to be one of the best preparations for a broad business life; and thorough English and high school training is indispensable." Another resolution emphasized the responsibilities of black business people with the statement that: "Negroes going into business should remember that their customers demand courtesy, honesty, and careful methods, and they should not expect patronage when their manner of conducting business does not justify it." At the same time, it was emphasized that "The mass of the Negroes must learn to patronize business enterprises conducted by their own race, even at some slight disadvantage." Finally, to promote black business growth, a resolution was also passed that called for churches, schools and newspapers to promote "the necessity of business careers for young people."[10]

It was also at this conference that Du Bois proposed the establishment of an organization of black businesspeople, a Negro Business Men's League, that would promote black business on local, state and national levels. Paradoxically, it was not Du Bois but Booker T. Washington who followed up on this proposal, when he founded the National Negro Business League in 1900. Consequently, Washington is given historic recognition for promoting black economic progress through business activity. Unlike Du Bois, however, the condition precedent for Washington's economic program for African Americans was at the cost of the loss of political and civil rights. But as Washington had said in his infamous 1895 "Atlanta Exposition Address": "No race that has anything to contribute to the markets of the world is long in any degree

---

[10] W. E. B. Du Bois, ed., "Resolutions of the Atlanta University Conference on the Negro in Business," *The Negro in Business* (Atlanta: Atlanta University, 1899) 50.

ostracized." Perhaps at that time, he meant the contributions to the world market of cotton produced by black labor, as opposed to Du Bois who said at the 1898 Atlanta conference in addressing the economic condition of Black America: "We must cooperate or we are lost. Ten million people who join in intelligent self-help can never be long ignored or mistreated."

BLACK BUSINESS AND THE TALENTED TENTH

Moreover, that same year, Du Bois in a commencement address to the Fisk University class of 1898 identified several areas of work, including the advantages and disadvantages of each, for black college graduates. The professional fields noted by Du Bois were law, medicine, the ministry, and teaching. His emphasis, however, was on the importance of a college education for men in business, particularly as a basis to ensure success in the economic development and expansion of the black community for as Du Bois explained: "The college man, who, making himself familiar with the best business methods of a business age, starts in to open this field, will not only earn and deserve a living for himself, but will make it easier for a thousand to follow his examples."[11]

Continuing, Du Bois emphasized that, while there was a large supply of black labor available for work and that while black industrial schools were providing skilled laborers, that it was up to "young men and women" who, with college training in business, could develop enterprises to provide "remunerative employment" for black laborers. In this business plan for black America Du Bois, noting that, while blacks had the capital to invest in industrial development, there was a lack of black business leadership but he emphasized, however, that

> What we do lack, and what schools like this [Fisk, as an example
> of a liberal arts university] must begin to supply in increasing
> numbers is the captain of industry, the man who can marshall

---

[11] W. E. B. Du Bois, "Careers Open to College-Bred Negroes," in Two Addresses Delivered by Alumni of Fisk University, in Commemoration with the Anniversary Exercises of Their Alma Mater, June, 1898 (Nashville: Fisk University, 1898) in Herbert Aptheker, ed., *Writings by Du Bois in Non-Periodical Literature Edited by Others* (Millwoods NY: Kraus-Thompson Organization Limited, 1982) 5.

and guide workers in industrial enterprises, who can foresee the demand and supply it—note the special aptitude of laborers and turn it to advantage—so guide with eye and brain the work of these black millions, that instead of adding to the poverty of the nation and subtracting from its wealth, we may add to the wealth of the land and make Negro poverty no longer a by-word.

Du Bois then emphasized in this 1898 commencement address the potential of the black consumer market as a basis for black business expansion, the first step in Du Bois's three-part business plan to improve the economic life of African American. The plan called for cooperative economic reciprocal relations of three groups, black consumers, black merchants, and black industrialists. The success of Du Bois's plan however, rested on black consumers. First, as he indicated, with the number of black people, who he referred to as, "eight million souls," providing a consumer market of $150 million to $300 million annually, "that part of this expenditure," he said, "at least, could be made through Negro merchants, if well-trained, educated, active men would only enter this field and cultivate it." Next, according to Du Bois's plan, the inventory for black merchants would come from goods produced by black industrialists, but Du Bois emphasized that "this field calls not for mere money-makers, or those who would ape the silly display and ostentation of certain classes of Americans: not does it call for men narrowed and shrunk by the soul-destroying commercialism of the hour." Rather than personal wealth accumulation, Du Bois's plan was that the goals for black captains of industry were to provide a living wage that would enable black workers to buy homes, educate their children, establish effective social service institutions, and "to make the Negro people able to help others even as others have helped us."

In 1898, then, the college-trained black businessman and black captain of industry were considered by Du Bois as the primary occupations that could provide the basis for the economic up-life of black Americans. Within five years, however, Du Bois began to view black businesspeople and especially black capitalists as the bane of black America. In his 1903 essay, "The Talented Tenth" Du Bois denounced money-making as a goal for black Americans for in that essay he said: "If we make money the object of man-training, we shall develop money-makers, but not necessarily men." Moreover, there was no mention of the importance of a liberal arts college education for future businessmen or even that of providing college level courses in business.[12] By 1903 Du Bois had removed the black businessman and captain of industry as the prime mover in his economic plan for black America. Perhaps this was because, as Bernard Boxhill said, that Du Bois's "criticism of the life of the money maker is philosophical. He believed that a money maker—presumably someone whose main aim in life is to become wealthy or economically secure—was certain to be dishonest, and in that case his life was likely to be poor."[13]

Moreover, in *The Souls of Black Folk* Du Bois continued his critique of black businesspersons, particularly in his chapter, "Of the Wings of Atalanta," where, within the construct of a somewhat peculiar context, Du Bois attempts to demonstrate that black business people represented an inherent danger to Southern race relations. First, Du Bois juxtaposes the change in the occupational structure of black leadership in the South with the loss of what he describes as: "a certain type of Negro,—the faithful, courteous slave of other days, with his incorruptible honesty and dignified humility." Du Bois attributes this loss to the rise of the new leaders of "Negro opinion," who, according to Du Bois were, "the businessmen, all those with property and money." He then adds that this group is replacing, "the Preacher and Teacher [who] embodied once the ideals of this people,—the strife for another and a juster world, the vague dream of righteousness, the mystery of knowing." Du Bois then cautions

---

[12] W. E. B. Du Bois, "The Talented Tenth," *The Negro Problem: A Series of Articles by Representative American Negroes of Today* (New York: James Pott & Co., 1903) in Herbert Aptheker, ed., *Writings by Du Bois in Non-Periodical Literature,* 17. Du Bois noted that by 1899, there were 2,329 black college graduates of whom 212 had graduated college before 1876. Also, that 2,079 were men, 250 were women and that 1,940 had graduated from "Negro" colleges while 389 had graduated from white colleges. Of that number, only 47, 3.6 percent were in business; 701 were teachers; 221 were clergymen; seventy-six were physicians; sixty-two were lawyers; fifty-three in the Civil Service; twenty-six were farmers; 222 were clerks and Secretaries of national societies; nine were artisans, nine were editors; and, five were in miscellaneous occupations.

[13] Bernard R. Boxill, "Du Bois on Cultural Pluralism," in Bernard W. Bell, Emily Grosholz, and James B. Stewart, eds., *W. E. B. Du Bois on Race and Culture: Philosophy, Politics, and Poetics* (New York: Routledge, 1996) 75.

that "these ideals, with their simple beauty and weird inspiration, will suddenly sink to a question of cash and a lust for gold."[14]

Continuing his diatribe on the black businessman Du Bois cautions, "What if the Negro people be wooed from a strife for righteousness, from a love of knowing, to regard dollars as the be-all and end-all of life?" In expanding this question he added, "What if to the Mammonism of America be added the rising Mammonism of the South...reinforced by the budding Mammonism of its half-awakened black millions?"[15] Incredibly, it seems that Du Bois was raising the spectre not only of the potential for a black business class to develop into a radical sector of opposition in their refusal to conform to a subordinate status, but he was also even suggesting that a black business class could offer economic competition to white businesspeople in the South. After all, in his 1898 Fisk address, Du Bois had established the consumer power of African Americans.

Moreover, with 90 percent of the black population living in the South at that time and with literally 90 percent of the black consumer dollar going to whites in business, the potential loss of the black consumer dollar represented a real threat to Southern white merchants. Indeed, in his *Black Reconstruction,* Du Bois would state that "The masters feared their former slaves' success far more than their anticipated failure."[16] Yet, is it possible, that in promoting his "Talented Tenth" program of a liberal arts trained cadre of black leaders, that Du Bois was seeking a tradeoff in giving up the pursuit of economic justice for blacks through black business leaders, as much as Booker T. Washington in his "Atlanta Compromise" address had in offering up the political and civil rights for blacks in his promotion of industrial education? For in closing this chapter, Du Bois emphasizes that the South needs institutions of higher learning, especially for blacks that will provide "ideals, broad, pure, and

---

[14] W. E. B. Du Bois, *The Souls of Black Folk* ([1903] New York: Penguin Books, 1989) 67.

[15] Ibid, 68.

[16] W. E. B. Du Bois, *Black Reconstruction: An Essay Toward a History of the Part Black Folk Played in the Attempt to Reconstruct Democracy in America, 1860-1880* (New York: Harcourt Brace, 1935) 633.

inspiring ends of living,—not sordid money-getting, not apples of gold."[17]

Was Du Bois implying, then, that if the South invested in higher education in the liberal arts for blacks, beyond industrial schools, then the South would be rewarded with a class of black leaders who would not challenge the racial status quo? As Du Bois indicated in his essay, "Of the Training of Black Men," in *Souls of Black Folk*, the cadre of liberal arts college trained black men presently in the South had already demonstrated that "With all their larger vision and deeper sensibilities, these men have usually been conservative, careful leaders. They have seldom been agitators, have withstood the temptation to head the mob, and have worked steadily and faithfully in a thousand communities in the South."[18] Doubtless, with great constraint and tact, Du Bois did not offer up the college trained Washington as an example.

Perhaps it seems from the above commentary that Du Bois, in promoting his "Talented Tenth" agenda was guilty of the very charges he made against Washington. After all, in his essay, "Of Mr. Booker T. Washington and Others," Du Bois specifically emphasized that "To gain the sympathy and cooperation of the various elements comprising the white South was Mr. Washington's first task."[19] And, could it be, too, that in giving up his black businessmen, Du Bois was able to strengthen his argument on the advantages to the South in supporting a liberal arts program for the college education of his "Talented Tenth," for in another one of his indictments, Du Bois emphasized that Washington's economic program for black America had become "a gospel of Work and Money to such an extent as apparently almost completely to overshadow the higher aims of life."[20] After all, Du Bois had attempted to establish that only college educated blacks could provide the conservative black leadership required in the South to keep the masses of laborers in line, a strategy that he hoped would win the kind of support for black liberal arts colleges that Washington was able to generate for the black industrial schools.

---

[17] Du Bois, *Souls of Black Folk*, 72.
[18] Ibid, 85-86.
[19] Ibid, 37.
[20] Ibid, 43.

Still, after having established that college educated black men, trained in the liberal arts of "pure" and "inspiring" goals, as opposed to "sordid money-making" could, because of their conservatism, make for the best choice as leaders of Southern blacks, Du Bois in his chapter, "Of the Sons of Master and Men," said, that for them to be effective leaders, that they must have power. Indeed, he even included black captains of industry in this group of leaders. As college educated-bred men, Du Bois said these men would be able to "take hold of Negro communities and raise and train them by force of precept and example." Moreover, this discussion was preceded by Du Bois emphasis that "We must accept some of the race prejudice in the South as a fact." Yet, Du Bois did not equivocate when he stated specifically in "On the Wings of Atalanta," that for these college-trained race leaders to be effective as brokers of accommodation and conciliation between the classes of blacks as well as races, that they must have the "power of the ballot."[21]

It appears then, that between 1898 and 1903, that Du Bois's two thoughts regarding the leadership of blacks, that of black businesspeople and his "Talented Tenth" represented an inherent contradiction in the progressive ideals for economic justice that informs Du Bois's "double consciousness." Problematized within the construct of "two warring ideals," the "lust for gold" and "sordid money making," as opposed to ideals that focus on a "juster world, the vague dream of righteousness," represented for Du Bois "two unreconciled strivings." In this instance Du Bois took what he believed was the high road. Some two years later in outlining the principles of the Niagara Movement that he organized to challenge Washington's accommodationist political agenda, Du Bois was emphatic in his position that economic advancement for blacks was clearly tied to political power. In the 1905 Niagara Movement Declaration of Principles sixteen racial iniquities were listed. The first two expressed opposition to the denial of suffrage and civil liberty. These were followed by a statement on economic deprivations which in part said: "We especially complain against the denial of equal opportunities to us in economic life...it tends to crush labor and small business enterprises."[22]

---

[21] Ibid., 140.

[22] W. E. B. Du Bois, "The Niagara Movement," *Voice of the Negro*, 2 (September 1905): 619-22. Also see, Manning Marable, *W. E. B. Du Bois: Black Radical Democrat* (Boston: Twayne, 1986).

BLACK ECONOMIC COOPERATION

Moreover, in an attempt to reconcile his "warring ideals," Du Bois began to change his position regarding the future direction of black economic development. Doubtless, his 1907 Atlanta conference with its theme, "Economic Cooperation Among Negro Americans," was perhaps the second precipitating factor after his "Talented Tenth" agenda that prompted Du Bois to move away from promoting black capitalists and captains of industry, as the nucleus for black economic advancement, and to push for "black business cooperation." The proceedings of the conference were expansive in the historic information provided that documented the extent to which blacks had had a long history of cooperative economic self-help with its origins in Africa that survived in the Diaspora, beginning with the African Slave Secret Burial Societies, mutual aid and benevolent societies and fraternal organizations. Included were specific reports on several types of black cooperative enterprises, the church, schools, beneficial and insurance societies, and banks. In addition, information was provided on cooperative black transportation enterprises, cooperative real estate and fraternal building and loan associations, as well as cooperative manufacturing groups.[23]

Yet, at that time, Du Bois's interest in black economic cooperation was closely tied to his announcement in 1907 that he was a "Socialist of the Path" for he indicated that he believed neither in the abolition of private property nor "that government can carry on private business as well as private concerns."[24] Du Bois, however, continued his belief in the democratic process. Although the Niagara Movement failed in 1909, many of its goals were assumed by the National Association for the Advancement of Colored People (NAACP) established in 1910. As the organization grew in influence and power and, while the NAACP announced that it would work to improve employment conditions for blacks, the promotion of black business development in a separate economy, however, was not one of its goals. But as editor of its official publication, *The Crisis,* Du Bois used this position to promote his

---

[23] W. E. B. Du Bois, ed, *Economic Co-Operation among Negro Americans,* Atlanta University Publications, no. 12 (Atlanta: Atlanta University Press, 1907).

[24] W. E. B. Du Bois, "Negro and Socialism," *Horizon* 1 (February 1907): 7-8. This was the short-lived journal published by the Niagara Movement.

economic agenda, which included black economic cooperatives as well as the expansion of black business in a separate economy.

Even as late as 1912 Du Bois had not given up on black capitalism. At that time, Durham, North Carolina, represented the model for a successful "separate" black economy, including in its development not only black economic cooperation through consumer support for black business, but also a committed and responsible class of black capitalists, who invested in the community in their financial support for black community institutions. But what Du Bois considered as the most important factor that accounted for the success of Durham's black capitalists was that the racial environment in that city was conducive to black business advancement. Du Bois described this racial business policy as one of white encouragement of black economic activity "by active aid and passive tolerance."[25]

Increasingly, Du Bois's interest in black business activity was revitalized. Still he noted that the financial accomplishment of blacks in business were limited not only in the number of black businesses but also because of their slender resources, even the financial institutions in terms of their capital assets. Still, whenever information was available, Du Bois used *The Crisis* to publish articles on the diversity of business enterprises established by blacks. At the same time, he also used *The Crisis* to promote black economic cooperatives. In 1915, Du Bois published an article that announced his new five-part program for the economic advancement of blacks. While he advocated cooperation as a basis for a planned black economy, he also cautioned against the rise of black capitalists for he said:

> Under economic co-operation we must strive to spread the idea among colored people that the accumulation of wealth is for social rather than individual ends. We must avoid, in the advancement of the Negro race, the mistakes of ruthless exploitation which have marked modern economic history. To this end we must seek not simply home ownership, small landholding and savings accounts, but also all forms of co-

---

[25] W. E. B. Du Bois, "The Upbuilding of Black Durham," *The World's Work* (January 1912): 334-338, in Lewis, ed., *W. E. B. Du Bois: A Reader*, 257

operation, both in production and distribution, profit sharing, building and loan associations."[26]

Some two years later, in 1917 a black cooperative society was founded, with Du Bois charting its progress through various articles in *The Crisis*.[27] Interest among blacks in cooperatives intensified during the Great Depression and continued even through World War II.[28] Yet, Du Bois's resolute promotion of a separate black economy stood in contradistinction to the integrationist goals of the NAACP. In refusing to compromise his position not only on the reality of a segregated economy but also on the iniquities inherent in racial capitalism, Du Bois was forced to resign as editor in 1934. In the American mind cooperatives were associated with socialism, despite their increase in numbers, even during World War II.[29] Indeed, an article published in the *Chicago Tribune* in 1945 reported that several large corporations charged co-ops as "Breeders of Socialism."[30] In the 1930s the NAACP in concern for its image as well as what it viewed as the best course of action to defeat segregation, using the American legal system to challenge racial iniquities, felt as threatened by Du Bois's promotion of a black segregated economy, as it did by being identified with leftist ideologies. Still, after leaving the NAACP in 1934, Du Bois continued his promotion of black economic cooperatives and in his 1940 autobiography *Dusk of Dawn* presented an economic plan which he called the "Co-operative Commonwealth."[31]

In November 1941, at a meeting of the presidents of "Negro-Land Grant Colleges," a response to the continued impoverishment of the masses of blacks, Du Bois presented a proposal for the direction that these colleges could take to address some of the poverty problems.

---

[26] W. E. B. Du Bois, "The Immediate Program of the American Negro," *The Crisis* (April 1915): 310-312.

[27] *The Crisis*, August 1917, 168 and December 1919, 48, 50. Subsequently five stores were established that had the consumer support of 75,000 blacks. Also see, Joseph Demarco, "The Rationale and Foundation of Du Bois's Theory of Economic Cooperation," *Phylon* 35 (March 1974): 5-15.

[28] Walker, *History of Black Business in America*, 230-33.

[29] Ibid., 422, n., 44.

[30] *Chicago Tribune*, 9 May 1944.

[31] W. E. B. Du Bois, *Dusk of Dawn* (New York: Harcourt, Brace and Company, 1940) 216.

Interestingly, in this proposal Du Bois attempted to reconcile the college education program of his "Talented Tenth" with economic realities, which for Du Bois proceeded from Marxist doctrine that "economic activity is fundamental to survival." What was most startling in Du Bois's program was his renunciation of the liberal arts basis of the education of his "Talented Tenth." Indeed, as Du Bois proceeded in presenting his proposal, it was as though he had reinvent himself and his educational philosophy for Du Bois said in explaining the Marxist basis of his program that:

> Many persons object to this economic interpretation of life.... They say that we ought to think of religion, ethics, science and art first and then come down to prosaic income. But students of human action are replying that while ethics, science and art are the more important aspects of life...in the situation facing man today the world over, earning a living is and must be the first object of organized life."[32]

Still, Du Bois had not given up on his emphasis that a "Talented Tenth" must provide leadership. But in a startling reversal of what he had emphasized as the core curriculum for this group in 1903, Du Bois in 1941 said that not until the problems of poverty were eradicated, "can we concentrate... on the spiritual and esthetic aspects of living." Finally, Du Bois was forced to confront not only the reality of the expediency of economic survival that Washington had at the turn of the century, but also in doing so, compromised his program of liberal arts for black college education, which had focused on the humanities. In this instance, however, while Du Bois continued to criticize business education for blacks, he now emphasized that there was a critical need, specifically for "an increasing number of men especially trained in economic and social development." In this respect, then, Du Bois distinguished training in economics as distinct from training in business, which as he said corrupted blacks, explaining that through no fault of their own blacks

---

[32] W. E. B. Du Bois, "A Program for the Land-Grant Colleges," from *Proceedings of the Nineteenth Annual Conferences of the Presidents of Negro Land Grant Colleges November 11-13, 1941*," (Chicago: n.p., n.d) 42-57 in Aptheker, ed., *Writings by Du Bois in Non-Periodical Literature*, 193.

trained in business had "little choice of career in business and industry except exploitation and legal theft among their own ignorant masses."[33]

It would seem that Du Bois would have emphasized the importance of ethics as fundamental to training in business. Yet, Du Bois's main concern was that black colleges must address the immediate economic needs of the community, a point he had emphasized in a 1933 article entitled, "The Negro College": "The university must become not simply a center of knowledge but a center of applied knowledge and guide of action. And, this is all the more necessary now since we easily see that planned action, especially in economic life, is going to be the watchword of civilization"[34]

In this instance, the focus of Du Bois's presentation at this 1941 meeting of the presidents of land grant colleges was to generate support for his proposal, which called for these colleges to launch a scientific study to identify the economic needs of the black communities and then subject the findings to analysis. Du Bois had always indicated that very little attention had been given to his Atlanta University studies. With the advancement of scholarship and a greater receptivity to the study of blacks, doubtlessly Du Bois hoped that there would be greater receptivity to such a study undertaken in light of new sociological theory and methodology. Indeed, there was interest in a study of the Negro, which was launched in 1938 with Gunnar Myrdal as the Director of the project, with the findings published in 1944 as *An American Dilemma*, a monumental study of some 1500 pages.[35]

Yet, increasingly, during WWII Du Bois began to focus on international concerns. With the end of the war, the rise of the Soviet Union, and the drive for decolonization, Du Bois's condemnation of capitalism, including black capitalists, intensified, as he began to view the

---

[33] W. E. B. Du Bois, "A Program for the Land-Grant Colleges," from *Proceedings of the Nineteenth Annual Conferences of the Presidents of Negro Land Grant Colleges November 11-13, 1941*," (Chicago: n.p., n.d) 42-57 in Aptheker, ed., *Writings by Du Bois in Non-Periodical Literature*, 198.

[34] Du Bois, "The Negro College," in Lewis, *W. E. B. Du Bois: A Reader*, 72.

[35] Gunnar Myrdal, *An American Dilemma: The Negro Problem and Modern Democracy* (New York: Harper & Brothers Publishers, 1944).

attainment of peace within the context of bringing an end to the structural violence inherent in racial capitalism.[36]

Indeed, even before the war's end Du Bois's 1944 article (published in Rayford W. Logan's book, *What the Negro Wants*) "My Evolving Program for Negro Freedom" presented what he referred to as the "third modification" of his economic agenda for African Americans. He noted that after his return from Russia in 1926 and as a result of his more careful reading of Marx that he was even more adamant in his opposition to blacks as capitalists. As he explained, "the solution of letting a few of our capitalists share with whites in the exploitation of our masses, would never be a solution of our problem, but the forging of eternal chains, as Modern India knows to its sorrows."[37]

Moreover, by 1948 Du Bois not only revised his construct of the "Talented Tenth," but also restated it into a doctrine he called the "Guiding Hundredth," which he presented in his "The Talented Tenth Memorial Address." At that time Du Bois was eighty years old and acknowledged that his construction of the "Talented Tenth" was based on the knowledge that was available up to the end of the nineteenth century and on his assumption that "with knowledge, sacrifice would automatically follow." Du Bois was thirty-five when he wrote the "Talented Tenth," but said that because of his "youth and idealism, I did not realize that selfishness is even more natural than sacrifice." As to the "Guiding Hundredth," Du Bois emphasized that foremost in their education should be the acquisition of expert knowledge of economics as it affected American Negroes. Certainly this was realistic but notwithstanding Du Bois continued to insist that fundamental to this group's success "would be its willingness to sacrifice and plan for such economic revolution in industry and just distribution of wealth, as would make the rise of our people possible."[38]

---

[36] See, Gerald Horne, *Black and Red: W. E. B. Du Bois and the Afro-American Response to the Cold War, 1944-1963* (Albany NY: State University of New York Press, 1985).

[37] W. E. B. Du Bois, "My Evolving Program for Negro Freedom," from Rayford W. Logan, ed., *What the Negro Wants*, 31-70 in Aptheker, ed., *Writings by Du Bois in Non-Periodical Literature*, 235.

[38] W. E. B. Du Bois, "The Talented Tenth Memorial Address," *The Boule Journal* (October 1948): 5.

For the remainder of his life Du Bois continued to denounce business education as opposed to education in economics. In a speech given in 1953 by Du Bois entitled "On the Future of the American Negro," he said: "At the very time that economics, that is the study of work and income, is of foremost importance for our well being, economics is not being studied in our schools. Neither in the elementary schools nor in colleges are students learning about the philosophy of money and exchange production and trade, wealth and saving."[39] Some five years later, at the age of ninety Du Bois in a 1958 article on blacks and socialism that "We teach Business as a science when it is only the art of legal theft. We regard advertising as a profession even when it teaches the best way to lie....We want high wages even if most of the world starves."[40] Some six years earlier in 1952, Du Bois had written: "Not even a Harvard School of Business can make greed into a science." [41]

Throughout his life, Du Bois emphasized the attainment of economic justice for blacks, as he developed and modified his various programs on black business activity. His denunciation of blacks as capitalists in his 1903 publications did not abate, but became more specific in Du Bois's economic analysis. Writing in 1921 Du Bois said, "today to a very large extent our laborers are our capitalists and our capitalists are our laborers," but he also predicted that at the rate of black economic progress, "fully separated classes" might develop.[42] Some thirty years later in 1956, Du Bois wrote that blacks were "flying apart into opposing economic classes....This division is only in embryo, but it can be sensed.... Negro businessmen...today form the most powerful class among Negroes and dominate their thought and actions."[43] Increasingly in Du Bois's economic thought, class—not race—would become a

---

[39] W. E. B. Du Bois, "On the Future of the American Negro," *Freedomways* 5/1 (Winter 1965): 117-124, in Virginia Hamilton, ed., *The Writings of W.E.B. Du Bois* (New York: Thomas Y. Crowell Company, 1975) 232.

[40] W. E. B. Du Bois, "The Negro and Socialism," in Helen Alfred, ed., *Toward a Socialist America* (New York: Peace Publications, 1958) 179-191; in Aptheker, ed., *Writings by Du Bois in Non-Periodical Literature,* 289.

[41] W. E. B. Du Bois, *In Battle for Peace: The Story of My 83rd Birthday* (New York: Masses and Mainstream, 1952) 171.

[42] W. E. B. Du Bois, "The Class Struggle," *The Crisis* 22 (June 1921): 55-60. Also see, W.E. B. Du Bois, "The Negro and Communism," *The Crisis* 38 (September 1931): 313-15.

[43] W. E. B. Du Bois, "[Negro Business]," *National Guardian,* 23 January 1956.

divisive force in the lives of African Americans. Yet, while Du Bois could acknowledge that race limited the unity of black and white workers, paradoxically, he did not view race as a factor that shaped capitalist attitudes toward labor. In his economic thought on racial capitalism, he viewed the destructive class tendencies inherent in capitalism as crossing racial lines in the exploitation of the working classes, surely two warring ideals in the "double consciousness of Du Bois's economic thought.

Yet, if there was a problem with Du Bois's economic analysis, which was informed by his reading of Marxism, it was that the masses of blacks were not concerned. Few had read Marx, even fewer cared about his economic determinism. What they knew about Marxism was its emphasis on the unity of a working class and, in the minds of the masses of blacks, they were as exploited by white labor as by white capital. As Du Bois said: "I do not believe that it is possible to settle the Negro problem in America until the color problems of the world are well on the way toward settlement. I do not believe that the descendants of Africans are going to be received as American citizens so long as the peoples of Africa are kept by white civilization in semi-slavery, serfdom and economic exploitation."[44]

DU BOIS, PROPHECY, AND RACIAL CAPITALISM

Yet, ironically, at the dawn of the twentieth century Du Bois in his economic analysis of world capitalism was as prophetic in his predictions of the future basis of wealth holding in America as a nation and how race impacted on the limited economic position of blacks, as he was in 1903 when he predicted that the problem of the twentieth century would be the problem of the color line. Indeed, in 1920 in his *Darkwater: Voices Beyond the Veil*, Du Bois predicted that just "as the intricacy and length of technical production is increased, the ownership of these things becomes a monopoly, which easily makes the rich richer and the poor poorer."[45] At the dawn of the twentieth century, the ownership of America's technological innovations in industrial production resulted in

---

[44] *Pittsburgh Courier*, 25 April 1936.

[45] W. E. B. Du Bois, *Darkwater: Voices Beyond the Veil* (New York: Harcourt Brace, 1920) 100.

tremendous iniquities in wealth. In 1900, when Du Bois was thirty-two years old, just one percent of the population owned more of the nation's wealth than the remaining 99 percent. Du Bois died in 1963, but wealth distribution changed very little in the post-Civil Rights era. Moreover, just as Du Bois had predicted, the revolution in technology, which he described as "technical production," in this instance, telecommunications and computers, had by 1998 resulted in the top 1 percent of the nation's households holding more wealth than the entire bottom 95 percent.

Moreover, despite the gains made by black Americans since the Civil Rights era, especially in educational attainment, occupational mobility, and a rising middle-class, racial iniquities in wealth holding remained. Simply put, in 1995 the median black household had a net worth of $7,400, including home equity, which amounted to about 12 percent of the $61,000 in median wealth for whites. In addition, in 1998, the black median household income was $25,351, some 60 percent of the median white income of $42,439. What is significant for black household incomes at the end of the twentieth century is that it had changed very little since the 1954 Brown decision, when black household incomes in 1959 were 59 percent of white household incomes.[46]

The reality, then, is that in the history of the economic life of African Americans, black wealth accumulation, compared to that of whites, at the end of the twentieth century has differed very little from what it was in the thirty year period following the 1964 Civil Rights Act from that of black wealth holding in the thirty-year period following the Civil War. But even more crucial is Du Bois prophetic assessments of racial capitalism in limiting black business expansion for as he emphasized in his 1898 *Philadelphia Negro*: "One of the great postulates of the science of economics—that men will seek their economic advantage—is in this case untrue, because in many cases men will not do this if it involves association, even in a casual and business way, with Negroes. And this fact must be taken account of in all judgments as to the Negro's economic progress."[47] In the 1990s, blacks comprising almost 13 percent

[46] Chuck Collins, Betsy Leondar-Wright, and Holly Sklar, *Shifting Fortunes: The Perils of the Growing American Wealth Gap* (Boston: United for a Fair Economy, 1999).

[47] W. E. B. Du Bois, *The Philadelphia Negro* (New York: Lippincott, 1899) 141-46.

of the nation's population showed business profits that amounted to only
1 percent of the nation's total business receipts.

It would seem, then, that in intellectual discourse on Du Bois, given
the abysmally-placed economic position of blacks, that greater
consideration should be given to Du Bois's economic thought on black
business. Yet, a century earlier Du Bois recognized the immediate reality
of racial capitalism, which limited black access to white financial markets
by which a strong business foundation could be built. At the 1898 Atlanta
conference he emphasized the extent to which industrialization and the
rise of big business was destroying the small businessperson:
"Commercial life is slowly changing. The large industry, the department
store and the trust are making it daily more difficult for the small
capitalist with slender resources." Commercial life continued to change
in the twentieth century by a revolution in high technology. In this
context, then, Du Bois in his economic thought proved that he was very
much a man of the twentieth century, even beyond his death in 1963, in
that he very early recognized the extent to which technology would
propel capitalism and provide the basis of economic advancement and
the expansion of wealth in America not only in the industrial age but also
in a post-industrial age

Moreover, it is not that the economy has not prospered, but while in
1989, when the United States had sixty-six billionaires, 31.5 million
people lived below the official poverty line. By 1999, the nation's
prosperity had resulted in the rise of 268 billionaires. Indeed, if there was
equality in American wealth holding, with blacks comprising almost 13
percent of the population, there should have been, at the minimum,
twenty-six black billionaires. There is not one billionaire of sub-Saharan
African descent although the leading black wealth holder in the United
States, Oprah Winfrey is worth $725 million. Even when Winfrey
achieves a billion dollars in wealth, doubtless she or any other person of
African descent will ever match the wealth accumulated by America's
leading wealth holder William Gates, with $102 billion.

Unless, black Americans can become like Reginald Lewis, Michael
Jordan, Oprah Winfrey, Sean "Puff Daddy" Combs, or Russell Simmons,
even a Henry Lewis Gates or a Maya Angelou, it seems we offer little or
no economic advantage to those who own and control wealth in America,
since as ordinary workers, few of us offer, as Du Bois indicated, any

"economic advantage" to the nation's wealth holders.[48] Yet, paradoxically, black genius in the arts in the post-Civil Rights era has produced more black millionaires than Du Bois ever anticipated because of the "economic advantage" provided whites who control the production and distribution of black artistic expression in contradistinction to Du Bois, since his view was that "The emotional wealth of the American Negro, the nascent art in song, dance, and drama can all be applied, not to amuse the white audience, but to inspire and direct the acting group itself."[49]

Still, it is not that African Americans have not prospered or advanced. Indeed, there has been an increase in income for college graduates, but only 15 percent of African Americans are college graduates and, interestingly, in a nation propelled by free enterprise in business, a significant proportion of black professionals are supported by the government in our work for federal, state, and municipal agencies. Even the economic success of many of our post-Civil Rights era black businesspeople, as well as professionals in law and medicine, is the result of federal and state affirmative action policies. Simply put, African Americans live in a capitalist free enterprise economy and the wealth of America is—in its business productivity—racial capitalism.

Whether blacks are capitalists or not at the dawn of the new millennium is moot. African Americans live in a capitalist economy and few, including our intellectuals, have taken the moral high ground. Even with racial capitalism limiting the possibility of economic equality for the masses of blacks, few black Americans have rejected the individual acquisition of wealth as a goal. Moreover, few African Americans, even those with limited economic vision, have viewed the future for either themselves or their children as "workers of the world." But even so, the "digital divide" underscores the potential economic limitations confronting African Americans at the dawn of the twenty-first century. In regards to the economic status of American labor at the dawn of the new millennium Du Bois, however, was also prophetic of their position in a

---

[48] Juliet E. K. Walker, "Oprah Winfrey, The Tycoon: Contextualizing the Economics of Race, Class, Gender in Black Business in Post-Civil Rights America" in Alusine Jalloh, ed., *African American Entrepreneurship* (Rochester: Rochester University Press, forthcoming 2001).

[49] Du Bois, *Dusk of Dawn*, 219.

post-industrial economy. He emphasized in his 1920 *Darkwater* that, "The world market most widely and desperately sought today is the market where labor is cheapest and most helpless and profits are most abundant."[50] As the American economy has moved to an advanced service sector economy, a result of developments in high tech industries propelled by microelectronics and digital electronic technologies, including computers, telecommunications, and aerial communication (digital wireless personal communication systems), the nation's industrial workers have seen the movement overseas of America's industrial jobs.

America ranks first in an expanding global economy, paced not only by its technological innovations, but also, paradoxically, by its new venture in imperialism and neocolonialism. As American multinationals develop and expand their markets in an increasingly global economy, how, then, can African American multinationals, while seeking profits reconcile their competitive incursions in Africa and the Diaspora International Economy, without being considered within the frame of Neocolonialist? The question has been asked: "Does this mean, then, that blacks in the United States, as Americans, and, as they seek international markets, South Africa, as an example, particularly in competitive enterprises, such as black hair care products and publishing, as examples, can be viewed or placed in the class of neocolonialists?"[51] Yet, while Du Bois predicted the exploitative expansion of capitalism in a post-industrial society within his construct of the impact of technological innovations in a capitalist society, early on he took the position, in this instance, in response to Garvey's "Back-to-Africa" black capitalist economic program that: "Africa belongs to the Africans. They have not the slightest intention of giving it up to foreigners, white or black"

---

[50] Du Bois, *Darkwater*, 48.

[51] Juliet E. K. Walker, "Neocolonialism in the African Diaspora?: Black American Business Competition in South Africa, Luster Products, Inc (USA) v Magic Style Sales, CC (SA) Case, 1990-1996," in Alusine Jalloh, ed., *African-American Entrepreneurship* (Rochester: Rochester University Press, forthcoming 2001)

CONCLUSION

Certainly, the achievement of full economic equality for African Americans is critical. In the early twentieth century, Du Bois's political thought in its emphasis on the achievement of civil and political rights was expressed foremost with his 1905 Niagara Movement, which provided the foundation for the subsequent achievement of black political and civil rights in the 1960s. Still, the Civil Rights movement launched by Du Bois in the early twentieth century is not complete. At the dawn of the new millennium, the achievement of economic equality, also foremost in the economic thought of Du Bois, clearly remains the goal for African Americans. Moreover, very little has changed. While by no means can the Reverend Jesse Jackson, whose life of activism has been in the promotion of Civil Rights of black Americans, be compared to Booker T. Washington, but interestingly, Jesse Jackson in his access to Wall Street and White Corporate America is using his power and influence as a broker to negotiate economic advancement for African Americans as did Booker T. Washington in his relations with white philanthropists and industrials almost a century earlier. Paradoxically, too, Booker T. Washington was confronted with the rising tide of Jim Crow, while Jesse Jackson is challenging the retrenchment of affirmative action in his efforts to increase black employment in White Corporate America and to provide black investment companies with greater access to Wall Street.

Consequently, while there has been advancement in the economic life of black Americans, very serious racial iniquities persist. In wealth holding blacks have yet to achieve economic parity with whites. Moreover, in America's increasingly multiracial society, blacks are losing economic ground to other minorities.[52] At the dawn of the new millennium, then, the achievement of economic equality has yet to be achieved by African Americans. Yet, while the nation's wealth is

---

[52] Juliet E. K. Walker, "The Future of Black Business: Can It Get Out of the Box," in Lee A. Daniels, ed., *State of Black America 2000 Report* (New York: National Urban League, 2000) 199-226.

measured in business profits, ultimately as Du Bois said: "We should measure the prosperity of a nation not by the number of millionaires but by the absence of poverty, the prevalence of health, the efficiency of the public schools and the number of people who can read and do read worthwhile books."[53]

---

[53] W. E. B. Du Bois, "On the Future of the American Negro," *Freedomways* 5/1 (Winter 1965): 117-124

"THE SWEETNESS OF HIS STRENGTH":

DU BOIS, TEDDY ROOSEVELT, AND THE BLACK SOLDIER

MARK BRALEY

In their 1996 book, *All That We Can Be: Black Leadership and Racial Integration the Army Way,* Charles C. Moskos and John Sibley Butler make the case that, at least in the Army, the military has led the way in creating an America free of racial discrimination, an America in which men and women are rewarded according to merit, an America in which, to borrow Martin Luther King, Jr.'s famous line, people are judged not by the color of their skin but by the content of their character. The Army, they argue, "is an institution unmatched in its broad record of black achievement. It is a world in which the Afro-American culture is part and parcel of the institutional culture. It is the only place in American life where whites are routinely bossed around by blacks"[1]

W. E. B. Du Bois was alive to witness only the first fifteen years of this celebrated progress. For most of his ninety-five years the military service held out the hope of progress which the nation continually dashed. Throughout American history African Americans have looked at military service as a way to improve their social status and to prove themselves

---

[1] Charles C. Moskos and John Sibley Butler, *All that We Can Be: Black Leadership and Racial Integration the Army Way* (New York: Basic Books, 1996) 2.

worthy of equal rights to white Americans.[2] The logic is obvious. As Manuel Mansart, the hero of Du Bois's trilogy, *The Black Flame*, naively tells his wife on the eve of America entering WWI, "Don't you see, we are now citizens of this country. The nation is depending on us as its sons. This means the end of segregation. A black man worthy to die for his country is worth living for it, too."[3] Perhaps Manuel's sanguine view of military service represents the view Du Bois held in 1918 when he was tempted by his friend and NAACP associate Joel Spingarn to join Army intelligence in a special unit created to "undertake a 'far-reaching constructive effort to satisfy the pressing grievances of colored Americans.'"[4] Spingarn himself had already received a commission in the army as a major and had taken up the establishment of a separate officer training camp for blacks as his personal cause. Although neither he nor Du Bois would have advocated a segregated facility, the Army would not have it any other way. Spingarn enlisted Du Bois's editorial voice to raise African-American support for the camp.[5] About a year later, in June 1918, Spingarn broached the idea of Du Bois donning the Army green, and Du Bois, perhaps seeing this as a chance to become the catalyst for

---

[2] Confirmation can be found in any number of sources. For one example see Philip S. Foner, *History of Black Americans* (Westport Ct: Greenwood Press, 1975) vols. 1 and 3. In volume 1 we learn that both the colonists and the British offered slaves freedom in return for enlisting in their respective armies, though the numbers were limited and the practice was not uniform throughout the colonies north and south (324-44). The same held true during the War of 1812 (482-92). Volume 3 covers black military involvement in the Civil War. Foner reports that Frederick Douglass "insisted that it was time for 'Action! Action! not criticism.' He condemned those blacks who opposed taking up arms as being 'weak and cowardly,' and he urged his people to 'fly to arms and smite with death the power that would bury the government and your liberty in the same hopeless grave.' To be free, they must themselves strike the blow. Now they could prove their manhood and demonstrate their equality with the white man in fighting prowess and love of country. The gratitude of the country would be accorded to the Negroes and prejudice against them greatly diminished if they proved by force of arms that they deserved an improved status" (357-58).

[3] W. E. B. Du Bois, *The Ordeal of Mansart* (Millwood NY: Kraus-Thomson, 1976) 45.

[4] Herbert Aptheker, ed., *The Correspondene of W. E. B. Du Bois, Selections, 1877-1934*, (Amherst: University of Massachusetts Press, 1997) 1:227.

[5] See *The Crisis* 14 (June 1917): 60-61, "Officers," in *Selections* 137-38.

broader social change by working from within the halls of power, allowed himself to be talked into saying yes.[6]

As Mark Ellis has shown in his essay, "'Closing Ranks' and 'Seeking Honors': W. E. B. Du Bois in World War I," shortly after agreeing to take the commission, Du Bois wrote and published his famous "Close Ranks" editorial, calling for African Americans to "forget our special grievances and close ranks with our own fellow white citizens and the allied nations that are fighting for democracy."[7] The response to the July 1918, *Crisis* editorial in much of the African-American community was swift and overwhelmingly negative, accusing Du Bois of selling out. Ellis concludes that Du Bois's primary motivation in writing the editorial was "to strengthen his application for a commission" and that it "did not square with his known rejection of accommodationism."[8] In "The Damnable Dilemma": African-American Accommodation and Protest during World War I," William Jordan responds to Ellis by arguing that the "Close Ranks" editorial was a conscious accommodationist move on the part of Du Bois. The decision, he argues, "was an understandable and probably sensible one, made possible by Du Bois's pragmatism and ideological flexibility, guided by an understanding of the dangers of militancy amid pro-war frenzy, and encouraged by the government's wartime racial strategies."[9] Combined with Elliot M. Rudwick's characterization of Du Bois's accommodationist actions and statements during WWI as part of "the great Du Boisian paradox" (now integrationist, now segregationist), Ellis's and Jordan's statements leave us with no certain sense of Du Bois's views about the merits of military service for African Americans.[10]

Just what did Du Bois think about military service as a means to racial uplift? How does the black soldier figure into his thinking? How are military service and the black soldier represented in his writings and to

---

[6] See David Levering Lewis, *W. E. B. Du Bois: Biography of a Race, 1868-1919* (New York: Henry Holt, 1993) 552-560, for an account of this entire episode.

[7] *Selections,* 159.

[8] Mark Ellis, "'Closing Ranks' and 'Seeking Honors': W. E. B. Du Bois in World War I," *Journal of American History* 79/1 (June 1992): 96, 124.

[9] William Jordan, "'The Damnable Dilemma': African American Accommodation and Protest during World War I," *Journal of American History* 81/4 (March 1995): 1583.

[10] See Elliott M. Rudwick, *W. E. B. Du Bois: A Study in Minority Group Leadership* (Philadelphia: University of Pennsylvania Press, 1960) 207.

what end? William Jordan is right when he argues, echoing Cornel West's
The American Evasion of Philosophy, that Du Bois was a pragmatist who
was willing within limits to shift his thinking if he thought doing so stood
a chance of bringing the desired outcome. The "Close Ranks" episode
provides us with only one coordinate in trying to pin down Du Bois on
this issue. I choose to begin, instead, with *The Souls of Black Folk* and read
it as part of a dialogue with one of the most avid spokesmen for
American military might during one of our nation's most bellicose
periods, Theodore Roosevelt at the turn of the nineteenth century. I will
argue that with regard to the military, the black soldier, and, by
extension, war, Du Bois was fairly consistent throughout his life. Despite
his militant reputation, he was generally opposed to war, and while he
never failed to support the black soldier, his soldier was a reluctant one,
not by nature given to violence, pushed to fight, and always fighting on
two fronts simultaneously. While military service presented the
opportunity to establish both black manhood and American identity on
terms understood and accepted by the general populace, Du Bois's
concept of manhood relegated military experience to one part of a larger
and more pacifistic sense of identity. Over against Roosevelt's "big stick"
Du Bois poses the peaceful assertiveness of Alexander Crummell.

I begin where so many studies of Du Bois's thought, regardless of the
issue, begin, that is, with his famous concept of double consciousness
from *The Souls of Black Folk*:

> One ever feels his two-ness,—an American, a Negro; two souls,
> two thoughts, two unreconciled strivings; two warring ideals in
> one dark body, whose dogged strength alone keeps it from being
> torn asunder.
> The history of the American Negro is the history of this
> strife,—this longing to attain self-conscious manhood, to merge
> his double self into a better and truer self.[11]

One can't help but notice the martial metaphor of this passage. "Two
warring ideals" battle for control of one body. The conflict is internal, a

---

[11] See W. E. B. Du Bois, *The Souls of Black Folk* in *Writings* (New York: Library of
America, 1986) 365.

socially created psychological one, but the paradox is that this internal strife might be resolved by shifting the energies of the battle to an external opponent. As a tactic, resolving internal strife by turning to an external antagonist is nothing new. Shakespeare's Henry IV, for example, intends to do just that at the beginning of *Henry IV, Part 1* when he tells Westmoreland that those who "Did lately meet in the intestine shock / And furious close of civil butchery, / Shall now, in mutual well-beseeming ranks, / March all one way and be no more opposed / Against acquaintance, kindred, and allies" (I. 1. 12-16). Instead, Henry will lead them against the pagan infidel in the Holy Land. More apropos to the discussion of Du Bois's hopes for the healing power of military service is Richard Slotkin's analysis of the WWII movie, *Bataan*, in his book *Gunfighter Nation*. As he convincingly argues, the movie, with its multiethnic platoon fighting Japanese soldiers they refer to as "monkeys," strives to make the "ideological point...that the test of war will produce unity out of division."[12] The Hollywood answer to the friction caused by internal national divisions along ethnic, racial, and class lines was to gather a diverse group and pit them against a dehumanized enemy. Du Bois did not characterize the "enemy" that way,[13] but the mechanism of internal healing through battle with an external enemy still holds as a possibility to be explored.

We might be concerned that the internal strife that both Henry IV and Slotkin refer to is within the state and not within the individual, as is the case with Du Bois's concept of double consciousness. Du Bois, however,

---

[12] Richard Slotkin, *Gunfighter Nation: The Myth of the Frontier in Twentieth-Century America* (New York: Anthenuem Press, 1992) 322.

[13] Not only did Du Bois not refer to the Japanese in World War II in such a derogatory way, he in fact praised the Japanese as a colored people asserting their own rights in the world. Even when he refers to the Germans in advocating black participation in WWI, he refrains from dehumanizing labels. See, for example, W. E. B. Du Bois, "World War and the Color Line," *The Crisis* 9 (November 1914): 28-30, in W. E. B. Du Bois, *Selections from* The Crisis, *1911-1925, Writings in Periodicals Edited by W. E. B. Du Bois*, edited by Herbert Aptheker, (Millwood: New Jersey: Kraus-Thomson, 1983) 1:83-85. There Du Bois, after warning that "the triumph of Germany means the triumph of every force calculated to subordinate darker peoples," writes, "[t]he writer speaks without anti-German bias; personally he has deep cause to love the German people. They made him believe in the essential humanity of white folk twenty years ago when he was near denying it" (84).

continually made the leap from the individual to the larger entity, as the subtitle to his autobiography *Dusk of Dawn* attests. *An Essay Toward the Autobiography of a Race Concept* assumes that to understand Du Bois is to understand something about the race, and vice versa. The key to that internal resolution for the individual was in the desired outcome: "self-conscious manhood." One could argue that for men in America, going to war has been the surest way to achieve and to demonstrate one's manhood. At least that has been (and to some extent continues to be) a prominent part of America's national mythology, a mythology charted and deconstructed so well by Richard Slotkin in his frontier trilogy. As he puts it in *Regeneration Through Violence,*

> The first colonists saw in America an opportunity to regenerate their fortunes, their spirits, and the power of their church and nation; but the means to that regeneration ultimately became the means of violence, and the myth of regeneration through violence became the structuring metaphor of the American experience.[14]

One could add to the list of things to be regenerated, as Theodore Roosevelt did (as Slotkin shows in *Gunfighter Nation*), both individual and national manhood. But for the African-American man, as Du Bois's framing of the double consciousness bind suggests, going to war has not been simply a project of establishing one's manhood; it has been the arena for proving one's American-ness. And if the Du Bois of *Dusk of Dawn* looking back on his commissioning episode in WWI is to be believed, the power of military service to create a sense of American identity is considerable. Du Bois remarks in his 1940 autobiography, "I became during the World War nearer to feeling myself a real and full American than ever before or since."[15] Over the course of his lifetime Du Bois had had many opportunities to experience that sense of inclusion and identity. Born in 1868, in the wake of America's most devastating conflict, he lived through the Spanish-American War, World

---

[14] Richard Slotkin, *Regeneration Through Violence: The Mythology of the American Frontier, 1600-1860* (New York: HarperPerennial, 1996) 5.

[15] See W. E. B. Du Bois, *Dusk of Dawn: An Essay Toward an Autobiography of a Race Concept* in *Writings,* 741.

Wars I and II, and the Korean War. In 1963, the year he died, the United States was increasing the number of advisors in Vietnam from 12,000 to 15,000.

The specific period leading up to the writing and publication of *Souls of Black Folk* provided plenty of reason for Du Bois to focus on the military and the black soldier. The turn of the century was one of the most militaristic moments in United States' history. Just five years prior to *Souls'* publication, America had charged through the Spanish-American War. In that case it hadn't simply been, as Lincoln, speaking of the Civil War in his second inaugural, had said, that "the war came."[16] Rather, during this period war was sought out. In thirty-five post-bellum years leading up to the century's end, the Civil War remained a visible part of American culture. War monuments were going up everywhere, celebrating the soldiers of both sides of the conflict. Mark Twain was rescued from financial ruin in 1885 with his publication of Grant's memoirs. In 1887 and 1888 the Century Company published its popular *Battles and Leaders of the Civil War*, one of the sources for Stephen Crane's *The Red Badge of Courage*, which appeared first in newspapers in 1894. One monument sure to have captured the attention of African Americans, Augustus Saint-Gaudens's memorial to Robert Gould Shaw and the black soldiers of the Massachusetts 54th Regiment, was erected in Boston in 1897. Despite the shift of America's energies to industrial development and a belief in what Samuel P. Huntington calls "business pacifism" (222), the war had been such a searing experience for the United States that it remained a prominent part of public discourse.

Du Bois's own family background is another important coordinate in assessing his attitude toward military service. Du Bois did have a military pedigree of sorts, one that, David Levering Lewis points out, Du Bois tinkered with in his various autobiographies. His great-great maternal grandfather, Tom Burghardt, had served for three days during the Revolution. Or as Du Bois reports in the *Autobiography*, "He enlisted to serve for three years."[17] Significantly, Du Bois notes that Tom Burghardt's service freed him and his family from slavery, evidence of the efficacy of

---

[16] See Du Bois, *Souls of Black Folk* in *Writings*, 686.

[17] W. E. B. Du Bois, *The Autobiography of W. E. B. Du Bois: A Soliloquy on Viewing my Life from the Last Decade of its First Century* (New York: International, 1968) 62.

military service for bringing about racial uplift.[18] He counted his great grandfather, Jack or Jacob Burghardt, on both sides of Shays's Rebellion and claimed, at least in *Darkwater*, that Jack had participated in the war of 1812.[19] Du Bois's father had served in the Union Army as evidenced by a photo of him in uniform, but it's unclear whether Du Bois ever learned that Alfred had deserted his unit, New York's 20th Regiment of the United States Colored Troops.[20] In the *Autobiography* he links his own birth to the birthday of America's first commander-in-chief: "In 1868 on the day after the birth of George Washington was celebrated, I was born on Church Street, which branched east from Main in midtown."[21] In this sentence Du Bois symbolically draws about himself the mantle of the Revolution, the aura of a prophetic birth, and the plain clothes of anytown America. But it was the first of these, the mantle of the Revolution, that he sought to promote in 1908 when he attempted and failed to be admitted to the Sons of the American Revolution based on the exploits of Tom Burghardt.[22] His feelings about war aside, Du Bois understood the authenticating value of a military lineage. Lewis suggests that one of the motivations for Du Bois to establish himself as a Son of the American Revolution was a desire to exorcise the taint of his father Alfred. Whether that taint was the result of Alfred's failure to do his duty as a soldier or as a father, Lewis doesn't make clear. To some, that distinction might not have mattered. A father who had failed to do his part in the war had also to that extent failed as a father.

During the last quarter of the nineteenth century, Theodore Roosevelt, too, sought to exorcise a paternal demon, but he felt none of the ambivalence toward war that Du Bois felt and had perhaps a bigger hand in shaping America's martial ethos than anyone else of the period. Roosevelt adored his father but, according to biographer H. W. Brands, felt "troubled by his father's failure to serve" in the Civil War.[23] On the

---

[18] W. E. B. Du Bois, *Darkwater: Voices from Within the Veil* in Eric J. Sundquist, ed., *The Oxford W. E. B. Du Bois Reader* (New York: Oxford University Press) 486; Du Bois, *Autobiography*, 62.

[19] Lewis, *W. E. B. Du Bois*, 13; Du Bois, *Darkwater*, 486.

[20] Lewis, *W. E. B. Du Bois*, 22.

[21] Du Bois, *Autobiography*, 61.

[22] Lewis, *W. E. B. Du Bois*, 374-75.

[23] T. H. Brands, *TR: The Last Romantic* (New York: Basic Books, 1997) 19.

other hand, it was a great source of pride to him that several of his predecessors on his mother's side had answered the call to arms, though that call had come from the Confederacy. His uncle James Bulloch in fact had been an admiral on the warship *Alabama*, responsible for sinking or capturing over sixty Union vessels.[24] Roosevelt's asthmatic condition as a youth and his family Civil War heritage combined with a host of cultural influences to produce the man who espoused "the strenuous life" and a muscular, imperialist America.

Roosevelt's collection of essays and addresses, *The Strenuous Life* came out in 1902, the year before Du Bois's *Souls*. In significant ways, *The Souls of Black Folk* can be read as a response to Roosevelt's work. In fact, as I said in the opening, looking over the period from about 1890 up to 1903, the two men almost seem to be in dialogue with one another. Superficially, they have much in common. Both were elitists of sorts, Roosevelt by birth, Du Bois by force of will. Both attended Harvard (Roosevelt graduating a decade earlier than Du Bois), and both were taught by William James. Of that great philosopher of individualism and pragmatism Du Bois said, "he was my friend and guide to clear thinking."[25] He was Roosevelt's vertebrate biology professor.[26] Both held a firm belief in the power of the individual will to shape history, what Shamoon Zamir refers to as a belief in heroic vitalism.[27] For Roosevelt the belief in the hero would undergird his philosophy of the strenuous life; for Du Bois one could trace his notion of the Talented Tenth to his belief in individual excellence. In celebrating privately his twenty-fifth birthday in Berlin, he forecasts just such a heroic role for himself: "These are my plans: to make a name in science, to make a name in literature and thus to raise my race."[28] Paradoxically, the idea of race was also fundamental to the way both Du Bois and Roosevelt saw the world. As Du Bois put it in "The Conservation of Races," "the history of the world is the history,

---

[24] Ibid., 19-20.

[25] Du Bois, *Autobiography*, 143.

[26] Brands, *TR*, 72.

[27] Shamoon Zamir, *Dark Voices: W. E. B. Du Bois and American Thought, 1888-1903* (Chicaco: University of Chicago Press, 1995) 30-32.

[28] W. E. B. Du Bois, "Celebrating His Twenty-Fifth Birthday," in Herbert Aptheker, ed., *Against Racism: Unpublished Essays, Papers, Addresses, 1887-1961* (Amherst: University of Massachusetts Press, 1985) 29.

not of individuals, but of groups, not of nations, but of races." And each race, he says, has its "particular message...which shall help to guide the world nearer and nearer that perfection of human life for which we all long." [29] Roosevelt takes a Spencerian, racist bent, arguing in *The Winning of the West*, "it is of incalculable importance that America, Australia, and Siberia should pass out of the hands of their red, black, and yellow aboriginal owners, and become the heritage of the dominant world races."[30]

We might take TR's four-volume history of the American West as the starting point for the dialogue. Roosevelt opens his narrative with a history of the spread of the English-speaking peoples, essentially a paean to the Anglo-Saxon race:[31]

> [I]t may be fairly said that in America and Australia the English race has already entered into and begun the enjoyment of its great inheritance. When these continents were settled they contained the largest tracts of fertile, temperate, thinly populated country on the face of the globe. We cannot rate too highly the importance of their acquisition. Their successful settlement was a feat which by comparison utterly dwarfs all the European wars of the last two centuries.[32]

In 1890 Du Bois may not have known of or read *The Winning of the West*, (indeed, the four volumes were published over a period of seven years beginning with the first two volumes in 1889) but his Harvard commencement address that year may be read as a response to Roosevelt's Anglo-Saxon thesis. Du Bois's speech entitled "Jefferson Davis as a Representative of Civilization" is particularly important in the context of this essay because as Du Bois puts it, "The Anglo-Saxon loves a soldier—Jefferson Davis was an Anglo-Saxon, Jefferson Davis was a soldier." After apparently praising Davis for his, by Teutonic lights, noble qualities, Du Bois calls Davis's merits into question in ways that bring to

---

[29] W. E. B. Du Bois, "The Conservation of Races," in *Writings*, 817, 819.

[30] Theodore Roosevelt, *From the Alleghenies to the Mississippi, 1769-1776. The Winning of the West* (Lincoln: Nebraska: University of Nebraska Press, 1995 [1889]) 1:63.

[31] See Slotkin's discussion of Roosevelt's Teutonism in *Gunfighter Nation*, 44-47.

[32] Roosevelt, *From the Alleghenies*, 47-48.

mind Roosevelt. Davis's claims to fame, according to Du Bois, were "advancing civilization by murdering Indians," fighting in the imperialist land-grab that was the Mexican War, and finally, championing "a people fighting to be free in order that another people should not be free."[33] Although Roosevelt never fought for slavery, in *The Winning of the West* he writes, "The most ultimately righteous of all wars is a war with savages, though it is apt to be also the most terrible and inhuman. The rude, fierce settler who drives the savage from the land lays all civilized mankind under a debt to him."[34] Roosevelt would also be the motive force behind America's imperialist expansion at the turn of the century. Du Bois might just as well have substituted an older Roosevelt for Davis as his representative of civilization. Both embodied what Du Bois calls "the Strong Man," or "Individualism coupled with the rule of might."[35]

Du Bois offers for our consideration the complementary idea of "the Submissive Man." Whereas Davis was a soldier, "Not as the muscular warrior came the Negro, but as the cringing slave...the personification of dogged patience bending to the inevitable, and waiting."[36] Spoken five years before the Atlanta Cotton States Exposition, Du Bois's address seems to present a vision of the African American that anticipates that of Booker T. Washington. One could even argue that Du Bois's version is potentially more damaging. Washington counseled patience as part of a gradualist approach to uplift. Du Bois is apparently saying that submission and patience are essential qualities of the African American. His characterization of the African American seems to play right into the hands of all those theorists of race who had figured blacks as effeminate. As one example that, according to Thomas F. Gossett, would retain currency even into WWI was Count Arthur de Gobineau's *Essay on the Inequality of the Races*, in which Gobineau explains that of the three race types, the white race is the masculine race while "both the yellow and the black races are 'feminine' races." And, as Gail Bederman shows in *Manliness and Civilization*, Roosevelt would link his imperialist project to the relative manliness of races.

---

[33] W. E. B. Du Bois, "Jefferson Davis as a Representative of Civilization" in *Writings*, 811.

[34] Roosevelt, *From the Alleghenies to the Mississippi*, 3:45.

[35] Du Bois, "Jefferson Davis," 811.

[36] Ibid, 812-13.

Shamoon Zamir provides a useful caution in interpreting Du Bois's Submissive Man: "the meaning of submission in the speech is far from obvious," he says. "Du Bois is in fact proposing 'the submission of *the strength of the Strong* [Zamir's emphasis] to the advance of the all'.... Submission means, then, a kind of Christian-Hegelian recognition of duty and collective debt as the basis of the state."[37] I would go farther than Zamir in qualifying Du Bois's argument. Du Bois had, I suggest, an encyclopedic vision of the world. By that I mean, that a people, a nation, and even the world as a whole were ideally to be unities of fragments, each with their own unity, just as an encyclopedia (or a well-rounded education) would consist of the sum of its treatments of the various disciplines. We see this notion best elaborated in "The Conservation of Races," in which, as I've already mentioned, each race contributes to the world's social and moral development its own gift or message.[38] Hazel Carby, in her book *Race Men*, puts it this way: "Adopting a strategy of direct confrontation with the historical conditions under which he wrote, Du Bois asserted that processes of racialization could create *unified* communities existing in harmony with the national community."[39] The harmonious nation would be a unity of unities. In the Jefferson Davis piece Du Bois is not advocating replacing the Strong Man with the Submissive Man. The two are complementary—necessary to each other. Says Du Bois,

> The Teuton stands today as the champion of the idea of Personal Assertion: the Negro as the peculiar embodiment of the idea of Personal Submission: either, alone, tends to an abnormal developement [sic]....No matter how great and striking the Teutonic type of impetuous manhood may be, it must receive the cool purposeful "Ich Dien" of the African for its round and full developement [sic].[40]

But if this union is truly complementary, then not only does the Negro facilitate the round, full development of the Teuton, the Teuton

---

[37] Zamir, *Dark Voices*, 64.
[38] Du Bois, "Conservation of Races," 817.
[39] Hazel Carby, *Race Men* (Cambridge: Harvard University Press, 1998) 27.
[40] Du Bois, "Jefferson Davis," 813.

does the same for the Negro. If the African American corrects the "moral obtuseness and refined brutality" of the Teuton, perhaps the Teuton brings soldierly power or force to round out the development of the African American.[41] The two qualities in fact provide a basic description of the American soldier, who combines the qualities of service and a willingness to sacrifice for others with the ability to employ force as the means to that service.

Roosevelt's response may be found in his 1894 essay, "True Americanism." There he writes, "We have no use for the German or Irishman who remains such. We do not wish German-Americans and Irish-Americans who figure as such in our social and political life; we want only Americans."[42] His remarks are directed at immigrant populations, but presumably he would have opposed the idea of an African-American as well. As I've suggested "The Conservation of Races" in 1897 would have reiterated Du Bois's views on this matter. He asks, "What, after all, am I? Am I an American or am I a Negro? Can I be both? Or is it my duty to cease to be a Negro as soon as possible and be an American?....Does my black blood place upon me any more obligation to assert my nationality than German, or Irish or Italian blood would? His answer is firm: "We believe it the duty of the Americans of Negro descent, as a body, to maintain their race identity until this mission of the Negro people has been accomplished, and the ideal of human brotherhood has become a practical possibility."[43] The truth was that maintaining their race identity in America was not, in theory, going to be a problem. What Roosevelt was advocating was assimilation of immigrants in every way, not to exclude intermarriage. For white Americans that degree of African American assimilation was not acceptable. This was after all the heyday of Jim Crow, conveniently (for whites) assented to by Booker Washington.

The year 1898 provided a concrete test of the ability of the black soldier to become fully American through soldierly service. The Spanish-American War was Teddy's war. He had pushed hard for it and was greatly distressed by the thought that it all might be over before he could

---

[41] Ibid., 812.

[42] Theodore Roosevelt, "True Americanism," in Mario R. DiNunzio, *Theodore Roosevelt: An American Mind* (New York: Penguin, 1994) 170.

[43] Du Bois, "Conservation of Races," 821, 825.

get into the action.[44] He lobbied for and received permission to put together his own regiment of men drawn largely from the West he celebrated, but also from the ranks of his east coast Ivy League circle. Perhaps most interesting is the fact that the Rough Riders included both Mexican and Native Americans but no blacks.[45] Black soldiers were already segregated into the Buffalo soldier units of the 9th and 10th Cavalries and the 24th and 25th Infantry Regiments, all of which saw action in Cuba. By some accounts the black units saved Roosevelt's Rough Riders during the fighting. In *The Black Troopers, Or the Daring Heroism of the Negro Soldiers in the Spanish-American War*, published in 1899, the same year as Roosevelt's *The Rough Riders*, Miles V. Lynk, writes, presumably of the skirmish at Las Guasimas,

> "The Rough Riders" a New York cavalry regiment of whites popularly so called because it was composed of athletes and cowboys, was with the division in which the 9th, was serving. This regiment was considered the crack, white volunteer regiment, and was in charge of Lieut. Col. Theodore Roosevelt. These new recruits, not being used to guerilla war-fare, were ambuscaded by a handful of Spanish sharp shooters, and would have been exterminated had it not been for the timely arrival and quick work of the 9th and 10th cavalries.[46]

One of Roosevelt's own corporals is reported to have said virtually the same thing about the charge up San Juan Heights: "If it had not been for the Negro cavalry...the Rough Riders would have been exterminated."[47] Looking back near the end of his life, Du Bois, himself, wrote in *The Ordeal of Mansart,* "Negro regiments at El Caney had saved his Rough

---

[44] Brands, *TR*, 316-17; 340.

[45] According to Slotkin, the Indians in the regiment were segregated in their own company. See *Gunfighter Nation*, 103.

[46] Miles V. Lynk, *The Black Troopers, Or the Daring Heroism of the Negro Soldiers in the Spanish American War* ([1899] New York: AMS, 1971) 24-25.

[47] Theodore Roosevelt quoted in Willrad B. Gatewood, Jr., *Black Americans and the White Man's Burden: 1898-1903* (Chicago: University of Illinois Press, 1975) 59.

Riders from certain defeat. Later the 25th United States Negro regiment which he crucified, had held San Juan Hill for his undisciplined troops."[48]

Immediately following the war the Rough Riders had a much better publicist in Roosevelt himself. Although in his own account of the combat in Cuba, Roosevelt reported his men saying they would be willing "to drink out of the same canteen" as the black cavalrymen, that is only after he has narrated a damning incident that declares the superiority of the white soldier to the black infantryman:

> None of the white regulars or Rough Riders…showed the slightest sign of weakening; but under the strain the colored infantrymen (who had none of their officers [and who, by the way, were all white]) began to get a little uneasy and to drift to the rear…. This I could not allow, as it was depleting my line, so I jumped up, and walking a few yards to the rear, drew my revolver, halted the retreating soldiers, and called out to them that I appreciated the gallantry with which they had fought and would be sorry to hurt them, but that I should shoot the first man who, on any pretense, went to the rear….

After he tells us of his own men's intense interest and their vouching for Roosevelt being as good as his word, he concludes, "This was the end of the trouble, for the 'smoked Yankees'—as the Spaniards called the colored soldiers—flashed their white teeth at one another, as they broke into broad grins, and I had no more trouble with them, they seeming to accept me as one of their own officers."[49]

A couple of things are of interest here, both to do with hierarchy. One is that Roosevelt distinguishes between the infantry and the cavalry. The cavalryman has always had a romantic edge over the infantryman, the mobility and dignity of the horse and its connection to knights of the middle ages conferring a prestige on its rider—a prestige reflecting as well the rank and privilege of the nobility. Roosevelt is, of course, leading a cavalry regiment. The second point is that Roosevelt is quick to praise the

---

[48] Du Bois, *The Ordeal of Mansart*, 217.

[49] Theodore Roosevelt, *The Rough Riders* ([1899] New York: New American Library, 1961,) 35, 95-96.

black soldiers' fighting ability, but his anecdote reveals that the African-American soldier is lost without white leadership. Although there were a few army units around the country with black officers, they were very few in number and usually serving as chaplains. This leadership issue was critical going into World War I and, as we've seen, Du Bois would devote editorial space to the Army's proposal, at the instigation of Joel Spingarn, to create a segregated black officer training facility. In the meantime, *The Souls of Black Folk* and his essay "The Talented Tenth" took on directly the question of black leadership in a way that would dovetail with the issue of black officers.

As others have noted, one way to read *The Souls of Black Folk* is as Du Bois's self-anointing as the next leader of the African-American community. Arnold Rampersad, for example, writes, "*The Souls of Black Folk* is not a novel, but it has a major hero: the soul of W. E. B. Du Bois, his sufferings, his virtues, his gifts, offered as exemplary of the best achievement of the Afro-American people."[50] To ascend to that position meant, of course, dethroning the man acknowledged by white America and most of black America as the spokesman for the Negro, Booker T. Washington. In 1901 newly-seated President Roosevelt took the bold step of inviting Washington to the White House for dinner to discuss appointments of black civil servants. The ensuing furor convinced Roosevelt never to make that mistake again, but he and his successor William Taft, did continue to rely on the Wizard of Tuskegee to guide them on decisions concerning the African-American population. Du Bois would later blame the withdrawal of a Washington DC job as head of black public schools on the Roosevelt-Washington connection.[51] In effect, when Du Bois fires his critique at Washington in chapter three of *Souls*, he is also taking aim at Roosevelt. Roosevelt's validation of Washington's position as the leader of black America simultaneously rendered a judgment on black manliness and leadership abilities. By taking on Washington's educational and political approaches, then, Du Bois was also indirectly attacking Roosevelt's concepts of both black and white manhood.

---

[50] Arnold Rampersad, *The Art and Imagination of W. E. B. Du Bois* (New York: Schocken Books, 1990) 88.

[51] Du Bois, *Dusk of Dawn*, 622.

At first glance there's not much in *The Souls of Black Folk* that addresses the soldier at all. In fact, in "Of the Dawn of Freedom," although he begins with the problem of the liberated slave in the Civil War and speaks of Congress's grudging enlistment of black soldiers; he quickly buries those soldiers in order to pursue other issues. Instead of the black soldier, a triad of figures emerges from Sherman's march through Georgia: "the Conqueror, the Conquered, and the Negro." Neither "soldier nor fugitive," the Negro is here presented as "that dark human cloud that clung like remorse on the rear of those swift columns." Though Du Bois knew well the role black soldiers had played in securing their own freedom during the Civil War, they are here erased in favor of the image of "black men emasculated by a peculiarly complete system of slavery, centuries old."[52] Ironically, at this moment when leadership is desperately needed, the soldier does reenter as a kind of savior:

> [N]ow, suddenly, violently, they [millions of newly freed black men] come into a new birthright, at a time of war and passion, in the midst of the stricken and embittered population of their former masters. Any man might have hesitated to assume charge of such a work, with vast responsibilities, indefinite powers, and limited resources. Probably no one but a soldier would have answered such a call promptly; and, indeed, no one but a soldier could be called, for Congress had appropriated no money for salaries and expenses.[53]

But in this case the soldier is white—Major General Oliver O. Howard, who takes charge of the Freedmen's Bureau and does the best he can in a cause that dies, as Du Bois says, with the birth of the fifteenth Amendment.

If in "Of Booker T. Washington and Others" Du Bois fills the void left by General Howard with a soldier of a different standard for manhood, violence is not the measure. Du Bois outlines a heritage that begins in the eigthteenth century with "the one motive of revolt and revenge" and runs through the insurrections of Gabriel, Vesey, and Nat Turner. "John

---

[52] Du Bois, *Souls of Black Folk* in *Writings*, 48, 50.
[53] Ibid.

Brown's raid is the extreme of its logic."[54] As becomes clear in chapter 6, "Of the Training of Black Men," whatever support Du Bois may have been willing to give the black soldier, he did not espouse violent rebellion; he was not in that sense a forerunner to Malcolm X, advocating change "by any means necessary." Rather, Du Bois implies in chapter 6 that the training he envisions is a means of *containing* violence, and implicit in his presentation of the problem is a warning to his white readers. Three "streams of thinking" open the chapter, each followed by an ominous afterthought. The third "and darker thought" represents that of Du Bois's African-American audience, "the things themselves," who dare to dream of "the chance of living men." Its accompanying afterthought is the fear that the world is right and that they are "less than men." The fears accompanying the first two thoughts, however, are what I want to focus on. Both imply violence. Shadowing the call for "worldwide cooperation" that will unite men of all colors is the threat of "force and dominion," in other words, enforced harmony by those already in power. Most significant for Du Bois's white audience was the second alternative. For those who believe the second stream of thought, that the black man is "a clownish, simple creature...foreordained to walk within the Veil" (90), the fear is that some blacks may yet "become men." Any program to keep them from "breaking through" is an act of "sheer self-defence." Later, he warns "Southern Gentlemen" explicitly, "as the black third of the land grows in thrift and skill, unless skilfully guided in its larger philosophy, it must more and more brood over the red past and the creeping, crooked present, until it grasps a gospel of revolt and revenge and throws its new-found energies athwart the current of advance." [55] Although Elliott Rudwick and August Meier have pointed out that Du Bois "occasionally advocated retaliatory violence," the heritage of leadership that Du Bois outlines in chapter 3 begins in but moves away from the logic of Vesey, Turner, and Brown.[56] While he wants to keep the vision of potential violence in the back of his white readers' minds, the way of riot and rebellion is not his way.

---

[54] Ibid., 65-66.

[55] Ibid., 90-91.

[56] Elliott M. Rudwick and August Meier, "Black Violence in the Twentieth Century: A Study in Rhetoric and Retaliation," in *idem.*, eds., *Along the Color Line: Explorations in the Black Experience* (Urbana: University of Illinois Press, 1976) 226.

Following the early historical phase of violent revolt in Du Bois's account is the period in which Frederick Douglass is the dominant voice for African Americans. By Douglass's own account, his emancipation required a resort to violence (recall that he exchanged slavery for manhood first by learning to read and write but second by physically beating his overseer, Mr. Covey). Nevertheless, in Du Bois's brief history, Douglass represents a leadership of self-assertion with the violence held in check. The means of uplift is politics not war. The history of African-American leadership culminates in Du Bois's outline with Booker T. Washington. Washington's program, of course, represents a step backward, not only renouncing violence but also abandoning self-assertion and self-respect.

In this history of African-American leadership it is not the case that in eschewing violence, Du Bois turns away from the black soldier. When he imagines a different life for Josie's brother Jim in "Of the Meaning of Progress," a life with cultured parentage and a social caste to uphold him, he imagines him as either "a venturesome merchant or *a West Point cadet*"[57] [my emphasis]. In military terms, Du Bois's alternative to Washington's program, which would have been the means for developing solid, dependable soldiers—men who follow orders—is a program that develops solid, dependable officers—men who give orders. The military component of the Talented Tenth would have been West Point graduates. In imagining Josie's brother, the fruit of "cultured parentage," at West Point, Du Bois was surely aware of the elite nature of that institution. By 1903, exactly two African Americans had graduated from West Point since the first, Henry O. Flipper, graduated in 1877. The last of those three, graduating in 1889, was Charles W. Young, destined for distinguished service in Cuba, the Philippines, and later with the 10th Cavalry under General John J. Pershing in Mexico against Pancho Villa. As the United States geared up for World War I, the Army, under pressure from Woodrow Wilson, who was kowtowing to Southern interests, retired him rather than put him in charge of training black officers for service. Du Bois and Young had become friends at Wilberforce University in 1894; consequently, Du Bois knew first-hand of

---

[57] Du Bois, *The Souls of Black Folk*, in *Writings*, 78.

Young's qualifications to be a member of the Talented Tenth.[58] The military's strong resistance to black officers during this period would likely have been one reason that Du Bois makes no mention of military service in "The Talented Tenth" or in "Of the Training of Black Men" in *Souls*; again, however, he would later take up the cause of black officer training in the *Crisis*.[59] Of Du Bois's respect for Young, Lewis writes, "In the increasingly likely event that the United States entered the European war, Du Bois counted on General Young to lead the Talented Tenth into battle."[60]

In 1903, such a hoped for scene of military valor was still fifteen years off. We see a different kind of leader in *The Souls of Black* Folk. In the book's movement from the leadership highlighted in "Of the Dawn of Freedom" to that outlined in "Of Alexander Crummell" we see an enlightened white soldier replaced not by a soldier but by an enlightened, educated black man. Crummell—the man who could have been the leader African Americans needed but who died, "a soul that has missed its duty"—is not only not a soldier, but Du Bois also distances his model leader from Teddy's war.[61] In the Crummell chapter we find the second of two allusions to the Spanish-American War—both of them negative. The first appears in "Of the Quest of the Golden Fleece," where Du Bois links the war to the worldwide economic exploitation of people of color, as he will later do in his *Atlantic Monthly* essay, "The African Roots of the War." Here he writes, "The Negro farmer started behind,—started in debt. This was not his choosing, but the crime of this happy-go-lucky nation which goes blundering along with its Reconstruction tragedies, its Spanish war interludes and Philippine matinees, just as though God really were dead."[62] This is war as theater, something we veterans of the Gulf War, live from CNN, can relate to. It is war emptied of honor and the power to sanction manhood. The other allusion to the Cuban excursion comes, in "Of Alexander Crummell." Here again Du Bois

---

[58] Gerald Aston, *The Right to Fight: A History of African Americans in the Military* (Novato: Presidio, 1998) 95-98; Aptheker, ed., *Correspondence*, 1:221-22.

[59] Along with "Officers" (in note above), see *The Crisis* 13 (April 1917): 270-71, "The Perpetual Dilemma" in *Selections*, 134-35.

[60] Lewis, *W. E. B. Du Bois*, 517.

[61] Du Bois, *Souls of Black Folk*, in *Writings*, 169.

[62] Ibid., 125.

leaves little doubt about his assessment of the war. Crummell, he says, "was born with the Missouri Compromise and lay a-dying amid the echoes of Manila and El Caney: stirring times for living, times dark to look back upon, darker to look forward to."[63] The wars in Cuba and the Philippines seem almost to be the reasons for Crummell's death.

In truth, with Crummell, Du Bois refigures the warrior. Crummell was himself an advocate of the Talented Tenth. If Roosevelt's motto was "speak softly and carry a big stick," Crummell, who "intoned his prayers with a soft, earnest voice," might have recommended speaking softly and saying a big prayer. Regardless of the weapon wielded by Crummell, to sum up both the tragedy and the majesty of Crummell's life Du Bois turns to the imagery of war. In the process he transforms Roosevelt's bellicose image of manliness into a gentler vision of manhood. One of Roosevelt's essays in *The Strenuous Life* was "The American Boy," in which he recommends, in part, a life of physical activity and the simulated strife of athletics to develop the manliness required of a manly nation. Here, Du Bois's answer to that is to remind us of the difficulties of facing "the whirl of living," the "riddle" of life. "And if you find that riddle hard to read," he writes, "remember that yonder black boy finds it just a little harder; if it is difficult for you to find and face your duty, it is a shade more difficult for him; if your heart sickens in the blood and dust of battle, remember that to him the dust is thicker and the battle fiercer." Alexander Crummell shows us how to face that battle:

> Out of the temptation of Hate, and burned by the fire of Despair, triumphant over Doubt, and steeled by Sacrifice against Humiliation, he turned at last home across the waters, humble and strong, gentle and determined. He bent to all the gibes and prejudices, to all hatred and discrimination, with that rare courtesy which is the armor of pure souls. He fought among his own the low, the grasping, and the wicked, with that unbending righteousness which is the sword of the just. He never faltered, he seldom complained; he simply worked, inspiring the young, rebuking the old, helping the weak, guiding the strong.[64]

---

[63] Ibid., 165.
[64] Ibid., 170.

In "Of the Dawn of Freedom" General Howard is a white soldier leading African Americans into the halls of education. Alexander Crummell is an educated black man who shows whites and blacks alike how to go into battle. Indeed in one of his own addresses, Crummell argued on behalf of the black scholar-leader, saying,

> Just here arises the need of the trained and scholarly men of a race to employ their knowledge and culture and teaching to guide both the opinions and habits of the crude masses. The masses nowhere are, or can be, learned or scientific. The scholar is exceptional, just the same as a great admiral like Nelson is, or a grand soldier like Caesar or Napoleon.[65]

Crummell's own choice of models are here decidedly military figures; Du Bois alludes to another figure in describing Crummell early in the chapter: "Four-score years," Du Bois writes, "had he wandered in this same world of mine, within the Veil."[66] What American can hear "four-score" and not think of Abraham Lincoln, reluctantly shepherding a nation through the ordeal of civil war—a war waged for the sometimes warring ideals of liberty and union?

In *The Souls of Black Folk*, Du Bois framed an alternate vision of manly self-assertion to the one promoted by President Roosevelt. As he made clear in his "Credo" of 1904 the violence of war was to be avoided. "I believe," he wrote, "that War is Murder. I believe that armies and navies are at bottom the tinsel and braggadocio of oppression and wrong; and I believe that the wicked conquest of weaker and darker nations by nations of whiter and stronger but foreshadows the death of that strength."[67] And yet he would continue to support the black soldier. Roosevelt's last word in their "dialogue" came in 1906 following the incident in Brownsville, Texas, in which members of the 25th Infantry

---

[65] Alexander Crummell, "Civilization: The Primal Need of the Race," in John H. Bracey, Jr., August Meier, and Elliott Rudwick, eds., *Black Nationalism in America* (Indianapolis: Bobbs-Merrill, 1970) 142.

[66] Du Bois, *The Souls of Black Folk* in *Writings*, 513.

[67] W. E. B. Du Bois, "Credo," in David Levering Lewis, *W. E. B. Du Bois: A Reader* (New York: Henry Holt, 1995) 105.

allegedly shot up the town, killing at least one man. Following an investigation, during which the soldiers refused to identify the guilty parties, Roosevelt dishonorably discharged every member of the unit stationed at Brownsville—167 men, dismissed as less than men. From that time on, Du Bois rarely mentioned Roosevelt without in the same breath recalling his treatment of the soldiers of the 25th.[68]

Du Bois's last word came over fifty years after the Brownsville incident in *The Black Flame*. During the course of that massive historical novel Roosevelt gets another dose of criticism, but Du Bois's final word on Roosevelt's militaristic approach to world affairs is not contained in the few brief mentions of the former president but rather in the novel's treatment of war in general. Manuel Mansart's descendents participate in each of America's big conflicts during the twentieth century prior to Vietnam (and Du Bois manages to foreshadow even that conflict)—WWI, WWII, and the Korean War.

In his treatment of WWI, the pattern of fighting an external opponent in order to heal the internal conflict gets played out literally. Douglass Mansart, eldest son of Manuel finds himself in the trenches of World War I.

> Shuddering with tears he bayoneted young, struggling German boys and despised himself as he did it....Douglass staggered on, blind with blood and deaf with unendurable thunder. Then the mists cleared. Ahead a company of German Hussars came advancing like automatons of Fate. Beside him clustered a hundred black boys from his own company, but immediately ahead and between them and the Germans, scurried a bunch of their own white Southern officers. Both stared back, both stared ahead. Douglass saw distinctly that sneering officer who had ordered him home from Nancy. Deliberately he raised his rifle; deliberately the rifles of the other black boys were raised too; and then all fired: the Germans, the French and the black soldiers.

---

[68] See, for example, *The Crisis* editorials "Mr. Taft," 2 (October 1911): 243 and "Politics," 4 (August 1912): 180-81 in *Selections* 30, 40.

Between the fires the frightened Southern white officers dissolved into bits of flesh and blood.[69]

For one moment in the midst of that European strife, the combatants come together to eliminate the representatives of American racial bigotry, but Douglass's self-loathing undercuts any sense of the curative powers of military service.

During World War II, Manuel's grandson Revels, Jr., joins the Tuskegee Airmen, only to become disillusioned with war: "Suddenly he was sick of it all. Even enemies were human. This, then, was war! He was not punishing enemies. He was not striking against armed and evil men. He was starving little children, raping young girls and crucifying their old fathers and mothers."[70] On his last mission Revels flies his plane skyward until he runs out of fuel, then flies his plane into the ground.

Finally, there is Adelbert, one of Manuel's grandsons, who survives the Korean war minus an arm and his faith in America. After the war, disgusted with his country, he goes to Paris where he meets a "colored" woman—a Vietnamese revolutionary in Paris to assassinate a Vietnamese diplomat who is trying to reestablish colonial ties with France. She carries out her mission successfully and Adelbert helps her escape to Ghana where together they will fight the oppression of the world's colored peoples.[71]

Pointing to Alexander Crummell—in "the sweetness of his strength"—Du Bois, back in 1903, had offered an alternative to Roosevelt's concept of manhood as one attempt to get out of the bind of double consciousness.[72] Eventually he cut through the bind, which was itself a primary motivation for military service, by refusing to allow American-ness to be one of the defining terms and by making Negro identity a subset of being "colored." No longer was the goal to be both "an American and a Negro." His pan-Africanism, which had its beginnings at least as far back as 1919 with the first Pan-African Congress, broke down the national categories that gave the concept of state-regulated military service any sense of legitimacy. If one's allegiance

[69] Du Bois, *The Ordeal of Mansart*, 53–54.
[70] See *World of Color*, 197.
[71] See chapters 17 and 18 of *Worlds of Color*, 272–304.
[72] Du Bois, *The Souls of Black Folk*, in *Writings*, 513.

is to and one's self-identity emerges from a pan-African entity, then it makes no sense to be a soldier for America or for any other country, for that matter. Adelbert is the logical heir to Crummell's soldier for racial justice—a revolutionary for world unity with allegiance to no country, an anti-imperialist, sick of war, but willing to fight for what he believes in.

W. E. B. Du Bois and The Intersection of Race and Sex in the Twenty-First Century

Rufus Burrow, Jr.

Introduction

The sense of twoness, the double-consciousness of being both African and American that W. E. B. Du Bois wrote about in 1903, still exists to harrass and hound African Americans in the early months of the twenty-first century. There are very few signs of abatement. However, there are numerous indicators that unless bold, creative steps are taken, the problem of the color line will persist as a major obstacle to genuine human relations and community-building throughout this century.

This discussion takes as a given the continuing dilemma of racial discrimination in this country. To some degree every person of black African descent experiences racism and its effects everyday of their lives. *Every* African American experiences—often when we least expect it—an almost *uncontrollable rage* as a result of the many subtle ways that racism affects our lives. James Baldwin grappled with this in 1955, characterizing black rage as a disease, accompanied by a fever, which frequently recurs without warning. Baldwin reminded us that once the disease is contracted by African Americans, they then live the remainder of their lives *on guard,* never knowing when the fever will recur and again threaten life. Baldwin wrote about this in *Notes of a Native Son.*

It can wreck more important things than race relations. There is not a Negro alive who does not have this rage in his blood—one has the choice, merely, of living with it consciously or surrendering to it. As for me, this fever has recurred in me, and does, and will until the day I die (Baldwin, *Notes of a Native Son* 84-5).

No African American completely escapes the agony of this rage, for *the problem of the twentieth century and the four centuries preceding it, is now the problem of the twenty-first century.*

Because we are Americans who also happen to be descendants of Africans, we are still treated differently than the descendants of those who *ripped* our ancestors from the African continent and forced them into what was arguably the most dehumanizing form of slavery in the history of civilization.[1] Slavery itself was not foreign to Afrika, but the white man's type of slavery was.

This presentation focuses on the role that W. E. B. Du Bois played in defending the humanity and rights of women in general, and black women in particular. However, I consider this topic in light of my belief that Du Bois was—knowingly or not—in complicity with black sexism. Such a charge sounds strange in light of his forthright, relentless defense of the rights of black women. However, I think it possible to show that despite his early claim that he desired to sacrifice for the liberation, uplift, and progress of his race, his conceptual framework was, as Hazel Carby so aptly put it, "gender-specific." There was, Carby argues, a complete failure on the part of Du Bois and present day black male intellectuals, "to imagine black women as intellectuals and race leaders."[2] That, is, the dominant voice and leadership was to come from African American

---

[1] The nineteenth century black radical abolitionist Christian, David Walker, argued that slavery in the United States was the most cruel of any nation in history. See Walker, *David Walker's Appeal* ([1829] New York: Hill and Wang, 1965) 7-8.

[2] Although I was familiar with some of Carby's work as a cultural critic, I was not, at the time I prepared this selection, aware of her published Du Bois lectures in which she argues this point systematically and brilliantly. See Hazel V. Carby, *Race Men: The W. E. B. Du Bois Lectures* (Cambridge: Harvard University Press, 1998) chap. 1. Wilfred Samuels of the University of Utah informed me of this work at the Symposium Celebrating the Centennial Anniversary of the Publication of *The Souls of Black Folk* hosted by Mercer University, March 23-25, 2000.

males. Yet I admit at the outset that I am not as concerned to establish Du Bois's sexism as I am to suggest the need for us to expand his "double-consciousness" idea in the new millennium to include black women's consciousness, or more specifically, the problem of black sexism. The argument of some black men (and women) to the contrary, what we know as sexism is not a recent phenomenon in the African-American community. I then discuss briefly some implications of the beloved community ideal for black male and black female relations in the twenty-first century.

SEXISM AND THE AFRICAN AMERICAN COMMUNITY

The term "sexism" was not in common usage in Du Bois's day. However, his frequently used phrase "the damnation of women," surely approximated what we mean by sexism today. Du Bois persistently declared that womens' basic human and civil rights were denied solely because of their gender, and that such a practice was inconsistent with claims of human rights documents such as the Declaration of Independence and the Constitution of the United States.

Not surprisingly, many men—of all races—pretend either not to know what sexism is, or that such a beast even exists. We should allow for the possibility that some men may honestly not know what sexism is, or that it in fact exists. However, many males who *are* aware of the existence of sexism have yet another means of denial at our disposal. Very many of us are quick to say: "I concede that sexism exists, and I even have a sense of what it might be. But sexism must be a fairly recent phenomenon in the black community." Many African-American males have found this line of thought appealing. After all, many of us have only recently acknowledged that sexism exists in the black community. "So if sexism exists at all," some have reasoned, "it has come about only recently, say, within the last thirty years."

There was a time, e.g., the 1970s, when African-American men (and many black women) were quick to acknowledge the existence of sexism in the white community. Sexism was "white peoples' problem." Black men reasoned that black women had been deceived by white feminists, and that their energies should be devoted not to the issue of women's rights, but to the fact of racism, which dehumanizes all blacks.

This has not been an uncommon stance among black males, whether of religious or non-religious persuasion. Essentially we were saying that sexism is a white problem, and as such, it has nothing to do with black people and their struggle against racism. It is only in recent years that many men have acknowledged the existence of sexism in every community. But it is interesting to note that many African-American men are not willing to concede that we are complicit in sexism in the black community.

Sexism. What is it? It is a type of prejudice *plus* power that men and some women exercise *over* women of all races and classes, and without fear of retribution. Therefore, sexism is much more serious than mere prejudice against women. Sexism is the subordination, or we might say with Du Bois, "the damnation of women," primarily by men, *plus* the power to enforce it in order to make it appear that sexist practices are not even occurring, when in fact they are. That, in part, is why the white-male-controlled legal system places so much of the onus on the woman to *prove* that she is being sexually harrassed on the job, for example. The point is to cause women to feel that *perceived* sexual harrassment is but a figment of their imagination.

Although sexism manifests itself in individual men and women, the term is used here to mean *a complex system of ignorance, power, and exploitation used to oppress, abuse, and dehumanize women.*[3] Generally white men effectively control the life-chances of all women. African-American men have neither the power nor other resources needed to *systematically oppress and exploit* white and other women outside the black community. Nor do they possess the power, economic, and other resources to systematically exploit the masses of African-American women, although some degree of exploitation surely occurs. In addition, *by definition any male can be prejudicial toward any woman of any race.*

Black men do have *some* power within the context of the black community; power that is sufficient to effectively control some of the life-chances of black women. This cannot be denied. But beyond the black community, African-American men do not possess the power and

---

[3]This is essentially Manning Marable's way of defining racism, but I think that aspects of it may be appropriate for characterizing sexism as well. See his *Speaking Truth to Power* (Boulder CO: Westview Press, 1996) 87.

resources to *systematically subordinate and oppress* white and other women.

Although there are numerous individual sexists, some of whom, like myself, work hard and relentlessly to *recover* from it, my focus is on sexism in its institutional forms. This is important because it is possible for an individual male to be a recovering sexist, vigilant in eradicating vestiges of sexism in his speech and practice, but still be vulnerable to the charge of sexism. The reason for this is quite simple. As long as men benefit materially and otherwise from sexism, we are open to the charge of being in complicity with it. We are especially vulnerable to this charge if we *choose* not to fight against sexism in all areas of life. Indeed, it is precisely here that I have a contention with W. E. B. Du Bois. There is absolutely no question that he was the quintessential champion of black women's rights. However, Du Bois failed to name or to see himself as a beneficiary of black women's oppression. The *naming* and *seeing* are crucial, especially for one with the public stature and influence of Du Bois. In addition, the failure to name and to see himself as being in complicity with sexism are just as telling. This prompts me to wonder whether some unacknowledged undercurrent regarding the role of black women, for example, was at work shaping and informing Du Bois's way of being, thinking, and acting.

At any rate, black sexism, as the term is used in this discussion, is the intentional *and* unintentional systematic subordination of black women by black men. I must name this black sexism rather than mere prejudice against black women because in a number of black institutions, e.g., black churches, African-American men do possess sufficient power to enforce our prejudices against black women.

In many black churches, black women are allowed to occupy nearly every office except that of senior pastor. She can be an evangelist, director of Christian education, Sunday school superintendent, usher, cook, deacon, or elder. The one thing she cannot be in many churches is the senior pastor.[4] Indeed, in some black churches women are not even allowed to enter the pulpit area.

---

[4]See discussion in C. Eric Lincoln and Lawrence Mamiya, *The Black Church in the African American Experience* (Durham: Duke University Press, 1990) chap. 10, "The Pulpit and the Pew: The Black Church and Women."

A few years ago I attended an installation service of a former student. A number of persons were invited to give remarks. I watched as several men went to and spoke from the pulpit. Then came a black woman, who was aware that in some black churches women are not allowed to enter the pulpit. I observed as the woman stood spellbound as she looked at the pastor for a nod of approval or disapproval. The pastor literally took a few moments to silently deliberate on the matter, and then gave his nod of approval.

On another occasion I attended a workshop on black women in ministry, led by the womanist theologian Jacquelyn Grant. Professor Grant told the participants of an experience she had in a large black church in Chicago. Like a number of the black men who were in attendance, she wanted to place her tape recorder near the pulpit to tape a particular speaker. As she approached the pulpit her progress was impeded by a male official of the church who whispered to her: "Women are not allowed in the pulpit area." He then offered to place the recorder there for her.

SEXISM IS NOT A NEW THING IN THE AFRICAN-AMERICAN COMMUNITY

Sexism is neither "a white thing" only, nor a recent menace in the black community. In fact, it may be dated to at least the nineteenth century in this country, although there is evidence that it long antedates American slavery, and is traceable to the African continent. For example, Darlene Clark Hine and Kathleen Thompson tell us that although many African tribeswomen had more autonomy and authority than their European counterparts, neither group of women ever exercised dominant power over men. According to these historians, patriarchy and the practice of the "branding of women as 'other'" was not one that African men encountered for the first time in the American colonies.[5]

Marie Pauline Eboh argues similarly. She maintains that historically the status of women on both the African and Western continents has been similar. "Women in these continents," she writes, "have sweated

---

[5] Darlene Clark Hine and Kathleen Thompson, *A Shining Thread of Hope: The History of Black Women in America* (New York: Broadway Books, 1998) 11; chaps. 1-2.

heavily under the woe-begone patriarchal burden of male superiority and dominance on the one hand, and female subjugation (lack of voice and choice) on the other hand." Accordingly, Eboh maintains that in both African and Western nations women are essentially relegated to the private sphere of the home as homemakers, whose "sole purpose in life was to marry and beget children...."[6]

However, there is no unanimity of thought on the subject. Vashti M. McKenzie, for example, maintains that the "practice of female inferiority and subservience" was less prevalent on the African than the Asian and European continents. From antiquity African women were more often partners in family and community. There was an equality between African men and women that was not as readily apparent in other parts of the world.[7] McKenzie agues further that African women were the full equals of men, and that this egalitarianism between the sexes was the original condition before African culture was tainted by Asian, Arab, and Western European male-dominated cultures and ideologies.

Perhaps the most that can be said is that there is no unanimity of thought on the subject. One cannot speak with final authority about the entire African continent regarding the historical relation between women and men. One might be able to make some determination regarding the practice in a particular African nation and culture, but one should then be slow to make generalizations to be applied to all others.

With this background in mind we can now examine Du Bois's relationship to women's rights and black sexism. What do we learn from *The Souls of Black Folk* (hereafter *Souls*) which may be appropriated for community-building between black women and black men in the twenty-first century?

DU BOIS AND THE CHAMPIONING OF WOMEN'S RIGHTS

As early as 1907 Du Bois called for the full political equality of *all* women. On 11 March of that year he responded to a letter from M. B. Marston in

---

[6] Marie Pauline Eboh, "The Woman Question: African and Western Perspectives." *African Philosophy: An Anthology*, ed., Emmanuel Chukwudi Eze (Malden: Blackwell Publishers Ltd., 1998) 333.

[7] Vashti M. McKenzie, 14-15.

which he noted his support of women's rights: "I sympathize too with the women in their struggle for emancipation. I believe in full rights for human beings without distinction of race or sex. At the same time I hesitate to say anything concerning women's rights because most women in the United States are so narrow that anything I should say would be misinterpreted."[8] The "narrowness" to which Du Bois referred had to do with the racism among many white feminists.

In at least three significant ways Du Bois contributed to the liberation of women from patriarchy and subordination to men. First, he supported the woman suffrage movement through numerous supportive statements and articles. In addition, as editor he devoted three issues of the *Crisis*, September 1912, August 1915, and November 1917, respectively, to this issue. Second, Du Bois gave practical assistance to the efforts of women to get themselves heard and taken seriously. Third, more than any other male peer Du Bois focused on the plight of black women and their contributions to racial and sexual liberation.[9]

It is an indisputable fact that not long after the publication of *Souls*, Du Bois saw clearly the linkage between race, class, and sex. Even before the publication of *Souls*, Du Bois reported appreciatively on resolutions issued by the National Afro-American Council in 1899 which urged against the degradation and rape of women of any color, by men of any race.[10] In fact, even in *Souls* he addressed the tragedy of the rape of black women by white men (86). In 1910 he wrote that black women were without protection of law and custom, but were "derided as lewd" (Wilson, ed. 315). Du Bois early exhibited a clear sense that not only were women's human rights violated by men, but their bodies as well.

In *Darkwater: Voices from within the Veil* (1920), a book published seventeen years after *Souls*, Du Bois included a powerful chapter, "The Damnation of Women," which focused on the trials and struggles of women in general, and more particularly, black women. There he wrote that "the uplift of woman is, next to the problem of the color line and the

---

[8] Aptheker, *The Correspondence of W. E. B. Du Bois: Selections 1877-1934*, I:127.

[9] Bettina Aptheker, "On 'The Damnation of Women': W. E. B. Du Bois and a theory for Woman's Emancipation" in *Woman's Legacy: Essays on Race, Sex, and Class in American History*, ed. B. Aptheker (Amherst: University of Massachusetts Press, 1982) 78-79.

[10] H. Aptheker, *A Documentary History of the Negro People in the United States*, 2:777

peace movement, our greatest modern cause" (181). It was not his
intention to subsume the woman question under race, class, or the issue
of peace. A sociologist and historian, Du Bois knew that social facts such
as race, sex, and class were intermingled, though each was a problem to
be addressed in its own right. However, it remains a puzzle that although
Du Bois early linked race and sex, he failed to do so in a way that
blacks—especially men—could see the fact of the damnation of black
women with as much clarity as they saw the fact of racism.

To speak only of Du Bois's double-consciousness theme today cannot
be deemed either reasonable or morally plausible. Because of the long-
standing existence of sexism in the African-American community, it is
important for the survival whole of that community that we expand the
twoness theme to include the consciousness of black women and their
experience of sexism. Indeed, if poverty and being a lesbian happens also
to be aspects of her experience and reality, the black woman may be the
victim of at least five tightly meshed, multilayered, interlocking
oppressions: racism, colorism, sexism, economic exploitation, and
heterosexism.

Sensitive to the plight of women, Du Bois believed that if the fact of
racism were eliminated, this in itself would go a long way toward the
achievement of women's rights. He therefore worked simultaneously and
persistently on both liberation fronts. In addition, he was keenly aware
that even white feminists were frequently racists, and he did not hesitate
to tell them so.[11]

In the public sphere Du Bois rejected all attempts to subordinate
women to men. For him, part of the tragedy of "the damnation of
women" was the long held, wrongheaded belief that women exist not for
themselves, not as beings of intrinsic value, but for the pleasuring of men
(*Darkwater,* 163). As such, their value was not inherent, but imputed to
them by men. Presumably, the value that women do have is a result of
their worth to one or more men. To Du Bois it was indisputable that

---

[11]See Du Bois's letter to Miss M. B. Marston on 11 March 1907. Noting his sympathy
for women's struggle for emancipation, Du Bois declines at the time to say much
concerning women's rights for fear of being misunderstood. But he then writes: "The
Negro race has suffered more from the antipathy and narrowness of women both South
and North than from any other single souce" (Aptheker, ed., *The Correspondence of
W. E. B. Du Bois 1877-1934,* 1:127).

women should have the right to motherhood at their own discretion. Therefore, he early lent his support to birth control based on "reason and common sense...."[12]

Du Bois rejected the popular male practice of "benevolent guardianship" and the corresponding belief that men know what is best for women (*Darkwater*, 140). He also repudiated the belief that women and blacks did not really need the ballot, since white men are presumably better qualified to make political decisions for them.[13] Du Bois had neither stomach for nor patience with those who thought they knew the pain of the oppressed (whether blacks or women) better than they, and consequently that they are better able to speak for them.

It was not enough to talk about women's rights in abstract terms. Du Bois knew well the special problems that the black woman experienced—that she was at least doubly oppressed by virtue of her gender and race. "The world that wills to worship womankind," he said, "studiously forgets its darker sister."[14]

In the public arena Du Bois was especially concerned about the double oppression of black women. He did not hesitate to challenge black male chauvinism,[15] an effort for which he should be applauded. However, it must also be pointed out that he seemed to have little sense of his own complicity in black sexism, the way in which he benefited from it, and the masculine gendered language through which he discussed all issues, including women's rights.

What we need to be clear about is that one can champion the humanity, dignity, and rights of others without also being aware of or willing to acknowledge his own complicity in the problem, and how he benefits from it. This, I think, was Du Bois's unacknowledged dilemma.

---

[12]See letter from Margaret Sanger to Du Bois in 1925, and his response which included an enclosed statement of his support, per Sanger's request, in Aptheker, ed., *The Correspondence of W. E. B. Du Bois: Selections 1877-1934*, 1:301, 302.

[13] Foner, ed., *Speeches and Addresses*, 232.

[14]Du Bois, *Darkwater*, 165. The reference here seems to be to what came to be known as the "nineteenth century cult of motherhood," whereby the white woman was portrayed in literature and in other areas as the perfect woman and mother, whose place was in the home. Angela Davis gives an excellent analysis of this phenomenon, pointing out the socio-political implications. See Angela Y. Davis, *Women, Race & Class* (New York: Random House, 1981) Chap. 2.

[15] Marable, *W. E. B. Du Bois*, 84.

It was and continues to be the dilemma of both liberal and progressive whites who champion blacks' desire to be liberated from racism. Frequently the most sensitive whites write and speak eloquently on racism, but they do so in a way that implies that they are writing or speaking about the racism of other white people. They effectively take themselves out of the equation altogether, seldom if ever acknowledging, writing, and talking about their own racism; how it makes them feel; and what they intend to do about it.

A similar phenomenon seems to be at work regarding progressive males of all races who write on the fact of sexism or the damnation of women. Du Bois, a staunch advocate of the humanity, dignity, and rights of black women, fell short in this regard. He neither named sexism as a fundamental problem for the black community, nor did he seem to be aware of his own complicity in it.

DU BOIS AND BLACK SEXISM

Du Bois never declared himself either to be a sexist, or to be in complicity with black sexism. Nor did he explicitly address the fact of the origin of sexism and the oppression of women, which has a much longer history than racism. Fifty years after the publication of *Souls*, Du Bois declared that "back of the problem of race and color, lies a greater problem which both obscures and implements it..." (xiv) namely, the problem of class. Interestingly, he had by this time a more acute awareness of the economic connection with racism after the publication of *Souls*, but we do not see the same clearness of awareness of the linkage between race and sexism. That is, while Du Bois saw with clarity the class linkage with race and named it, he did not also explicitly name sex as part of that "greater problem which both observes and implements it."

Karen Baker-Fletcher maintains that the foremost male champion of women's rights, i.e., Du Bois, was not free of sexist or male chauvinist practices even in the public arena regarding black women intellectuals such as Anna Julia Cooper.[16] There might well be something to this. In an insightful introductory essay in Anna Julia Cooper, *A Voice From the*

---

[16] Karen Baker-Fletcher, *A Singing Something: Womanist Reflections on Anna Julia Cooper*, 49.

South, Mary Helen Washington implies that Du Bois may have been guilty of sexism regarding Cooper, a recipient of the Ph.D. degree from the Sorbonne in 1925. Washington observes that Du Bois and other leading black intellectuals of the late nineteenth-century "formed the prestigious American Negro Academy 'for the promotion of Literature, Science, and Art,'" limiting the membership to "men of African descent."[17] At the urging of Alexander Crummell in 1894, what became the Academy in 1896 was to be composed of fifty of the best black scholars who would address every aspect of African life and culture on the continent and in diaspora. These would be in the forefront of blacks' struggle for political power and equality.[18]

In any event, Mary Helen Washington has expressed concern that Du Bois and other members of the academy exhibited no mutual respect for black women intellectuals.[19] She therefore writes: "In spite of the reverential way [Cooper] referred to her male colleagues—her distinguished counterparts rarely returned the compliment in print. Cooper's relationship with Du Bois underscored how women got left out of black political life."[20] However, Cooper, Anna H. Jones, Bishop Alexander Walters, and Du Bois were all selected by a committee to represent African Americans at the international Pan African conference in London in 1900.[21]

Nevertheless, there is another reason to give pause vis-á-vis Du Bois's position regarding women. What of his treatment regarding his wife and daughter? Was his private behavior consistent with his public career and practice? Was he aware of the extent to which he benefitted from his late Victorian stance on the role of women in the home? Like most men of his day, Du Bois believed himself to be the head of the household, with all of the benefits pertaining thereto. The woman was expected to be the primary caregiver to children and the home. David L. Lewis has written about this aspect of Du Bois's complex double life.

---

[17] Mary Helen Washington, "Introductory Essay," in Anna Julia Cooper, *A Voice from the South,* (New York: Oxford University Press, 1988) xl.

[18] Marable, *W. E. B. Du Bois,* 34, 35.

[19] Carby makes a similar criticism of Cornel West and others of the so-called new black intellectuals. See *Race Men,* 194n6.

[20] Washington, "Introductory Essay," xl.

[21] Marable, *W. E. B. Du Bois,* 39.

Nina Yolande Du Bois's role as an effaced and dutiful wife was
not entirely of her own choosing…A theoretical feminist whose
advocacy could erupt with the force of a volcano (as in "The
Burden of Black Women" in the November 1907 *Horizon*, or in
"The Damnation of Women" in the 1921 collection of essays,
Darkwater), *Du Bois proved to be consistently patriarchal in his role
as husband and father. The all-too-commonplace truth is that he
increasingly acted as a well-intentioned tyrant at best and a bullying
hypocrite at worst.…*If his expectations of Nina were narrow, they
remained exacting. She had the duty not to hinder his own
private and public involvements and to follow his prescriptions
for their daughter's intellectual development. His expectations of
Yolande were as exalted as they were unrealistic (emphasis
added).[22]

Essentially Du Bois expected her to be a housewife, and to raise their
daughter in light of what *he* thought best for child rearing. His wife's
place was in the home. Period.

In response to a concern raised by Mary Nell Morgan,[23] I need here to
comment on Lewis's statement that in the home Du Bois behaved like "a
well-intentioned tyrant at best and a bullying hypocrite at worst."
Morgan takes issue with this, claiming that it was too harsh an assessment
of Du Bois, and that his wife willingly accepted the role of primary parent
and caregiver in the home. Morgan presented no specific evidence to
support her claim. However, she inquired further as to whether Du Bois's
relationship with his second wife, Shirley Graham, was different.

First, Lewis made no claim that Du Bois was physically abusive toward
his first wife and their daughter. As far as we know he was not. However,
abuse in marital relationships may take other forms, e.g., verbal, silence,
denial of affection, or domineering behavior. Second, we need to

---

[22] Lewis, *W. E. B. Du Bois.* 435, 451.

[23] Morgan was a participant in the Du Bois symposium at Mercer University, 23-25
March 2000. She teaches in the Political Science Department at SUNY, Stony Brook. The
symposium, "W. E. B. Du Bois, Race and the New Millennium: A Symposium Celebrating
the Centennial Anniversary of the Publication of *The Souls of Black Folk*," was directed by
Chester J. Fontenot, Baptist Professor of English and Chair, English Department.

remember that Nina Du Bois was also college bred, and precisely at a time when the college educated black woman was still a rarity. Very many black women who were as privileged in those days devoted their lives to teaching or some other vocation in their effort to contribute to the uplift of the race. It is quite possible that Mrs. Du Bois accepted the role of primary parent, but one wonders whether her husband also pressured her to make such a decision.

I raise this point particularly in light of Du Bois's own admission that although he considered himself to be a good provider for his wife and daughter, they were "incidents" in his "main life work," which was not in the home, but "out in the world."[24] Although we may be tempted to believe that remaining in the home, doing household work, and rearing their daughter was Nina Du Bois's "choice," there is as yet no evidence against Lewis's claim that her decision had more—or at least as much—to do with her husband's contradictory feminism and his *expectation* that she be confined to the home and the task of child rearing.

My third response is that it would not be surprising if Du Bois's relationship with Shirley Graham was qualitatively different from that with his first wife, who died in 1950. Du Bois was eighty-three when he overcame his "reluctance"[25] and married Graham, who was forty-five, in 1951. By virtue of sheer difference in age one may speculate that this was a different relationship in kind than that between Du Bois and his first wife. A much older, and perhaps much wiser man regarding the marital relationship, Du Bois was not likely as demanding regarding role differences. In addition, an activist, musicologist, novelist, and playwright, Graham herself was quite accomplished by this time and clearly was not the homebound type. Furthermore, there were no children to be raised. In light of these and other matters one should expect that Du Bois's and Graham's was a different type of marital relationship.

Since Lewis's first volume only treats the first fifty years of Du Bois's long life and career, he does not here discuss the marriage to Shirley Graham. However, based on what was said in the above paragraph we can speculate that what will appear in the subsequent volume of the

---

[24] Du Bois, *The Autobiography of W. E. B. Du Bois*, 281.
[25] Marable, *W. E. B. Du Bois: Black Radical Democrat*, 180.

biography[26] will be commensurate. In addition, that Du Bois was understandably lonely by this time in his life "because so many boyhood friends had died, and because a certain illogical reticence on my part had never brought me many intimate friends,"[27] lends support to the thesis that he and Graham had a qualitatively different relationship than he and Nina.

Regarding the role of women in the home one may be tempted to say that Du Bois was merely a man of his time. He simply behaved at home in a way that was consistent with much of the late Victorian practices of his day. One might even be tempted to say that it was permissible in those days to live by one set of rules in the privacy of one's home and another in public.[28] Therefore Du Bois could fight for the rights of women in the public arena, while fairly ignoring their dignity and rights within the context of the home. This notwithstanding, there is no way to square such inconsistent behavior with that of the genuine humanitarian. Such a person, it seems to me, would be ever vigilant in seeking coherence between his public and private behavior. To have fought gallantly for the rights of women in the public sphere, while ignoring their humanity and dignity in his own home, leaves Du Bois open to the charge of hypocrisy.

A staunch advocate of feminist principles in the public arena, Du Bois was off the path in the private sphere. We see another instance of this in his treatment of his daughter. According to biographer Lewis:

> Daughter Yolande was to be sacrificed time and again to the cruelest of double standards. On the one hand, her life, like her mother's, was controlled by the head of the family—a man whose faith in his own wisdom was serene and always unequivocal; but, whereas other late-Victorian husbands and fathers were determined to shelter their womenfolk from overexposure to education and public life, Du Bois's marching orders commanded Yolande to become superlatively educated and emancipated.[29]

---

[26]In the acknowledgments of volume 1 Lewis writes of how the initial plan of a single volume biography on Du Bois turned into a two-volume one (xii).

[27] Quoted in Marable, *W. E. B. Du Bois*, 180.

[28] Chuck Collins, Betsy Leondar-Wright, and Holly Sklar, *Shifting Fortunes: The Perils of the Growing American Wealth Gap* (Boston: United for a Fair Economy, 1999) 230-31

[29] Lewis, *W. E. B. Du Bois*, 451.

Lewis's description portrays for us a different side of Du Bois the man and champion of women's rights. His insistence that Yolande be educated in a certain way and that his wife follow his dictates to the letter was indicative of male control over women. Here we see a major inconsistency between Du Bois's public "theoretical" feminism and his private treatment of his wife and daughter. Publicly he was the undisputed male champion of women's rights, despite his unacknowledged masculine gendered language. Privately Du Bois was—intentionally or not—abusive and patriarchal toward his wife and daughter.

RACE, SEX, AND THE BELOVED COMMUNITY

No community can be all that it is capable of being if half of its population is systematically dehumanized. Such persons are effectively denied the chance to contribute to community-making to the fullest extent of their capability. In the long run, unless this is corrected, we all—the entire human family—lose.

The friendliest, most enlightened male still benefits from sexism. As long as sexism exists there will be a preference for men *over* women in every sphere of life and in all basic life-chances. As long as men are preferred by virtue of our gender it means, among other things, that there will be less competition from representatives of the other half of the human family. To have such an advantage is a major benefit in one's bid for a meaningful existence.

In this new millennium there must be hope that African Americans possess both the will and the ability to overcome obstacles to full personhood and citizenship in the United States. We cannot be all that it means to be persons and what it means to be community if we deny to others what these mean. For to be a person means to be deeply in touch with our interrelatedness with each other and with the rest of creation.[30] To be a person is to be intimately in touch with the God in self and in others to the extent that we respect the humanity and dignity of every person as a matter of course. To be in complicity with sexism in the African-American community and to do nothing to eradicate this

---

[30] Ashanin, 142.

menace is to be guilty of disregarding the humanity and dignity of black women, and ultimately of all persons.

The question that remains is whether African Americans have the will, courage, and moral resolve to uncover gendered thinking and behavior and to dismantle sexist structures in our community. It is a God-given right that African American women be fully human and all that that entails. W. E. B. Du Bois believed to the end that "the rights of humanity are worth fighting for...."[31] He was most especially concerned that African Americans exhibit the courage to fight for their rights, but since he was aware of the oppression of black women, even within their race, he would be just as adamant today that we—black men and black women—fight for their rights. This is the only assurance we have that anything that may have even a semblance of the beloved community among African Americans will emerge.

The beloved community is one in which persons will intentionally live in ways that affirm the humanity and dignity of self, the neighbor, and nonhuman aspects of creation. In this type of community persons will respect each other's personhood regardless of race, sex, age, sexual orientation,[32] and class. The creation of such a community will not be possible if the experience of any group is made to appear less valuable than that of any other. The beloved community will remain a faint dream, or at best an abstraction, as long as any group of persons is denied full humanity, dignity, and basic life-chances.

Du Bois's "double-consciousness" theme did not include the consciousness of black women and their experience of sexism in the black community. Du Bois was a humanitarian who sought the truth wherever he could find it. I therefore find it difficult to imagine that in the light of the challenges being made by many African-American women regarding

---

[31] Quoted Northrup 8.

[32] I make a distinction between "sexual orientation" and "sexual preference." The latter may imply choice, followed by a corresponding lifestyle. Sexual orientation on the other hand implies a particular lifestyle as well, but because it is *orientation* it is given in the process of creation, and thus the lifestyle is not chosen. That is, one *discovers* at the core of one's being that "this is who one is." One has as much choice in this as he has in the color of his eyes at birth or even his heterosexuality. The only chance that one has at happiness is to live to the fullest who she discovers herself to be. See Clark Williamson's excellent biblico-theologico-ethico discussion in *Way of Blessing Way of Life: A Christian Theology* (St. Louis: Chalice Press, 1999) 172-84.

the fact of sexism that he would not want to expand the double-consciousness theme to include black women's consciousness were he alive today.

Racism and sexism are not merely sociological and historical problems. As a theological social ethicist, I can say that they are fundamentally moral-theologico problems. If it is the case that persons are at bottom both autonomous and communal beings, then any practice which disregards their individual value and also makes community unnecessarily difficult to achieve must be deemed immoral. It must be immoral because every individual is imbued with the fragrance of the God who calls them into existence *to be together*. Because God willingly, thoughtfully, and lovingly calls persons into being, they have inviolable worth. In addition, practices, e.g., racism and sexism, which alienate races and genders from each other must be deemed immoral. The reason for this claim is the Jewish-Christian, personalistic, and African traditional conviction that God creates persons in and for community. Persons are not created to live apart, but in relationship.

W. E. B. Du Bois was not only a careful scholar, but a committed activist. We learn from his example that there are times, e.g., when one faces off with racism and sexism. On such occasions one has to declare herself to be *for* or *against*, and then have the courage to back it up through deeds. There must be no muting of the trumpet in such cases. There comes a time when one must declare that he is for racism, or against it; that he is for sexism, or against it. If he is against these he must show himself to be acceptable to reasonable people and to the God of the universe by doing all in his power to work toward their eradication. In the case of sexism he begins the process by first naming his own complicity in it and his desire to recover from it.

There is no such thing as moral neutrality. To be a person is to be an agent, i.e., to have the capacity to do or to act. This means that even when persons pretend not to act, not to take a stand for or against racism and sexism, they in fact act anyway. We make a moral choice, even when we decide not to decide. Persons are created in such a way that we are *forced to face our freedom*, whether we like it or not. Or, to quote Jean-Paul Sartre, "...man is *condemned to be free*. Condemned, because he did not create himself, yet, in other respects is free; because, once thrown into the world, he is responsible for everything he does" (emphasis added).[33] As persons we choose, even when we pretend that we don't. Sartre reminds us that for one to do something and pretend that the devil or some other force or circumstance made him do it, is to act in "bad faith."[34]

Today there is not only a continuing vast racial divide in the United States. The chasm between the sexes is just as broad and deep. For the African-American woman, however, the problem is exacerbated. Du Bois knew that even if serious efforts were made by whites and blacks to address the problem of the color line, there would be much lingering bitterness. It is no less the case regarding the sex line.

I have argued for the need to expand the double-consciousness theme to include the brooding that rightly occurs among growing numbers of African American women regarding past and present wrongs which they have suffered as a result of black sexism. If there is to be a chance of whites and blacks; of black women and black men working together constructively to achieve some semblance of the beloved community, and toward that "larger, juster, and fuller future" that Du Bois wrote about in *Souls*, they must find the means and the will to work together toward that end.

Although at some point black women and black men will have to find ways to *trust* each other, black women are challenged to remember to look first and foremost to themselves, and to know that no group, however liberal, progressive, or otherwise well intentioned is "so good, so true, and so disinterested as to be trusted wholly with the political destiny of its neighbors...." Du Bois reminds us that "the best arbiters of [one's] own welfare are the persons directly affected..." (*Souls*, 129). Just as African Americans would be unwise to uncritically trust their present and future interests to well meaning white people, black women would be unwise to uncritically entrust to African-American men their most important interests.

Du Bois was a fighter to the end of his days. The spirit of resistance to oppression is in part the legacy he leaves to us in the twenty-first century. What he said about the need to meet the issue of racial oppression head-

---

[33] Jean-Paul Sartre, "Being and Nothingness." Approaches to Ethics: Reprsentative selections from Classical Times to the Present, ed. W. T. Jones et. al. (NewYork: McGraw-Hill, 1977), 403, emphasis added.

[34] Sartre, "Being and Nothingness," 408-14.

on and to fight it with all our might is just as applicable, if not moreso, to the sex line, or what Carroll Watkins Ali refers to as "that peculiar oppression" to which African American men have subjected black women.

> Awful as race prejudice, lawlessness and ignorance are, we can fight them if we frankly face them and dare name them and tell the truth; but if we continually dodge and cloud the issue, and say the half truth because the whole stings and shames; if we do this, we invite catastrophe. Let us then in all charity but unflinching firmness set our faces against all statesmanship that looks in such directions.[35]

Du Bois believed firmly and always in the unlimited possibilities of humans' ability to be better than they are, if they set their minds and commit their resources to the task. "*There is in this world no such force as the force of a man determined to rise,*" Du Bois said. "The human soul cannot be permanently chained."[36]

Somehow we need to develop the courage to name *the sexism beast* in the African American community if it is truly our desire to develop among us relationships that are characterized by respect and acknowledgment of the other's dignity. Once we have named the beast and our complicity in it, we must then pull out all stops to slay it. Only by so doing will we open the way to the beloved community.

---

[35]Quoted in Lewis, *W. E. B. Du Bois: Biography of a Race 1868-1919*, 434, from Du Bois, "Starvation and Promise," *The Crisis* 2 (June 1911): 62-64.

[36] Foner ed., *Speeches and Addresses*, 217.

THE SENTIMENTAL DU BOIS:

GENRE, RACE, AND THE READING PUBLIC

BILL HARDWIG

Shorn of the hypnotic rhythmicity that blacks are said to bring to their woe [in blues music], white statements of black needs suddenly acquire the sort of stark statistical authority that lawmakers can listen to and politicians hear. But from blacks, stark statistical statements of need are heard as strident, discordant, and unharmonious. Heard not as political but only against the backdrop of their erstwhile musicality, they are again abstracted to mood and angry sounds.
—Patricia J. Williams

Nobody ever reads that fat volume on "The Philadelphia Negro," but they treat it with respect, and that consoles me.
—W. E. B. Du Bois

He who would tell a tale must look toward three ideals: to tell it well, to tell it beautifully, and to tell the truth.
—W. E. B. Du Bois[1]

---

[1] Patricia J. Williams, *The Alchemy of Race and Rights: Diary of a Law Professor* (Cambridge: Harvard University Press, 1991) 152; Mia Bay, "'The World Was Thinking Wrong About Race,'" *The Philadelphia Negro* and Nineteenth Century Science," in *W. E. B. Du Bois, Race, and the City:* The Philadelphia Negro *and Its Legacy*, ed. Michael

When W. E. B. Du Bois's novel *The Quest of the Silver Fleece* was first published in 1911, African American letters were undergoing a quiet revolution. In a little over the past decade, Charles Chesnutt had published his stories of the color line and his novels about post-Reconstruction racial dynamics, Paul Lawrence Dunbar's poems and his novel *The Sport of the Gods* had been released, and James Weldon Johnson's *Autobiography of an Ex-Colored Man* was to be published the next year. The noisy revolution of the Harlem Renaissance was just around the corner. However, in the 1890s, before this explosion of popularity for male writers, it was the writing of African American women that made an impact. Anna Julia Cooper's *A Voice from the South* and Frances Harper's *Iola Leroy* were both published in 1892, Alice Dunbar-Nelson's collections of stories were published in the 1890s, and Pauline Hopkins's three serialized novels were all published in the *Colored American Magazine* in the first couple years of the new century. Not surprisingly, most of these female authors relied on and borrowed from the firmly established traditions of what has been termed "women's writing," that is, sentimentalism. Certainly, writers such as Pauline Hopkins and Frances Harper found sentimentalism's focus on the inclusion of previously excluded groups and individuals through a refined morality to be helpful in their claim for racial equality.

This essay argues that in *The Quest of the Silver Fleece* Du Bois relies on sentimental strategies for many of the same reasons as do these black women. These strategies can be directly contrasted with his scientific sociology, which centers on a masculinized rhetoric of statistically verifiable versions of truth. Patricia Williams writes that "from blacks, stark statistical statements of need are heard as strident, discordant, and unharmonious."[2] Taking into account the history of resistance to scientific theories of racial equality, I argue that Du Bois tries in his fiction to access the different plane of truth offered by sentimentalism, one that works by way of empathy, rather than "strident" and "discordant" statements of oppression. In making this argument, I invoke and analyze the traditional gender alignments associated with

---

Katz and Thomas Sugrue (Philadelphia: University of Pennsylvania Press, 1998) 41; Du Bois, Introductory Note to *The Quest of the Silver Fleece*, i.

[2] Williams, *Alchemy of Race and Rights*, 152.

genre—sentimentalism as a women's genre and realism as man's "work"—in order to question the usefulness of these distinctions. After all, if we hold these distinctions to be "true," how do we account for Du Bois' sentimental strategies? I think we can begin to answer this question by looking at how *The Quest of the Silver Fleece* has been received by black and white critics alike.

Why do most critics characterize *The Quest of the Silver Fleece*, when they mention it at all, as melodramatic, dated, and an unsuccessful foray into fiction by a sociologist, but never as a formulaically sentimental novel, one that adopts the strategies and models provided by previously successful "sentimental" writers, such as Susanna Rowson, Harriet Beecher Stowe, or Frances Harper? How would its reception have been different if Du Bois published the novel with his wife's name, Nina Gomer Du Bois, instead of his own? Would it have been more popular or reached a different audience? What if it were written by Jane Addams or some other prominent socially-committed white woman? Would it have a different history of reception?

Perhaps a more interesting question is, how would we (as supposedly "detached" and "objective" scholars of literature) view *The Quest of a Silver Fleece* nearly a century later, if we believed it were written by a black woman or a white woman? Quite possibly we would laud it for its sentimental subversion of racial hierarchy, its subtle and covert undermining of the color line, its adaptations of the conventions of marriage and the sentimental narrative more generally. Instead, we tend to talk about this novel (to the extent that we discuss it at all) as an aberration from an otherwise accomplished writer or as a flight of fancy from an otherwise serious man. We ignore, for the most part, how important this project was for Du Bois, how much it meant to him as he was writing it. Instead critics comment on his one dismissive reference to the book in his 1940 autobiography, *Dusk of Dawn*: "In 1911, I tried my hand at fiction and published 'The Quest of the Silver Fleece' which was really an economic study of some merit" (269). This history of reception illustrates both the ways in which the novel suffers from our prescriptive ideas of what men and women should write, but also of the limitations of gender imposed upon women writers who are expected to produce works of "fancy" and other "non-serious" works.[3]

REFORMING THE TRUTH: SOCIOLOGY AND PHILANTHROPY

Early in his career as a promising sociologist, Du Bois seeks to contest racial classification by means of a rigorous scientific research. In the preface to his 1896 study of chattel slavery, *The Suppression of the African Slave Trade*, he writes: "I...trust that I have succeeded in rendering this monograph a small contribution to the scientific study of slavery and the American Negro" (v). Three years later, in his sociological study of Philadelphia's urban scene, *The Philadelphia Negro* (1899), Du Bois similarly comments, "I am glad that, almost without exception, there was a disposition to allow the full truth to be known for the sake of science and social reform" (iv). In both of these prefaces Du Bois cites his contributions to science, specifically the science of race, as the most significant aspect of his work. Both of these lengthy texts give more than lip service to the importance of science, as they abound with hundreds of tables, charts, and maps. The very onslaught of facts and numbers (particularly in *Philadelphia Negro*) serves as a visual reminder to the turn-of-the-century reader of how Du Bois sought to construct his thesis around "fact," rather than amorphous racial theory.

---

[3] Obviously, binary gender categories create problems for writers not wanting to write in stereotypically gendered ways (men who use the tropes of sentimentalism or women who borrow from realism's methodology, for example). However, the unique limitations that I am claiming are imposed on women arise in large part from the wholesale dismissal of "sentimentalism" as a serious literary category. This tradition of dismissal was well established by the time Hawthorne wrote about the "scribbling mob of women," continued in Howells's lamentation that "men of letters" must resign themselves to the fact that "the fate of the book is in the hands of women," and extends into more recent evaluations of sentimentalism by Herbert Ross Brown and Ann Douglas. In Du Bois's time, sentimentalism was similarly disparaged. Notice the tone of repugnance Frank Norris uses in his 1901 "A Plea for Romantic Fiction": "Romance has been often put upon and overburdened by being forced to bear the onus of abuse that by right should fall to sentiment; but the two should be kept very distinct, for a very high and illustrious place will be claimed for Romance, while sentiment will be handed down the scullery stairs" (cited in Francesca Sawaya, "Sentimental Tentacles: Frank Norris's *The Octopus*," *Sentimental Men Masculinity and the Politics of Affect in American Culture*. ed. Mary Chaplin and Glenn Hendler [Berkeley: University of California Press, 1999] 259).

According to Mia Bay, until *The Philadelphia Negro*, the United States intellectual community had not produced many sociological studies of race that were meticulously documented with scientific study. Bay writes that 1890s sociology, "was based on theoretical speculation rather than on empirical research" (44). Such speculation tended to be racist and presented the scientifically documented "deficiencies" of African Americans. If works like Frederick Hoffman's *Race Traits and Tendencies of the American Negro* (1896) were not rigorously scientific by contemporary standards, they certainly were immensely influential and white readers generally took their findings to be the "truth" about racial difference. Seeing the power of works like Hoffman's *Race Traits*, Du Bois discerned the necessity to disprove scientifically their findings.[4] Consequently, in the opening chapter of *The Philadelphia Negro*, Du Bois writes, "We must study, we must investigate, we must attempt to solve; and the utmost that the world can demand is, not lack of human interest and moral conviction, but rather the heart-quality of fairness, and an earnest desire for the truth despite its possible unpleasantness" (3). We see in this short quotation Du Bois outlining his entire project; he will carefully study and chart the circumstances of the lives of black folk in Philadelphia. His results may not be pleasant or even agreeable to the reading public, but if they have "an earnest desire for the truth" they will read and believe Du Bois's study despite what he believes they will see as its "unpleasantness." With this disclaimer, Du Bois uses science to deflect the ramifications of his findings. By invoking the myth of neutrality and objectivity, Du Bois asks science to bear a heavy load here. If one doesn't like the "truths" in this text, his logic goes, blame society and not the author. After all, the author simply records the facts.[5] In short, through

---

[4] Since there were few examples of American social science based in empirical research, Du Bois modeled his work on European examples, drawing from Charles Booth's seventeen-volume *Life and Labour of the People of London* (1889-1892). Du Bois also learned from German political economist Gustav Schmoller (with whom he studied in Berlin), who outlined a scientific methodology that emphasized "the accumulation of facts" (Bay, "The World was Thinking Wrong about Race," 50-51).

[5] This line of reasoning reminds me of James Joyce's defense of *Ulysses*: "If *Ulysses* isn't fit to be read, then life isn't fit to be lived." While Joyce's novel and Du Bois's sociological studies may have very little in common from certain angles, both authors needed to justify their works in order to protect them from censorship/banning by

the appropriation of the regard given to science and the authority it wields, Du Bois could in part influence how philanthropists and legislators dealt with the issue of race. He could don the lab coat of scientific objectivity in order to resist prejudiced attitudes about racial difference. As Kenneth Mostern puts it, "Social science would...serve as the hegemonic tool by which he could fight racism."[6]

While the format and presentation of his ideas changed drastically in *The Souls of Black Folk*, where Du Bois mixes sociology, history, personal reflection and fiction, his commitment to science's rationality remains fundamentally unaltered. For Du Bois, the scientific documentation and interpretation of the facts about racial oppression within *Souls* were themselves radical acts. As Alvin Poussaint puts it, "His studies had convinced him of the infallibility of scientific research, not only as a source of truth, but as a conqueror of oppression" (xxxi). Science proved capable of conquering oppression, according to Du Bois, because of its ability to sharpen/improve one's rational faculties. Writing in *Souls* about the results of racism, he claims, "They must be recognized as facts, but unpleasant facts, things that stand in the way of civilization and religion and common decency. They can be met in but one way—by the breadth and broadening of human reason, by catholicity of taste and culture" (124). This quotation introduces the idea of the "unpleasantness" of the facts of racial prejudice for a second time. These facts impede civilization and religion, but they must be presented, as a picture of the "true" story of the roots of the nation's racial dynamics.

Du Bois contrasts this "rational" science with Booker T. Washington's plan for industrial education: "The saying that Education will fix prejudice is a truism" (124).[7] The rhetoric with which Du Bois criticizes

---

publishing communities/governments that did not want to hear the stories they had to tell. Both writers use the rhetoric of objectivity in making this defense.

[6] Kenneth Mostern, "Three Theories of the Race of W.E.B. DuBois." *Cultural Critique* 34 (1996): 40.

[7] For a thorough and thought-provoking account of this debate, see David Levering Lewis's *W. E. B. Du Bois: The Biography of a Race* (New York: Henry Holt, 1993), particularly chapters 9, "Social Science, Ambition, and Tuskegee," and 10, "Clashing Temperaments." Lewis explorers these leaders's differences in terms of their geographical and intellectual backgrounds: "If Du Bois's considerable and growing knowledge of the black South was, nevertheless, akin to a professional explorer's knowledge of Africa or the

Washington remains pertinent. Throughout the two chapters of *Souls* that address Washington in-depth, "Of Mr. Booker T. Washington and Others" and "Of the Training of Black Men," Du Bois consistently speaks of the emasculating effects of Washington's ethos of compromise. His most insistent complaint about Washington's approach to the nation's racial dynamic seems to revolve around his failure to allow men to be men, to assert their manhood. In the fourth paragraph of *Souls*, Du Bois announces that the primary effect of racism is the African Americans' "longing to attain self-conscious manhood" (45). It would be reductive simply to equate this notion with our concept of manhood today, and claim that Du Bois eliminated women from his vision and created a hyper-masculine framework through which he defined success. In part because of the fear of neurasthenia, around the turn of the century manhood came to represent vital civilization and the ability to adapt to changing social situations. Given this pervasive rhetoric of social Darwinism, one can easily see how the "attaining of manhood"—with its attendant associations with sophistication, refinement, and adaptability—stood as an important goal for African Americans.

In *Souls*, Du Bois's metaphors and descriptions invoke a very palpable and visceral notion of manhood. Discussing the "tremendous undertaking" of the Freedmen's Bureau attempt to legislate protection for the newly-emancipated slaves, Du Bois writes, "[A]t the stroke of a pen was erected a government of millions of men—and not ordinary men either, but black men emasculated by a peculiarly complete system of slavery" (62). If Du Bois demonstrated only a vague knowledge of Freud later in his life,[8] this quotation provides more than a little fodder for a discussion of the unconscious mind. We have here nothing less than the metaphorical connection between a fondled and erect penis and political agency ("manhood"). In short, the "stroke" of (to?) the "pen(is)" provides relief to the "emasculated," impotent African American men.

Amazon, Washington *was* the black South—the peasant South arrayed with honorary degrees" (256).

[8] In *Dusk of Dawn*, Du Bois refers briefly to Freud's work, claiming that the psychologist influenced his idea of a "racial unconscious" (Mostern, "Three Theories of the Race of W.E.B. DuBois." 52).

It is this manly declaration, this "stroke," that Booker T. Washington (in Du Bois's estimation) so noticeably lacks. Citing the differences between Northern and Southern sensibilities, Du Bois writes, "Mr. Washington's counsels of submission overlooked certain elements of *true manhood*" (82, emphasis mine). Later, he adds, "So far as Mr. Washington apologizes for injustice, North or South, does not rightly value the privilege and duty of voting, belittles the *emasculating effects* of caste distinctions, and opposes the higher education and ambition of brighter minds...we must firmly oppose [him]" (94, emphasis mine). The question I would like to pose is, why does Du Bois feel compelled to question Washington's *manhood* at almost every turn of his criticism of Washington's political views?

First of all, he clearly identifies the ability/necessity of "self-assertion" as a manly action that is necessary to avoid the emasculating legacy of slavery and racial segregation. Du Bois calls Frederick Douglass the "greatest American Negro leader," and lauds his ability as an older man to "still bravely [stand] for the ideals of his early manhood" (86). One can imagine Du Bois's appreciation for both Douglass's political self-assertion (his tireless speech-giving), and his manly refutation of Edward Covey.

Secondly, Du Bois's concept of manhood seems linked to his view of that social science must provide a brave and unblinking examination of unpleasant details. This, for Du Bois, is real roll-up-your-sleeves-and-get-dirty man's work. Lastly, Du Bois seems to pair manly scientific study and self-assertion with "productive" racial politics. That is to say, political action with regard to racial policy/reality, if not informed with a rigorous and assertive scientific sensibility, will prove "barren and unfruitful." Du Bois metaphorically links masculine agency with (re)productive potency in a way that suggests Booker T. Washington and other "submissive" race leaders are shooting blanks.

THE "TRUE" BEAUTY OF ART: THE TRANSCENDENCE OF CULTURE

As much as Du Bois seems committed to this notion of a masculinized science, the failure of *The Philadelphia Negro* and *Souls of Black Folk* to create any substantial impact in contemporary racial policy undoubtedly made Du Bois think twice about his methodology of activism. Some critics, such as Hale, see *Souls* as the turning point where Du Bois's perceives the impotence of racial "science" and shifts to race "propaganda." This shift, it seems to me, does not make sense in a larger context of Du Bois's work. After all, in 1911 his column for *The Crisis* Du Bois was still citing science as an effective "proof" of racial equality. Writing about the First Universal Races Congress and the subsequent publication of its findings, he claims, "[those who have 'said the last word concerning the races of men'] will realize that America is fifty years behind the scientific world in its racial philosophy....The leading scientists of the world have come forward in this book and laid down in categorical terms a series of propositions that [prove racial difference is not biological]" (13). So eight years after the publication of *Souls*, Du Bois still invokes science as the leading authority on, and "truth teller" about, race—science, for Du Bois, is not the problem. The backward and flawed methodology of American white scientists is to blame. Anthony Appiah claims that Du Bois rejects science around 1940 (with the publication of *Dusk of Dawn*), as he moves towards a Communist notion of social difference that relies less on race and race consciousness.[9] This date, nearly forty years after the publication of *Souls*, seems a more appropriate place to put Du Bois's questioning of the science of race.

Rather than saying that Du Bois rejects science around the time of the publication of *Souls*, I would like to argue that he adds a dimension heretofore undeveloped to his critique of American society. That dimension is Art. I capitalize this word to suggest that for Du Bois it signifies a transcendent act, one that can ever so briefly raise the artist above the veil of racial discrimination in an eternal union of "true artists." Du Bois also sees Art by black artists as serving a purpose for the here and now, as it stands as "proof" of the culture and soul of African Americans. Rather than seeing Art and Science as two irreconcilable

---

[9] Appiah quotes from *Dusk of Dawn*, where Du Bois writes, "'It is easy to see that scientific definition of race is impossible.' But we need no scientific definition, for 'all this has nothing to do with the plain fact that throughout the world today organized groups of men by monopoly of economics and physical power, legal enactment, and intellectual training are limiting with determination the unflagging zeal the development of other groups" (32-33).

spheres, this emphasis on "proof" connects and partially merges Du Bois's concepts of the two disciplines.

Perhaps the best way to understand Du Bois's gradual shift away from science would be to jump ahead to 1926, when in the climate of the Harlem Renaissance, Du Bois seeks to elucidate his conception of the black artist. Recognizing the difficulty in refuting "objective" science on its own ground, Du Bois increasingly began to describe his project as an artist in terms opposite to those of racialist science. In "The Criteria of Negro Art" he writes, "[W]hat have been the tools of the artist in times gone by? First of all, he has used the Truth—not for the sake of truth, *not as a scientist seeking truth,* but as one upon whom Truth eternally thrusts itself as the highest handmaid of imagination, as the one great vehicle of universal understanding."[10] As a social historian with a keen sense of science's role in the era's increasingly rigid racial classification, Du Bois aligns the truth of Art with universal laws of justice, placing it above the pedantic "truth" of science.

Even as he sees the "Truth" of literature as a means of resisting the "pseudoscience" of racial classification, Du Bois recognizes the way this search for Truth is racially-inflected in America. Although it is invariably distorted by a racialist public, for Du Bois Truth is a value that transcends race. As he states in *The Souls of Black Folk*, "[W]ed with Truth, I dwell above the Veil" (139). Here Du Bois employs the rhetoric of marriage to imply a divinely inspired or ratified union, an alignment that was meant to be. He looks to artistic Truth as a class signifier (as a rarified and selective quality closely aligned with classical education) that removes the stigma of race. Through his elite education at Harvard and the University of Berlin as well as his mastery of a Adler-esque sense of Great Ideas, Du Bois sees himself as wedding Truth, and in so doing, proving himself an equal of Shakespeare, Aristotle, and Aurelius, who "come all graciously with no scorn nor condescension." In these "gilded halls" of Truth, race is an irrelevant and coarse means of classification. By drawing upon what he figures as the objective equalizer—Beauty—Du Bois seeks to forge a class alliance with male white artists and intellectuals (an alliance that was not widely recognized by this white community).

---

[10] "Criteria" 66, emphasis mine.

GETTING HIGH ON ART, OR "TEARS, IDLE TEARS": THE AESTHETICS OF
LITERARY EVALUATION

Du Bois's invocation of High Art seems clear enough when we look at it
in the abstract—art as a symbol of refinement and erudition. However, it
becomes murkier when we think about what contemporary African-
American writing he would have categorized as High Art. If he saw art,
perhaps somewhat naively, as providing a portal into the foyer of white
elitism, which black artists did he see entering this door? Was his own
fiction an example of this art? What about Chesnutt's novels or Dunbar's
poetry? Or Pauline Hopkins's stories and serialized novels in the *Colored
American Magazine*? Or did he see High Art as an unattained goal, some
marker of progress that African American artists had, in his view, not yet
reached?

If we think of High Art as rarified and "cultured," demanding a
knowledge of elite and *avant-garde* movements and historical and artistic
references, then Du Bois's fiction seems more closely aligned to that
which has been traditionally denigrated as "low art" (or what Howells
mockingly termed "Tears, Idle Tears")—that is to say, sentimentalism.
The plot of Du Bois's first novel, *The Quest of the Silver Fleece* (1911),
unfolds almost entirely around the sentimental plot of would-be lovers
who are separated by social forces beyond their control. Predictably, the
novel ends with a reunion and a promise of marriage. In the novel,
Blessed Alwyn and Zora Cresswell meet at a Georgia school for African
Americans run by a Northerner, Miss Smith. They develop a close bond
when they decide to grow a secret crop of cotton (the silver fleece). When
the crop is stolen by the rich white land-owning Cresswells through legal
machinations that Bles and Zora have no control over or voice within,
and when Bles finds out that Zora was "not pure," the two separate and
independently travel North to re-invent themselves. While both
characters have successes in the North, they end up disenchanted and
return to rural Georgia to their roots. Zora uses the $10,000 she received
from her former employers, Mrs. Vanderpool, to help save Miss Smith's
school from the Cresswells's financial pressures, and eventually sets up an
African American collective farm, complete with communal farm land, a
hospital, and a store. After Bles becomes aware of Zora's new-found
virtue and strength, he accepts her offer of marriage and they,

presumably, live happily-ever-after. The plot unfolds on formulaically sentimental devices: a fallen hero (Zora) who, despite her lack of purity, exemplifies a sense of honor and dignity; the ratification of this sense of honor through a union with someone of higher standing (Bles); the perseverance of this heroine, who overcomes societal obstacles that appear to be unsurmountable.

When it was first released, some of the few critics that reviewed *The Quest of the Silver Fleece* likened it to Stowe's sentimental best-seller *Uncle Tom's Cabin.* A 1912 unsigned review in *The Nation* claimed that Du Bois "wished to write a sort of 'Uncle Tom's Cabin' to date, and he shows us the black man little better off than the black man of Mrs. Stowe, and a white man little more decent than the race of oppression she made abhorrent to the world sixty years ago."[11] Surely, part of the rationale for this review comes from the enormous success of Stowe's work. One could scarcely fictionalize racial dynamics in America for many decades after *Uncle Tom's Cabin* without being measured against the yardstick of Stowe's work. But I believe the reviewer was also responding, however unconsciously, to Du Bois's sentimental strategies within *The Quest of the Silver Fleece.*

As Kenneth Warren has argued, one basic difference between realism and sentimentalism is that in realism "the redemption of the individual lay within the social world," whereas in sentimentalism "the redemption of the social world lay with the individual."[12] If we apply this definition to Du Bois' novel, *The Quest* falls squarely within the realm of sentimentalism. Despite the seemingly insurmountable economic traps for black laborers and farmers, Du Bois's heroic individual, Zora, defeats these forces. If Du Bois's socialist sensibilities show up in the novel as the overwhelming economic pressures that lead to class and race divisions, then his sentimental strategy advances a hero capable of transcending or vanquishing these pressures.

The novel's theme of the heroic individual fighting a corrupt social world appears in a variety of ways. First we have the title, which alludes to Jason and the Argonauts' attempt to get the golden fleece—the coat of a magical flying ram. In fact, Du Bois originally titled his novel *The Quest*

---

[11] Cited in Aptheker, 120.
[12] Warren, 75-76.

of the Golden Fleece, until his editors at McClurg informed him that David Graham Phillips, a journalist and popular novelist, had published a book in 1903 entitled *Golden Fleece.*[13] Initially, Du Bois' allusion to Jason and the Argonauts seems fairly straightforward. In the Greek myth, Jason's uncle, Pelias, has usurped the throne of Iolcus, properly held by Jason's father. The heroic story of Jason begins with his attempt to regain his rightful throne. Such a story seems perfectly suited to critique the South's usurping of black labor under slavery and post-Reconstruction neo-slavery, as well as the theft of the profits reaped from this labor. African Americans, in this retooled myth, have been unceremoniously dispossessed of their throne, but, as the metaphorical alignment with Jason suggests, they will ultimately regain their rightful position within society. Some critics have even suggested a parallel between certain characters in the text and characters in the drama of Jason and the Argonauts.[14]

When we look at how Du Bois uses this story within the text, however, we get a different version of the Greek myth. Du Bois first mentions the narrative of Jason and the Argonauts in the fourth chapter, as Mary Taylor tells Bles the story while they ride to town together in a wagon. When she completes the account, Miss Taylor is disappointed that Bles's "hearing had apparently shared so little of the joy of her telling" (35). But, just as she finishes her thought, Bles looks out into the fecund cotton fields and says, "All yon is Jason's." Miss Taylor seems momentarily pleased that he listened to the story, but then expresses her confusion. "I thought it was—Cresswell's." Bles replies, "That is what I mean." Then comes the key interaction and rewriting of the myth: "'I am glad to hear you say that,' says Miss Taylor, "for Jason was a brave adventurer." "I thought he was a thief....The Cresswells are thieves now," retorts Bles.

Miss Taylor responds sharply to Bles's judgement of the Cresswells—despite her belief in "negro education," Miss Taylor finds any African-American criticism of white people unacceptable. Nonetheless, he has made his point. The Cresswells have stolen the

---

[13] Herbert Aptheker, *The Literary Legacy of W. E. B. Du Bois.* (White Plains, NY: Kraus International Publications, 1989) 110.

[14]3 David Levering Lewis, for example, sees Bles Alwyn functioning as Jason, while Zora's mother, Elspeth, is "emblematic of both Medea and the pagan African past" (*W. E. B. Du Bois: The Biography of a Race,* 445).

Golden Fleece. Bles's retelling of the story presents Jason as the thief. In this version, Jason does not act like a hero, nor a "brave adventurer," as we (and Miss Taylor) have traditionally been taught to see the story; he is the enemy, the criminal. In this seemingly minor shift of perspective within the myth, Du Bois has switched the power relations (Jason as wronged avenger to Jason as greedy thief), the discourse of rightness and righteousness, as well as who controls this discourse. If we extend the metaphor to the agrarian South, the people generally seen as heroic, just, and courageous (the Cresswells) become cowardly and depraved. Du Bois heightens this shift by having a white woman tell Bles the story. Clearly, the person "telling" and the person "hearing" are not coming to the story from the same perspective. Bles has internalized the story, rearranged and applied it to the specifics of what he knows, oppression in the rural South. Just as Bles revises the Greek myth, Du Bois implies, so too must his readers revise their ideas about Southern cotton plantations and their use of black wage slavery.

If in his revisionary myth of the golden fleece Du Bois switches the perspective from which we view the story of Jason and the Argonauts, *The Quest of the Silver Fleece* also comments on contemporary greed and capitalist practices. Arnold Rampersad has labeled the novel "an epic of cotton," in part because it focuses on the economic, social, and political consequences of cotton production in the turn-of-the-century South, from its growing and production to its distribution and manufacturing. Indeed, much of the novel focuses on the specific pressures that the land-owning aristocracy (the Cresswells) placed on the laborers in order to keep their wages down and to keep them tied to the land. After seeing first-hand the system of wage labor in the cotton field, the Northern-born teacher Miss Smith exclaims, "Why....It's slavery!" (134), even though they were forty-five years removed from the Civil War. Du Bois differs from many turn of the century African-American writers that focus on the racist practices of the white upper class by presenting this oppression as *primarily an economic issue*. Du Bois does not present the Cresswells as incorrigible hate mongers, as Chesnutt often does with his principal white characters. Instead he shows them as the key links in an economic system that breeds oppression and racism as tools to garner profits.

In this light, Zora's collective farm proves all the more threatening, as it hits the center of the entire racist structure—the white gentry's ability to corner the cotton market in the rural South. It also mirrors sentimentalism's theme that the capitalist preoccupation with profits produces sexist and racist oppression. Rather than spending it for personal gains, Zora uses the check she received from Mrs. Vanderpool to purchase as much of the swamp land located next to the Cresswells's mansion as she can in order to provide an actual "land of opportunity" for the black farmers: "We must have land," she says, "our own farm with our own tenants—to be the beginning of a free community" (362).[15] Here we see Warren's definition of sentimentality as the individual "redeeming" a corrupt social world. As Zora's dream begins to take shape, Du Bois's language waxes poetic, and he describes the work of the community with the larger-than-life fervor and zeal of a Virgilian epic: "The ringing of axes and grating of saws and tugging of mules was heard. The forest trembled as by some mighty magic, swaying and falling with crash on crash. Huge bonfires blazed and crackled until at last a wide black scar appeared in the thick south side of the swamp." As the workers rest "in utter weariness" they are "lying along the earth like huge bronze earth-spirits, sitting against trees, curled against dense bushes" (375). Perhaps the image of the "wide black scar" strikes us most today. With its metaphor of wounding, the clearing of the swamp takes on an ominous tone. But I think we need to put this description of a battle against the land in the context of other expansionist novels of the era, such as Willa Cather's *My Antonia*, which charts the "taming" of the glorious prairie lands. Both Cather's novel and *The Quest of the Silver Fleece* situate this "taming" in terms of the opportunities it provides for previously desperate and deprived people—eastern European immigrants in *My Antonia* and black laborers in Du Bois's novel.

In this passage about the clearing, Du Bois emphasizes an "earthy" and specifically African-American spiritual power. The forest trembles

---

[15] Incidently, Colonel Cresswell only agrees to sell it to her because of his belief that she will either fail to make her payments or that he can defraud her in the courts, thus reclaiming his land once it has been cleared and crops planted. He explains, "The only way to get decent work out of some niggers is to let them believe they're buying the land. In nine cases out of ten he works hard a while and then throws up the job. We get back our land and he makes good wages for his work" (363). Zora foils this plan by studying law at nights and writing an air-tight contract, which Cresswell doesn't even read, since he believes her incapable of writing a binding bill of sale.

"as by some mighty magic" and the workers appear like "huge bronze earth-spirits." It seems as if this image of an African American "free community" liberates Du Bois from white, normative examples of success and culture, if ever so briefly. In this economic collective, the "savage" spirituality becomes a treasure, a source of power. Outside of this utopia, it remains a dangerous taboo—one more example of the difference between blacks and whites, one more excuse to dismiss African Americans as sub-human.

From Jane Austen's heroines's dreams of a perfect match that allows them self-expression and freedom, to Charlotte's dream of a fuller life in a "true" Christian love in Susanna Rowson's *Charlotte Temple,* to Eliza's dream of a free life for her son George in *Uncle Tom's Cabin,* sentimental tales present an idealized notion of righteousness and truth. Without a doubt, the sentimental trope of a as-of-yet unfulfilled dream of justice dominates the entire novel. From the opening chapter entitled "Dreams" where Zora explains to Bles that "over yonder behind the swamps in great fields full of dreams, piled high and burning," to the novel's conclusion with Zora's dream of "a free community" (19, 362), dreams represent in this book a symbol of another plane of righteousness, one that transcends the corruption of present day America, one that rises above the veil of racism and oppression. The goal remains the same as in *Souls of Black Folk,* where Du Bois longs for "a juster world, the vague dream of righteousness, the mystery of knowing" (114). Dreams for Du Bois are more than fanciful imaginings; they are idealized versions of a better world, a transcendent world of equality and justice.

Of course, I do not mean to imply that Du Bois's sentimental fiction would fit seamlessly into a canon of white women writers, or even a canon of white women writers such as Stowe, who were committed to protest racial oppression. If Stowe's approach to the nation's racism was to create comfortable and comforting portrayals of African-American martyrs in order to create an empathy in her white reading audience, Du Bois strives for something else. While he undoubtedly draws from the sentimental tradition as a means of creating empathy, Du Bois creates black characters who demonstrate what we might call an indomitable will to power, as well as a sense of "black pride" that is almost wholly absent from turn-of-the-century portrayals of African Americans—sympathetic or not. In *Quest of the Silver Fleece* we see Du Bois forming a nascent sense of black consciousness that would dominate the Harlem Renaissance a decade later. Very early in the novel, Du Bois highlights the racial tension of the rural South by creating a confrontation between Zora and the standoffish white teacher, Miss Taylor, in which Zora yells, "I hates you" (43). Immediately after this conflict and in stark juxtaposition to Zora's across-the-board hatred of white people in positions of authority, Zora returns to Bles and says, "We black folks is got the *spirit*. We'se lighter and cunninger; we fly right through them; we go and come again just as we want to. Black folks is wonderful" (46).

At this point in the novel, Du Bois clearly presents Zora as in need of refinement, "a heathen hoyden" exhibiting an "impish glee" (44). Yet he signals her role as protagonist by having this "untrained" speech utter the book's most cherished ideas. First of all, Du Bois introduces (and italicizes) the idea of "*spirit*," which in this novel seems to represent both the religious and secular faith that propels the black community forward despite the overwhelming obstacles they face. Du Bois explicitly contrasts the "spirit"of the black community with white capitalist greed. Early in the novel, Zora is clearly a Pearl-like "child of the swamp" of "twelve wayward, untrained years." But part of her strength seems to come from her escape from "refinement" and its connections to normative white behavior. In other words, her lack of training gives her a perspective that the educated African Americans and white community do not have. She initially learns "life's lessons" not from the school run by white Northern women, but from her mother, Elspeth, a conjurer or "witch" who lives in a cabin in the swamp. With the aid of this education, Zora expresses Du Bois's belief that capitalist greed functions as a weight that holds people down. She contrasts the material possessions of the white community, "things—heavy, dead things," with the lighter and more cunning *spirit* of the black community.[16] So while Du Bois presents Zora

---

[16] While Du Bois presents material accumulation as a negative temptation, his idea stands in contrast to a Porgy and Bess "I got plenty of nuthin' and nuthin's plenty for me" mentality. After all, Zora and Bles work incredibly hard on their cotton field to raise capital for themselves. The difference lies in the goals for this accumulation. Zora and Bles wish to help the community, to provide services (such as a hospital, school, and communal food supply) that a just government would provide. Du Bois contrasts this wish with personal greed and consumerist desires.

as an uncontrollable "elf-girl" in need of discipline, he does not wish her to become an imitation of the white women.

In this respect, Du Bois's mission looks very different from Charles Chesnutt's. In *The House Behind the Cedars*, Chesnutt measures his heroine Rena's progress (both internally and externally) with the yardstick of normative white behavior. Rena improves as she becomes more like Southern white belles, thus proving that black people, at least light-skinned mulattos, are not inferior to even blue-blooded whites. Whereas Chesnutt constantly emphasizes Rena's light-skin and Mediterranean features, our first glimpse of Zora surrounds her with sounds of "savage music" and focuses on her blackness: "She was black, and lithe, and tall, and willowy. Her garments twined and flew around the delicate moulding of her dark, young, half-naked limbs....[H]er warm, dark flesh peeped furtively through the rent gown" (14-16). Du Bois has Bles Alwyn share in Zora's celebration of blackness, both in the physical sight of dark skin and the cultural and ethnic mores of the African American community. While in Washington, Bles sees a white woman exit a senator's office. As he notices her grace and her faint perfume, he thinks, "Colored women would look as well as that...with the clothes and wealth and training. He paused, however, in his thought: he did not want them like the whites—so cold and formal and precise, without heart or marrow" (235).

This sentiment is in direct contrast to Chesnutt's ideas, and the mention of marrow here seems to invoke ironically Chesnutt's most famous work, *The Marrow of Tradition*. Indeed, Bles catches himself and steps back from the desire to see black women mimicking white behavior. This replication of normative white behavior was precisely the goal of much of Chesnutt's work. In *The House Behind the Cedars*, the narrative's climax comes when Rena passes as white and is crowned the Queen of Love and Beauty at the medieval jousting tournament; she has proven her comparability to even the most refined white women. If Chesnutt wants to *equate* the refinement of the mulatto elite with that of the whites, Du Bois wants to demonstrate that black beauty and sophistication are *equal* to white refinement, but never attempts to equate the two. By this I mean that Du Bois wished to assert the right to social and economic equality for black Americans, but, unlike Chesnutt, he resists doing so by suggesting black people can be "just like" white people. He maintains a sense of ethnic difference, but seeks to remove the hierarchy beneath the expression of these differences.

In this sense, Du Bois alters the paradigm offered by sentimental novels. Sentimental novels often create sympathy by suggesting how an unfortunate or wronged protagonist actually mirrors the refinement and morality of her "superiors." This equating of the moral fiber of the protagonist with those in positions of power allows the reader to see that the protagonist actually deserves a "higher" station—s/he is one of them. For example, despite her error in trusting Montraville's promise to marry her when they arrive in America, Charlotte Temple demonstrates a spirituality and kindness that far surpasses those above her in society's hierarchy. The novel creates empathy not so much by questioning the notion of a hierarchy, but by suggesting Charlotte has been misassigned her spot within that hierarchy or that she deserves a promotion. To bring this issue back to Du Bois's theory about racial classification, we can look at Stowe's *Uncle Tom's Cabin*. In this novel, we are meant to empathize with Eliza, who demonstrates a piety, courage, and beauty that matches that of any of the white characters in the novel. Unlike dark-skinned Chloe or Dinah, Eliza simply does not belong as a slave. Her performative whiteness proves she cannot justly be enslaved. Despite her slightly less-than-white skin, Eliza, dear reader, can be as "white" (culturally) as you or me.

Eschewing this logic, Du Bois creates in Zora a sexualized "imp" of the swamp who through her faith in the *spirit* of the black community develops into a heroic "race leader." To contemporary readers, Zora comes off as a refreshing example of healthy black feminine power and sexuality. This strength and vitality leads some male critics to see Du Bois as a feminist. David Levering Lewis writes, "*The Quest* reflected the force and sincerity of Du Bois's feminism, his credo that the degree of society's enlightenment and of the empowerment of disadvantaged classes and races was ultimately to be measured by its willingness to emancipate women—and, above all, black women."[17] Rampersad similarly concludes, "[The] feminist identification of women as the superior of men in the leadership of the race is a major feature of *The Quest of the Silver Fleece*."[18]

---

[17] Lewis, *W. E. B. Du Bois: The Biography of a Race*, 449.
[18] Rampersad, 9.

If we are to take this view, however, we must wince as we learn that "the feral energies and intuitive culture of the swamp."[19] must be tamed at first by Bles, and later and to a greater extent by the wealthy white woman, Mrs. Vanderpool. In other words, before she can be a fitting heroine, despite her displays of strength and courage, Zora needs culture, refinement and instruction about how to become a lady. Whereas she initially mocks women like Vanderpool, her "education" teaches her she has much to learn from them. It seems strange, given Du Bois's political leanings during this period, that his hero would learn her most valuable lessons not from a socialist, but from a socialite.

If Zora "instinctively" knows the power behind the "*spirit*" of the black folk, she must study and master the ideals of purity, piety, and domesticity before she can be a proper leader.[20] As Zora and Bles develop an attraction to each other, Zora asks, "Bles, what's purity—just whiteness?" And so Zora's education begins. Bles responds with the lesson that will dominate much of Zora's actions throughout the remainder of the book: "[I]t means being good—just as good as a woman knows how" (98). Du Bois alters the notion of purity to some degree, defining it in terms of the knowledge of goodness, rather than an "untarnished" virginity until marriage. To this degree, he recognizes that, due to the prevalence of white men raping black women, black women at the turn of the century were not always in control of their own virginity. Even so, he often sees licentiousness in the black community as a plague that rises from African Americans being, in the words of his book *The Negro American Family*, "more primitive" (read "less cultured"). In this 1908 study, Du Bois focuses on what he sees as understandable yet aberrant sexual behavior of African Americans. He states, "While the tendencies are hopeful, still the truth remains: sexual immorality is probably the greatest single plague spot among Negro Americans, and its greatest cause is slavery and the present utter disregard of a black woman's virtue and self-respect, both in law court and custom in the South" (42).

---

[19] Lewis, *W. E. B. Du Bois: The Biography of a Race*, 446.

[20] I am borrowing here from Barbara Welter's definition of the "cult of True Womanhood." Welter outlines what she sees as the four fundamental tenets by which women were judged, which she labels the "four cardinal virtues—piety, purity, submissiveness, and domesticity" (21).

Much of the following sections of the novel picture Zora learning the appropriate lessons in order to become a "true woman," rather than an earthy elf-girl. The first step in Zora's education comes as Bles helps her dress appropriately and "subdue" her unruly "curled hair." The transformation creates "a revelation of grace and womanliness in this hoyden." She was developing a "brilliant, sumptuous womanhood," but it still contained "her early wildness and strangeness" (124-25). At this point of her transformation, Zora's sexuality remains a dangerous threat, and her developing body serves as a very visible reminder of this threat. She continues to "advance" under the tutelage of Bles and Miss Smith of the "negro school," and after a sickness that tamed her spunkiness, her education nears completion: "[S]he looked different: her buxom comeliness was spiritualized; her face looker smaller, and her masses of hair, brought low about her ears, heightened her ghostly beauty" (156). Her near-death experience creates an emaciated and "ethereal" beauty, one that straightens her hair and tempers her "buxom" sexuality, as if her high fever and prolonged illness cauterizes her overflowing passion and fecundity.

As she moves from a corporeal being to a spiritual one, Zora takes on much of the affect of the elite white women for and with whom she works. In the chapter entitled "The Training of Zora," Mrs. Vanderpool provides Zora the education befitting a refined white lady. If early in *The Quest for the Silver Fleece* Zora displays a prominent suspicion of white educators and white systems of education generally, she now enjoys the fruit from the tree of knowledge, and like Du Bois revels in her associations with European intellectual traditions: "She gossiped with old Herodotus....[S]he saw the sculptured glories of Phidias marbled amid the splendor of the swamp; she listened to Demosthenes and walked the Appian Way with Cornelia – while all of New York streamed beneath her window" (251). Du Bois transforms Zora from a wild hoyden to his version of a visionary artist that conquers the "Great Ideas" of Western Civilization.

What happened to the powerful swamp child and her triumphant claim that "black folks are wonderful?" What happened to the strong girl that single-handedly saved the cotton field from flood? In her place we have a sophisticated women in her finest dress, one who has developed a new-found respect for traditional notions of gentility.

AND THEY LIVE HAPPILY EVER AFTER?:
SENTIMENTAL CONCLUSIONS

In this essay, I have tried to demonstrate how turn-of-the-century African-American men have been denied the symbolics of American manhood and the strategies Du Bois used to resist this emasculation—both the masculinized rhetoric of scientific truth and the sentimental appeals to a different truth within his fiction. I have also argued that our understanding of Du Bois's sentimental novel *The Quest of the Silver Fleece* has been obscured by our associations of sentimentality (or at least American sentimentality) as women's work, and that we need a more fluid notion of gender roles to make sense of Du Bois's fiction. Hortense Spillers has suggested just such a fluid idea of gender, writing that the social dynamics at the turn of the century (and earlier) create in African-American men a unique position in the family dynamic and the American social system at large. She argues that since black men have not been permitted to occupy the social space allotted to "men," they have a unique opportunity to identify with the "female" within. In other words, social impotency, if reimagined and reconfigured, can be used as a strength (as a unique social position), rather than a damning weakness. She explains, "the black American male embodies the only American community of males which has had the specific occasion to learn who the female is within itself....It is the heritage of the mother that the African American male must regain as an aspect of his own personhood—the power of 'yes' to the 'female' within."[21] Such an idea raises compelling possibilities in relation to Du Bois's *The Quest of the Silver Fleece.* Is Du Bois, in writing a sentimental novel with an idealized heroine as its chief protagonist, attempting to access the "female within"? Is his novel an acknowledgment of "the heritage of the mother," or at least the heritage of the woman?

In a 1911 edition of the *Crisis,* Du Bois wrote an eulogy for Frances Harper: "[S]he was not a great writer," he begins, "but she wrote much worth reading. She was, above all, sincere" ("Writers" 20). Discussing this

---

[21], Hortense Spillers, "Mama's Baby, Papa's Maybe: An American Grammar Book," *Within the Circle: Literary Criticism From the Harlem Renaissance to the Present,* ed. Angelyn Mitchell (Durham: Duke University Press, 1994) 479-80.

statement, Frances Foster claims that Du Bois's luke warm review of Harper's writing should be contextualized because "Du Bois' predilection was for an elite literature more in the vein of Henry James" (xxxvi). While Foster's comment is certainly true with respect to Du Bois's philosophical ruminations about literature, this chapter has attempted to demonstrate the ways in which Du Bois's fiction has much more in common with writers of sentimentalism such as Harper than it does with James's rarified "art." In addition to their literary similarities, Du Bois and Harper have comparable biographies. Both leaders spoke tirelessly on the needs of education for African Americans; both were primarily political lecturers and activists who made brief forays into fiction writing.[22] Both writers' novels ultimately met with critical disfavor and were seen as "light" stories in contrast to the "urgency" of their political speeches and writings.[23] Of course, one of the most significant differences in their life stories is that despite its lack of critical favor in later years, *Iola Leroy* was, at the time of its publication, one of the best-selling African American novels ever. Also, *Iola Leroy* has undergone a critical renaissance in the past two decades, whereas Du Bois's novel still remains obscure and all-but-forgotten.

With all this being said, we are left with some large questions about the stakes involved in using the sentimental form for black men and women. Why has Du Bois's fiction been dismissed at the same time that

---

[22] Hazel Carby writes that after the Civil War, Harper was a full time lecturer and activist. She quotes an 1871 editorial in the *Christian Recorder* (a weekly of the AME church): "She has impressed many who were adverse to females entering the lecture field, that public speaking is her native element; the practical cast of her mind gives rare coloring and beauty to her lectures. Many more like Mrs. Harper are greatly needed, especially in the South, to remove the bad odor from the name 'Negro' (Hazel Carby, *Reconstructing Womanhood: The Emergence of the Afro-American Woman Novelist* [New York: Oxford University Press, 1987] 66).

[23] I have in mind Robert Bone's 1965 criticism of *Iola Leroy*. He writes, "*Iola Leroy* lacks the urgency of the other protest novels on the 1890s" (cited in Frances Smith Foster, "Introduction," *Iola Leroy, or Shadows Uplifted*. Schomburg Library of Nineteenth-Century Black Women Writers. [New York: Oxford Press, 1988] xxxvi). More recently, Houston Baker (*Workings of the Spirit: The Poetics of Afro-American Women's Writing* [Chicago: Univ. of Chicago Press, 1991].*Workings of the Spirit*, dismisses Harper's text as "bent on winning approval by embodying a subjecthood that has little reflective power at the mass black southern, vernacular level" (32). Similarly, there was and is very little discussion of Du Bois's *Quest of the Silver Fleece* as a protest novel at all.

his political writing has been increasingly celebrated? Why has Harper's political work been almost entirely forgotten (she is now known almost exclusively as a black woman *novelist*), while *Iola Leroy* is more popular today than any time since its initial popularity a century ago? Certainly, these questions can partially be answered by replying that Harper is a much, much better writer of literature than Du Bois, and Du Bois is an extraordinary political writer and thinker. But even taking these qualitative evaluations into consideration, I think the history of reception for the works of Harper and Du Bois points to preconceived gender expectations as well. Harper (as a woman) is supposed to write sentimental fiction, supposed to appeal to our sensibilities; Du Bois (as a man) is supposed to be a political activist, a leader through scientific analyses. In this social context, a woman political activist unsettles our expectations in the same manner as a man writing sentimental novels. This "switching of roles" doesn't—in American culture at the turn of the last century and this one—make sense.

As I Face America:
Race and Africanity in
Du Bois's *The Souls of Black Folk*

Kwaku Larbi Korang

In *Dusk to Dawn*—the work which Du Bois proposes as his "autobiography of the race concept"—there comes a moment when the autobiographer stages Africa in a mode of racial self-confrontation. "What is Africa to Me?" Du Bois asks, directly quoting the poet Countee Cullen. And he goes on to ponder: "As I face Africa what is it between us that constitutes a tie which I can feel better than explain?" A fairly long affirmation follows:

> Africa is of course my fatherland. Yet neither my father nor my father's father ever saw Africa or cared overmuch for it. My mother's folk were closer and yet their direct connection, in culture and race, became tenuous; *still, my tie to Africa is strong.* On this vast continent were born and lived a large portion of my direct ancestors going back a thousand years or more. The mark of their heritage is upon me in color and hair. These are obvious things, but of little meaning in themselves; only important as they stand for real and more subtle differences from other men. Whether they do or not, I do not know nor does science know today.
>
> But one thing is sure and that is the fact that since the fifteenth century these ancestors of mine and their descendants have had a common history; have suffered a common disaster and have one

long memory. The actual ties of heritage between the individuals of this group, vary with the ancestors that they have and many others... But the physical bond is least and the badge of color relatively unimportant save as a badge; the real essence of the kinship is its social heritage of slavery; the discrimination and insult; and extends through yellow Asia into the South Seas. It is the unity that draws me to Africa.[1]

The racial sentiments contained in the passage come directly from the heart and are powerfully expressed. And yet for all that they have not failed to lay the one who expressed them open to a charge of romantic hyperbole. In his invocation of Africanity, so the argument against him goes, Du Bois indulges in willful mystification to buttress a scientifically and ethically unsupportable race-feeling. This is the position especially taken by the Ghanaian philosopher Anthony Appiah as he puts Du Bois's thought at the center of a critique of Pan-Africanism's "Illusions of Race." Commenting on the passage quoted above, Appiah notes "the pathos of the chasm between the unconfident certainty that Africa is 'of course' [Du Bois's] fatherland and the concession that it is not the land of his father or his father's father." With an intent to show Du Bois's ways of error as he makes racial Africanity the presupposition of his being, thinking, and acting in and on the world, Appiah goes on to ask skeptically:

What use is such a fatherland? What use is a motherland with which even your mother's connection is "tenuous"? What does it matter that a large portion of his ancestors have lived on that vast continent, if there is no subtler bond with them than brute—that is, culturally unmediated—biological descent and its entailed "badge" of hair and color?[2]

---

[1] W. E. B. Du Bois, *Dusk of Dawn: An Essay Toward an Autobiography of the Race Concept* (New York: Schocken Books, 1968) 116-17.

[2] Anthony Appiah, *In My Father's House: Africa in the Philosophy of Culture* (New York: Oxford University Press, 1992) 41.

Africa America, the critic of Du Bois and his Pan-Africanist precursors insists, cannot lay claim to Africa on the basis of a mystique of a shared racial essence. What is more, there is no such thing as African civilization able to give cultural support to a Pan-African racialism as, say, Judaism validly supports the racialism of Jewish Zionism. And hence Appiah wonders if it would not have been more worthwhile for Du Bois to "ask if there is not in American culture—which undoubtedly *is* his—an African residue to take hold of and rejoice in, a subtle connection mediated not by genetics but by intentions, by meaning."[3]

This last criticism of Du Bois, as I am going to demonstrate in my reading of *The Souls of Black Folk,* is misplaced. There is indeed a residue of African meaning in America that Du Bois's early work intentionally sources, locating itself within it as the fountainhead of its critical energies. Before I get to that demonstration, however, I want to ask whether the America Appiah faults Du Bois for not claiming was incontestably his for the taking. In Beijing, China, on his ninety-first birthday, Du Bois would declare: "in my own country for nearly a century I have been nothing but a 'nigger.'"[4] The man may have had a legal claim to being American, it is true; but speaking with the authority on nearly a century of experience behind him, the Americanness of America's people of African descent remained, for a doubting Du Bois, a grave existential question. Looking at the spectacle of the history that had formed him/her in the New World, the attitudes that fixed him/her, could an American of African descent, securely say I AM? Not if his/her American experience consigned the black person to the nothingness of a "nigger."

Others before and after Du Bois make this the basis of problematizing and contesting the validity of a secure American identity for America's African-descended people. Thus Ralph Ellison, in *Invisible Man,* explores a condition of invisibility as a *lived* metaphor, one that captures the existential and experiential mode of being of people of African descent in America. For his part, James Baldwin laments that *Nobody Knows My Name,* the title of one of his collection of essays. And Richard Wright, in his ironically titled *Native Son,* pursues the difficult paradox of the black

---

[3] Appiah, *In My Father's House,* 41-42.
[4] Elliott Rudwick, W. E. B. *Du Bois: Propagandist of the Negro Protest* (New York: Atheneum, 1969) 293.

person who knows his Americanness only in his intimate alienation from it. We might recall, also, E.W. Blyden's diagnosis in 1881, in his *Christianity, Islam and the Negro Race*, of the situation of the Negro at the receiving end of the caste injuries of white America: "To be himself...is to be nothing—less, worse than nothing...."[5] And, finally, we may turn to the West Indian, Frantz Fanon, who, in an echo of the title of Du Bois's 1903 work, notes in his *Black Skin, White Masks* that "what we often call the black soul is the white man's artifact."[6] Yet Fanon, seizing his humanity through his racially marked and despised black body, would also go on to declare affirmatively: "O my body, make of me a man who always questions."[7]

Du Bois's embrace of his Africanity in a racial mode, then, is not to be dismissed as mere romantic posing and a morally bankrupt racism at that. Looking at *The Souls* and his other works, we see Africa deployed as a mode of self-presence and self-fashioning that partakes of—and anticipates—Fanon's humanistic invocation of his body. The despised body of Africa he bears provides Du Bois an ethical substratum; what is imposed as a badge of insult is humanistically recomposed by Du Bois into a badge of merit. Racial Africanity, then, is Du Bois's mode of relating to his own existence as affirmative possibility: it is that which allows him to say I AM. More than this, it is also about seizing on that possibility to deal with the constraints of indignity, insult, invisibility and dehumanization which are the legacy of the African descended people in their relationship with white America. In its Africanist mediation, the existential affirmation I AM also imposes the existential obligation I OUGHT. In between these two—I AM and I OUGHT—we might come to appreciate Du Bois's mature interpretation of his life not as the duration of the single, individual life but as "an autobiography of the race concept." What is implied in that is Du Bois, the individual, displacing himself into the race, the *I* making the advancement of the racial *We* its special existential responsibility. It is this expansive mode of selfhood—as Du Bois outlines in a diary entry shortly after his twenty-fifth

---

[5] E. W. Blyden, *Christianity, Islam and the Negro Race* (Edinburgh: Edinburgh University Press, 1967) 37.

[6] Frantz Fanon, *Black Skin, White Masks*, trans. Charles L. Markmann (New York: Grove Press, 1967) 14.

[7] Fanon, *Black Skin, White Mask,* 232.

birthday—that the young man who had grown up in Great Barrington, New England, imagines as his proper relationship with the future:

> The general proposition of working for the world good becomes too soon sickly and sentimental. I, therefore, take the world view that the unknown lay in my hands and work for the rise of the Negro people and all peoples of African descent, taking for granted that their best development means the best development of the world. These are my plans: to make a name in science, to make a name in literature, and thus raise my race.[8]

The pages of *Crisis*, the influential journal of the NAACP edited by Du Bois from 1910-1934, confirm his existential commitment to helping in the birthing of racial self-consciousness and working towards the uplift of his people. Take the 1912-1913 volume of *Crisis*, for instance, where Du Bois reports and comments on a letter written to the journal by two African-American men. A freight train wreck had delayed their rail journey in Kentucky, in the Jim Crow South, and these two black men had had the rare fortune of being served dinner in the railroad dining car. They were writing to enthusiastically report that the white patrons in the car had not objected to their elevation. Du Bois's editorial comments cut to the heart of what Cornel West refers to as the "African encounter with the absurd in America—and the absurd as America."[9] Du Bois notes:

> The editor read this [letter] and read it yet again. At first he thought it was a banquet given to black men by white; then he thought it charity to the hungry poor; then—it dawned on his darkened soul: Two decently dressed, educated colored men had been allowed to pay for their unobtrusive meal in a Pullman dining car "WITHOUT ONE SINGLE WORD OF COMMENT OF PROTEST!" And in humble ecstasy at being treated for once like ordinary human beings they rushed from the car and sent a letter a thousand miles to say to the world: My God! Look! See!

---

[8] Rudwick, W. E. B. *Du Bois: Propagandist of the Negro Protest*, 29.
[9] Cornel West, "W. E. B. Du Bois: An Appreciation," 1974.

What more eloquent [remark] could be made on the white South? What more stinging indictment could be voiced? What must be the daily and hourly treatment of black men in Paducah, Ky., to bring this burst of applause at the sheerest and most negative decency?

Yet every black man in America has known that same elation—North and South and West. We have all of us felt the sudden relief—the half mad delight when contrary to fixed expectation we were treated as men and not dogs; and then, in the next breath, we hated ourselves for elation over that which was but due any human being.

This is the real tragedy of the Negro in America: the inner degradation, the hurt hound feeling; the sort of upturning of all values which leads some black men to "rejoice" because "only" sixty four Negroes were lynched in the year of our Lord 1912.

Conceive, O poet, a ghastlier tragedy than such a state of mind![10]

The tragic ambivalence Du Bois points out here harks back to the oft-quoted diagnosis that he performs in the opening of *Souls*. The black person in America, according to Du Bois, lives in a world that does not guarantee him "true self-consciousness." For long, a racialization of social power in America has made its people of African descent the inferior relation: first under slavery and, since Emancipation, under Jim Crow. There has been a psychic and cultural cost to African Americans in these long years of being ground under by white America. Not only does the dominant world see and pronounce on the black person in certain ways, overwhelmingly negative; it does so without the latter's permission. But, then, even if the latter had any permission to give, it mattered little to the powerful white world any way. What the dominant world makes of the Negro is what the Negro is and will be. Hence Du Bois's own indignation, in *Souls*, with white sociologists for taking fantastic liberties with the Negro, "gleefully count[ing] his bastards and prostitutes," and generally reducing his existence to the lowest order of humanity. It is merely a local manifestation in the scientific community of a wider

---

[10] Quoted in Rudwick, W. E. B. *Du Bois: Propagandist of the Negro Protest*, 158.

structure of social perception and evaluation that makes the black person abstractly into a problem for and of America and not a concrete someone with problems, like everybody else, *in* America.

But what is worse, in Du Bois's diagnosis, the African American has come to see himself not on his own terms but as the other world sees him. For this reason the black person is burdened with a "double consciousness." And this captures the peculiar sensation he has of always taking the measure of his human selfhood through the eyes of the dominant world, of being accustomed to "measuring [his] soul by the tape" furnished by another. The black encounter with the absurd in and as America lies in having been reduced to being looked on by the white world in "amused pity and contempt." The black person is in an unhealthy relationship that reduces him from personhood to thinghood, a relationship that leaves him unable to deal with his American reality from a position that is authentically his own. For Du Bois, the reality of America for Africa in America is an unending struggle for human recognition; the necessary striving of the black person and race to stand up and be counted. This is the occasion of Du Bois's existential anguish: "Why did God make me an outcast and a stranger in mine own house?" (45).

Du Bois's biblical language may suggest that the state of affairs he describes is a God-given one and might have a metaphysical permanence. But if that is the case, *Souls* can only be read as a bleak text of despair. Du Bois is not a fatalist however, and I want to suggest that the African structure of feeling that he brings affirmatively to *Souls* confounds such fatalism. True, Du Bois does not make light of the depth of the crisis of consciousness which, as he sees it, frustrates and undermines the Negro's efforts in economy, polity, culture, and ethics in America.

> From the double life every American Negro must live, as a Negro and as an American...from this must arise a painful self-consciousness, an almost morbid sense of personality and a moral hesitancy which is fatal to self-confidence....Such a double life with double thoughts, double duties, and double social classes must give rise to double ideals, and tempt the mind to pretence or revolt, to hypocrisy or radicalism. (222)

And yet this crisis is not so much that he lacks soul power as that the Negro's American circumstances have conspired to make him *experience* himself lacking this power. Du Bois makes this qualification carefully in the following: "Here in America, in the few days since Emancipation, the black man's...hesitant and doubtful striving has often made his strength lose effectiveness, to seem like absence of power, like weakness. And yet it is not weakness..." (46). Black strength *seeming like* weakness: Du Bois's diagnosis marks a crucial distinction between true and false lack, between what is really not there and what is there but has lost direction, focus and potency—and hence might as well not be there. The distinction has a part in the way Du Bois will go on to historicize the African American cultural experience—"the soul-beauty of a race which his larger audience despised" (47)—into a recuperative strategy in *Souls*. And I want to suggest that Du Bois's question "What is Africa to Me?" is important in this recuperation of the strength of the black soul. Africanity, I will argue, is crucial in an understanding of the American and New World genealogy of morals and music, ethics and aesthetics, that Du Bois conducts in two later chapters of *Souls*: "Of the Faith of the Fathers" and "Of the Songs of Sorrow."

To recapitulate the story of a joyful letter to *Crisis* about a rare moment when two black men were permitted to cross the color line: we have heard Du Bois's critical judgment making such joy, induced in the pathologies of ambivalence afflicting Africa in America, morally repugnant and misplaced. How can one branch of the human race, the black one, justify the need to seek permission from another branch, the white one, to affirm its God-given humanity? The editor of *Crisis* may indict the white world and the American South, in particular, for being a large part of this ethical dilemma. But charity, for Du Bois, begins at home. His moral indignation is reserved for the Negro, too, for half acquiescing in a relationship that dictates the loss of his human bearings. Why else do black human beings absurdly "rejoice" because "only" sixty-four of their kind were lynched by white men in 1912? Were these black human beings not willfully blind to the human tragedy of their American existence? And was this not because they had developed an ethical spinelessness—the "upturning of all values," as Du Bois puts it? Where, then, within his own institutional sphere, are the self-made values, the black soul, that authenticates the Negro's humanity? And how has he come to squander this humanity made in the image of God? These questions, I suggest, are the basis of Du Bois's attempt to produce, from an evolutionary perspective, a historical sociology of the black church in *Souls*. Conducted in the mode of ethical self-critique, this historical sociology is designed to show what has been humanly lost by Africa in America. By implication, it also shows the humanity within their self-conception that, by self-application, black folks may hopefully (yet) recover and, reconnecting themselves with it, overcome the fatal division within their racial soul.

Du Bois's account, in "Of the Faith of the Fathers," reveals, then, that even under the worst form of human degradation, slavery, Africans in America had access to and recreated their own authentic African values that kept them anchored to their humanity. The "institutional Negro church of Chicago," as he puts it, is but a development of "the heathenism of the Gold Coast" (213). The church, which is the "social center of Negro life in the United States," Du Bois argues, is the "most characteristic expression of the African character" of African Americans. This African character is first a matter, externally, of the "communistic" organization of the church. This organization, because of the peculiarities of slave history, was not to be on the basis of clan and tribe, blood and kinship. Instead the plantation organization conspired to give these African forms their own New World expressions. Du Bois points out that this was a "terrific social revolution": the white plantation owner had replaced the African chief, a sort of a paterfamilias, with "far more despotic powers" over his slave subjects ranged below him. But "some traces were retained of the former group life, and the chief remaining [African] institution was the Priest or Medicine-man" (216). It is a careful concession by Du Bois to autonomous African organization and its authority within the larger plantation system to which it was subordinated. The Priest or Medicine-man "early appeared on the plantation and found his function as the healer of the sick, the interpreter of the Unknown, the comforter of the sorrowing, the supernatural avenger of wrong, and the one who rudely but picturesquely expressed the longing, disappoint-ment, and resentment of a stolen and oppressed people" (216).

Over time, so Du Bois's narrative goes, with a Christianizing of African form, the Negro preacher had emerged in the role of bard, physician, judge, and priest to the African community of worship in the New World.

What troubles Du Bois in "Of the Faith of the Fathers" are the implications for the black person's inner life of the Christianizing of the African associational form that he describes. He implies that in its pre-Christian phase, African-American religious culture and expression kept faith with its African soul-foundation and remained a vibrant human force, a virile alternative to the anti-human forces of the plantation system. Its ethics was an ethics that kept the slave's degradation at a distance, thereby nurturing in him a spirit of revolt and resistance.

> Endowed with a rich tropical imagination and a keen, delicate appreciation of Nature, the transplanted African lived in a world animate with gods and devils, elves and witches; full of strange influences,—of Good to be implored, of Evil to be propitiated. Slavery, then, was to him the dark triumph of evil over him. All the hateful powers of the Under-world were striving against him, and a spirit of revolt and revenge filled his heart.

In spite of a certain persistence of the irrational within it, the African element accounts for the determination not give in, "the fierce spirit of revolt" (218), of New World African groups like the Maroons, the Danish blacks, etc. On the other hand, what happened in America was an upturning of the black person's values as an African religion based on a self-reliant ethic of revolt was Christianized, with the enthusiastic support of slave masters. Transformed into an ethic of passivity and compensation, African religion was thus Americanized. As a result, according to Du Bois,

> courtesy became humility, moral strength degenerated into submission, and the exquisite native appreciation of the beautiful become an infinite capacity for dumb suffering. The Negro losing the joy of this world, eagerly seized upon the offered conceptions of the next; the avenging Spirit of the Lord enjoining patience in this world, under sorrow and tribulation until the Great Day when he should lead his dark children home,—this became his comforting dream.

All fatalistic faiths, according to Du Bois, breed true believers side by side with sensualists, and the fatalistic Christianity of the plantation was no exception. Hence his conclusion that "Many of the worst characteristics of the Negro masses of to-day had their seed in this period of the slave's ethical growth." And by this he accounts for the Negro's present-day "shiftlessness," the "sullen hopelessness" that replaces his one-time "hopeful strife" (*Souls*, 219).

Du Bois was a black nationalist and an advocate of African race pride all his life. The modern political faith he professed as an African-American nationalist was certainly always at odds with any easy American accommodationism. With this in mind we can see that his historical reconstruction of the career of the black church sets his modernist agenda competing against a formidable tradition. Because of the peculiar institution of slavery, as Du Bois notes, the black church came before the black family. For centuries, then, this made the church the primary point of black socialization, the dominant institution providing the ethical foundations of black life. But the church he came to observe was also, in his view, an example of the American accommodationism that did not sit well with him. We might say that his critical reconstruction of its history, then, was to test a possibility of recovering for his brand of black nationalism the inner element of Africanity this church had, but lost. Tricked by Christian propaganda, the career of the Negro church is a falling off, a deviation from its true ethical first principles. Du Bois reaffirms these principles, albeit tempered in the New World, as African and autonomist in form. They are grounded in an Old World (African) humanism that is opposed to the American fatalism infecting and enervating the Negro (and his) church. It comes as no surprise then that he celebrates the revival of Africa, as an ethical postulate, in the religious practice of the freedmen who emerged with the abolition movement.

> The free Negro leader early arose and his chief characteristic was intense earnestness and deep feeling on the slavery question. Freedom for him became a real thing and not a dream. His religion became darker and more intense, and into his ethics crept a note of revenge, into his songs a day of reckoning close at hand...Through fugitive slaves and irrepressible discussion this

desire seized the black millions still in bondage, and became their one ideal of life. The black bards caught new notes, and sometimes even dared to sing,—

> "O Freedom, O Freedom over me!
> Before I'll be a slave
> I'll be buried in my grave
> And go home to my Lord
> And be free." (220)

Writing in a time when a rising tide of white supremacist reaction against Reconstruction had left Africa America deeply divided within itself, directionless, with many demoralized, and many more clutching on to a false hope, Du Bois makes of his Africa a prophecy:

> But back of this still broods silently the deep religious feeling of the real Negro heart, the stirring unguarded might of powerful human souls who have lost the guiding star of the past and seek in the great night a new religious ideal. Some day the Awakening will come, when the pent-up vigor of ten million souls shall sweep irresistibly toward the Goal, out of the Valley of the Shadow of Death, where all that makes life worth living—Liberty, Justice, and Right—is marked "For White People Only." (225)

In Du Bois's historical reckoning, not only has the African in America been a bondsman physically, his ethic of self-production and self-projection—the precondition of the integrity of the race—has always been embattled, psychologically speaking. The story of the faith of the fathers shows how, under siege from white America, it has been difficult for the black person to remain true to his own (African) first principles. But for Du Bois there is a difference between difficulty and impossibility. And this is why his recuperation of a New World African humanism in *Souls* is a self-critical affair, one that must inquire to what extent the race is fatally compromising its own historically set standards of humanity. Du Bois's presentation of Booker T. Washington and his infamous Tuskegee machine in *Souls*, then, can be seen as a secular counterpart of the critique of the black church that he does from his Africanist perspective. Washington's secular gospel to black America, in Du Bois's estimation, is a gross deviation from the New World African humanism which he insists must situate an ethics of social action for blacks and the leaders who would inspire them. And this is why Washington, as assessed by Du Bois, must cut a poor figure as a leader of the race compared to Alexander Crummell, the pan-Negroist defender of the African racial soul eulogized in the twelfth chapter of *Souls*. Crummell's Africanist commitments had grown out of a twenty year sojourn on the continent (1853–1873), in Liberia, where he had authored such titles as "The Relations and Duties of Free Colored Men in America to Africa" and *The Future of Africa* (1862). During this period he had collaborated with Blyden, regarded in the Old World as the founder of African nationalism. Blyden's belief that Africa was the spiritual repository of the world had not only given him a moral basis to conduct a relentless critique of crass materialism in the West but an argument also that Africa's racial heritage of spirituality needed vitally to be preserved for the world. The Pan-Africanist shadows of Blyden and Crummell are cast across Du Bois's "The Conservation of Races," the paper he delivered before the American Negro Academy in 1897. In that paper Du Bois is to be found arguing for "race organization...solidarity...unity" that will lead to the "realization of that broader humanity which freely recognizes differences in men, but sternly deprecates inequality in their opportunities of development."[11]

Crummell, it has been suggested, is Du Bois's "spiritual father,"[12] and, if anything confirms this, it is the moving tribute that the younger scholar pays the older in *Souls*. Crummell had written on his return to America, in *The Greatness of Christ and Other Sermons* (1882):

> The special duty before us is to strive for footing and for superiority in this land. For if we do not look after our own interests as a people, and strive for advantage, no other people will. What this race needs in this country is POWER...and that comes from character, and character is the product of religion, intelligence, virtue, family order, superiority, wealth and the

---

[11] Julius Lester, ed., *The Thought and Writings of W. E. B. Du Bois: The Seventh Son.* (New York: Random House, 1971) 1:183.

[12] Quoted in Manning Marable, *W. E. B. Du Bois: Black Radical Democrat* (Boston: Twayne Publishers, 1986) 34.

show of industrial forces. These are forces which we do not possess.[13]

Elsewhere, in "The Attitude of the American Mind Toward the Negro Intellect" (1897)—published in 1898 as the third in the series of the American Negro Academy's Occasional Papers—Crummell would declare:

> The Race must declare that it is not to be put in a single groove; and for the simple reason (1) that *man* was made by his Maker to traverse the whole circle of existence, above as well as below; that universality is the kernel of all true civilization, of all race elevation. And (2) that the Negro mind, imprisoned for nigh three hundred years, needs breadth and freedom, largeness, altitude, and elasticity; not stint nor rigidity, nor contractedness.[14]

We hear echoes of these sentiments and principles in the opening chapter of *Souls* in Du Bois's assessment of the implementation of the ideals of (black) Reconstruction: "The bright ideals of the past—physical freedom, political power, the training of brains and the training of hands,—all these in turn have waxed and waned, until even the last grows dim and overcast." Du Bois asks: "Are they all wrong,—all false?" and the answer he gives is: "No, not that, but each alone was over-simple and incomplete...the fond imaginings of the other world which does not know and does not want to know our power. To be really true, all these ideals must be melted and welded into one" (51).

The critical comments of Crummell and Du Bois, mentor and disciple, underscore their commitment to a general racial will-to-power, or what the latter, in *Souls*, repeatedly refers to as "black strivings." On top of this is their belief that it is black leadership in particular that holds this will-to-power in trust and that, from an ethical perspective on leadership and accountability, this will ought strictly to be non-

---

[13] Marable, *W. E. B. Du Bois: Black Radical Democrat*, 33.

[14] Alexander Crummell, "The Attitude of the American Mind Toward the Negro Intellect." in *The American Negro Academy Occasional Papers, No. 3*. Washington, DC, 1898) 16.

negotiable. Looking at the methods of solving African American problems in economy, polity, culture and society in piecemeal terms jeopardizes black power as a holistic demand. Thus in "Civilization, the Primal Need of the Negro Race," also delivered in 1897 before the American Negro Academy, Crummell, as the first president of the academy, castigates the false prophets of materialism within the black community. "By the soul only the nations shall be free," he declares, quoting the English Romantic, Wordsworth, as he comes out against those who advocate that property alone is the source of the power that would bring about the "elevation of the race." What use, Crummell demands to know, is a materialistically based power not backed by soul power? What would be the human worth of a race which, as he points out, has created no art, no science, no philosophy, no scholarship of its own?

> Neither property, nor money, nor station, nor office, nor lineage, are fixed factors, in so large a thing as the destiny of man; that they are not vitalizing qualities in the changeless hopes of humanity. The greatness of peoples springs from their ability to grasp the grand conceptions of being. It is the absorption of a people, of a nation, of a race, in large majestic and abiding things which lifts them up to the skies.[15]

The cultural demand made in the context of Irish modernism by James Joyce—"to forge the uncreated conscience of my race"—is the same one made here by Crummell. If leadership of the black community devolves on its educated portion—what Du Bois designates the "Talented Tenth"—this class of leaders was under the ethical obligation, in Crummell's view, to use their brain power to "transform and stimulate the souls of a race"; to "uplift all the latent genius, garnered up, in the by-places and sequestered corners of this neglected Race" (6, 7).

The terms of Du Bois's critique of Washington's program of a purely practical education for blacks and his appeasement of the political establishment both Northern and Southern emerge in outline here.

---

[15] Crummell, "Civilization the Primal Need of the Race," in *The American Negro Academy Occasional Papers* (Washington, DC, 1898) 3:5.

Washington may be a Southerner, but, as Du Bois points out, this is one Southerner who has thoroughly imbibed that Northern spirit of commercialism which makes material prosperity the fundamental goal of life. Du Bois never gets more sardonic than when he points out that, in the Washingtonian world-view, "the picture of a lone black boy poring over a French grammar amid the weeds and dirt of a neglected home" is the "acme of absurdities." "One wonders," Du Bois concludes, "what Socrates and St. Francis of Assisi would say to this" (81). Washington's vocational philosophy is conceived too narrowly and would deny the human being in the black person and make him into an instrument. Slavery had accomplished precisely that. Washington was perpetuating the automation of the black person except that under his scheme of neo-slavery, this black person was being offered gold in exchange for his soul. Much like Blyden, therefore, Du Bois is asking—as one of the former's West African disciples has put it: "What shall it profit a race if it should gain the whole world and lose its own soul?"[16]

The argument against Washington for his mismeasure of black humanity has a political dimension as well. In what has passed into history as the "Atlanta Compromise" of 1895, the man seen as the leader of black opinion, had surrendered to the whites the black demand for political and civil equality. Coming at a time when African Americans were being rapidly disfranchised in the South and reduced to internally colonized people by Jim Crow, Washington's gesture could only be seen from a black nationalist perspective as a monumental betrayal of the race. What had happened to the "determined effort [by blacks] at self-realization and self-development despite environing opinion"? (84). In recent black leadership Du Bois finds his great example of keeping the flame of self-determination burning in the career of Frederick Douglass and others who shared his persuasion. Although they held on to American assimilation as an ideal, they also believed that a nationalist "assertion of the manhood rights of the Negro by himself was the main reliance, and John Brown's raid was the extreme of its logic." Again, Du Bois does a genealogical reconstruction of African-American leadership and contrives to make his reader see Douglass as a spiritual

---

[16] J. E. Casely Hayford, *Ethiopia Unbound: Studies in Race Emancipation*, second edition (London: Frank Cass, 1969) 160.

heir of a legacy bequeathed by those before 1750 in whose veins, as he puts it, "the fire of African freedom still burned" (84). This legacy is also upheld and passed on by Gabriel (1822), Vesey (1831) and Nat Turner; by the black communicants who, rather than put up with insult to their color, withdrew from white churches in Philadelphia and New York and formed the religious institution they self-consciously called the African Church. Alas, in the case of the leader succeeding Douglass, this sacred African fire appeared to be in imminent danger of being doused.

One of Du Bois's critics, Thomas Sowell, makes the claim that Du Bois and Washington "were not nearly as far apart in substance as popular stereotypes sometimes suggest." For his part Wesley Pugh, writing in *Crisis* in 1974, notes that the conflict between the two was an "inflated controversy" and that "Their ideas were not basically contradictory."[17] Such misleading claims can be made, I want to argue, if we overlook the valency in Du Bois's argument of Africanity, entailing for him the preservation of black self-presence in America. A non-negotiable first principle, above all, racial Africanity supplies the ethical substance of Du Bois's critique of Washington, who is seen as sacrificing this principle on the altar of political and economic expediency.

I have no wish to understate the distance from the Gold Coast in Africa to African-American Chicago, to borrow Du Bois's own roots-to-fruits metaphor. After all, as he declares in the opening pages of *Souls*, even though he longs to "merge his double self into a better and truer self," he is not out to "Africanize America." There remains in America something of value that Du Bois's Africa might learn from. But we may not downplay Africa in the structure of feeling informing *Souls* either. In the same breath that he utters his disavowal, Du Bois affirms Africa in a declaration that he has no wish to "bleach his Negro soul"—which could only be made to African specification—"in a flood of white Americanism." He only seeks to make it "possible for a man to be both a Negro and an American…" (45). Philosophically, Du Bois wants to think both the exceptional and the universal together, and, politically, to strive to work between the two. This difficult proposition is a Pan-Africanist one, being an argument that Crummell's associate in Liberia, Blyden, in

---

[17] Quoted in Marable, *W. E. B. Du Bois: Black Radical Democrat*, 272-73.

his many writings had used to justify his racial conception of African nationalism. In his *Liberia's Offering*, published in 1862, Blyden writes:

> An African nationality is the great desire of my soul. I believe nationality to be an ordinance of nature; and no people can rise to an influential position among the nations without a distinct and efficient nationality. Cosmopolitism [sic] has never effected anything, and never will, perhaps, till the millenium. God has "made of one blood all nations of men," but he has also "determined the bounds of their habitation."[18]

We can read Blyden making two humanistic assertions here: (a) that there is natural law ("the ordinance of nature") which imposed a moral equivalence on all human beings without distinction; and that (b) in its universal reference, this same moral law left all equally deserving of the particular distinction of nationality. Looked at politically, Blyden is arguing for the inter-national foundations of national sovereignty. What should be of interest to us, insofar as Du Bois's black nationalism in America is concerned, is the ethical formula that emerges from this Pan-Africanist argument. Blyden's exceptional case for a racial Africanity is made on the grounds of what is *deservingly different and equally deserving*. In *Souls*, Du Bois shows us that one half of this Pan-Africanist equation, that of equal dessert, is not incompatible with the secular and Christian humanism enshrined in American republican idealism—with its progressive notions of Liberty, Fraternity, Justice. It is this half that he seeks to make accountable to the other half, a deservingly different African humanity in the commonwealth of American souls. For Du Bois, at the same time that the Negro "must be himself, not another" in order to "attain his place in the world" (49), the "ideal of fostering and developing the traits of the Negro [must be] in large conformity to the greater ideals of the American republic..." (52).

When Du Bois invokes *both* the Negro exception and American commonality in *Souls*, then, it is, so to speak, to bring the moral equivalence of racial Africanity before, and make a case for it in, the court of equal dessert. Thus, as we read his rendition of the story of Alexander

---

[18] Blyden, *Christianity, Islam and the Negro Race*, v.

Crummell, it is to see Du Bois testifying, on the grounds of humanity, that there is not anybody more deserving as a human being than this remarkable personage. As door after door of opportunity is shut in Crummell's face by the white establishment, Du Bois makes his story into an eloquent indictment of America. America, as he puts it in the chapter, "On the Death of a First Born," is a "land whose freedom is to us a mockery and whose liberty a lie" (228). Just as death cheats Du Bois of a son, with "The soft voluptuous roll which Africa has molded into his features," so the Veil, imprisoning Africa in America behind the bars of color, connotes social death for the race. This is a needless waste of its own special potential as much as it is a waste of America's overall human potential.

If we are to invoke a metaphor to sum up the historical and sociological chapters in *Souls* that deal with post-Emancipation black-white, North-South, and class-mass relations, then, we might say that, in them, what Du Bois calls "American civilization" is on trial. Presiding we might say is Liberty, that icon of America, with the scales of justice in her hand, that stands at New York harbor facing the outer world. This is the face that America chooses to show the world and, as people who enter the country through New York harbor can attest, to greet its immigrants. Ralph Ellison, in "What America Would Be Like without Blacks," notes that "one of the first epithets that many European immigrants learned when they got off the boat was the term 'nigger'—it made them feel instantly American."[19] Ellison makes this profoundly unsettling comment in 1970. Sixty-three years before, in *The Souls*, Du Bois takes the stand to protest the anti-human forces that exile his race from citizenship, showing how the constitutional principle of "We the [American] people" has been betrayed. There may be one republic, but what it fought for and won in the Revolutionary War, fought over again and reaffirmed in the Civil War, its republican idealism, seemed to stop where the Negro, who was a combatant in these conflicts, began.

In our metaphorical court of justice, then, the plaintiff is the Negro. Du Bois is the black spokesman, the public intellectual speaking on behalf of his race; and he is out to demonstrate that the so-called "the Negro problem" is "Merely a concrete test of the underlying principles of the

---

[19] Quoted in Cornell West, *Race Matters* (Boston: Beacon Press, 1993) 3.

great republic..." (52). Especially arraigned before this republican court of conscience, to continue with our metaphor, is the South. And it is there on charges of human rights abuse against blacks, of infringing their civil rights, of denying them economic and educational opportunity, of conspiring to keep them in a state of cultural retardation. However, the white North's policy of conciliating the white Southern elite makes the North an accomplice of Southern intransigence. Progressive the North has proved itself to be, and it must be commended for that, but it must also share some of the blame. Still, Du Bois understands that there are potential alliances to be forged between blacks and elements of goodwill in the South—and the North, too—and that his case is damaged by making the white South one mass of caste prejudice and racial intolerance. And his own people, he must also acknowledge, are not wholly blameless, either. Thus the intellectual, who is both prosecution and witness, must present his case evenly, his passion tempered by balance and, above all, reason. The intention registered in his procedure is to seek arbitration and reconciliation, not punishment, as he presents the case of the African branch of the all-American family before a reasonable "jury" of the whole nation. This is a "jury" whose composition is imagined according to the true principles of "We the people." On the very last page of *Souls*, we find Du Bois appealing to it in the name of "O God the Reader"; he thus vests it with power to change the way things are. "Let the ears of a guilty people tingle with truth, and seventy millions sigh for the righteousness which exalteth nations, in this drear day when human brotherhood is mockery and a snare" (278).

In "Of the Passing of the First Born," Du Bois makes a gloomy reference to African Americans as "a hunted race, clinging...to a hope that is not hopeless but unhopeful" (227-28). In his final chapter, "Of the Songs of Sorrow," however, Du Bois's mood is considerably less heavy. There a more or less optimistic politics intervenes and he is able to give his reader an all-American model of reconciliation. "I, too, sing America," declared the great African American poet Langston Hughes. An earlier incarnation of the same spirit is operative as Du Bois labors under the poetic burden of demonstrating in this chapter that the efflorescence of an African aesthetic under—and in spite of—the duress of New World slavery, transforming itself into something uniquely American, testifies to the resilience and originality of the souls of black folk. His analysis of the African American *Songs of Sorrow* insists on the passage of a soulful black aesthetic from its African priority to an American originality. Roots to fruits: Africa finds its consummation in America. Just as surely America finds its originality in the African self-presence within itself. Here in an aesthetic that is African American, African *and* American, Du Bois discovers an affirmative resolution, a transcendence of what is otherwise a pathological dilemma of double consciousness. A New World aesthetic in which Africa and America cohabit in a resolutive tension becomes a prophetic metaphor, an article of faith—that it may yet be possible to be both a Negro and an American. *The Souls* ends on the hopeful note, then, that the different racial voices of America might yet blend into a common song, and that one of the *dominant* strains in that song will be African.

Du Bois's Africa in *Souls*, we must grant ultimately, is an American quantum—it is not, contrary to what Appiah thinks, written purely on the body of another continent far removed from this one. No, what Du Bois makes of it is an enduring structure of self-presence within America, one whose resilience must be celebrated and whose possibilities continually weighed, in affirmation, against the constraints, the setbacks, to the black person's struggles for a place in the American sun. This is the basis for his ethical demand in *Dusk of Dawn* for "extraordinary moral strength, the strength to endure discrimination and not become discouraged; to face almost universal disparagement and keep one's soul; and to sacrifice for an ideal which the present generation will hardly see fulfilled" (209). In Du Bois's Africa, we can overhear the stirring cadences of one of the great African-American Songs of Sorrow: "We Shall Overcome."

W. E. B. DU BOIS:
MORE MAN THAN MEETS THE EYE

KALAMU YA SALAAM

W. E. B. Du Bois was one of the most prescient American intellectuals of the twentieth century. We know, honor, and respect his achievements and are often awed by the depth, breadth, and sheer volume of his work as a scholar, editor, man-of-letters, and activist. Certainly his *Souls of Black Folk* is one of, if not indeed, the most frequently cited book published in America.

Du Bois's *Souls of Black Folk* gave us two definitive and classic concepts: (1) double consciousness and (2) that the problem of the twentieth-century would be the color line.

There is no other intellectual who can match Du Bois in addressing the issues and concerns germane to Black folk in modern America. Indeed, the very weight and wonder of Du Bois's work contributes to a romanticizing, and often a misunderstanding, of Du Bois the man. The general picture many of us hold of Du Bois's personality is that of a proper, indeed almost puritanical, highly educated egg-head who was a bit aloof and even contemptuous of the common, working class African American. Despite all the evidence to the contrary, and partially because of a skewed appreciation of Du Bois's talented tenth formulation, we often think of Du Bois as a bit of an elitist snob. Nevertheless, a close reading of Du Bois reveals a man who enjoyed life and was surprisingly down to earth as well as radical in his personal views. This is the Du Bois I respect and admire.

Here are a few aspects of Du Bois that offer a fuller view of both the man and his views on life. Debates around sexism and gender politics continue to rage among our people today. How many of us are aware of Du Bois's progressive and insightful stance on women's rights.

In his book *Darkwater* published in 1920, the year before women's suffrage became the law in America, Du Bois's essay "The Damnation of Women" offered this radical reading of gender politics:

> All womanhood is hampered today because the world on which it is emerging is a world that tries to worship both virgins and mothers and in the end despises motherhood and despoils virgins.
>
> The future woman must have a life work and economic independence. She must have knowledge. She must have the right of motherhood at her own discretion. The present mincing horror at free womanhood must pass if we are ever to be rid of the bestiality of free manhood; not by guarding the weak in weakness do we gain strength, but by making weakness free and strong.[1]

Even in the twenty-first century these remain progressive positions; imagine how radical they were 80 years ago! But then Du Bois was always clear that we are engaged in a social struggle and not simply an intellectual quest; education is necessary but not sufficient, we must have action.

We have all heard or read Du Bois's famous propaganda quote taken from the October 1926 issue of *The Crisis*:

> Thus all Art is propaganda and ever must be, despite the wailing of the purists. I stand in utter shamelessness and say that whatever art I have for writing has been used always for propaganda for gaining the right of black folk to love and enjoy. I do not care a damn for any art that is not used for propaganda

---

[1] Nathan Huggins, ed., *Du Bois: Writings*. The Library of America 34 (New York: Literary Classics, 1986). All quotes are from this volume.

But I do care when propaganda is confined to one side while the other is stripped and silent.[2]

I would add that Du Bois understood that while all art is propaganda, not all propaganda is art. All art carries and proposes ideas and ideals, an ideology and worldview, thus, whether explicit or implicit, overt or covert, there is a propaganda aspect to all art. Du Bois was a man who had been educated at Harvard and in Berlin, a refined and well-bred intellectual, but he was no advocate of art for art's sake. While it is no surprise that Du Bois believed in the power of art and that he favored a partisan art, what we sometimes forget is that this great educator and intellectual was above all an activist who dedicated his life's work to the cause of freedom, justice, and equality.

While some choose to emphasis the propaganda element of Du Bois's work as a critique, I think Du Bois's emphasis on the artist as activist gives us a deeper understanding of the man—for he was no mere mouthpiece for someone else's ideology, here was a man who committed himself to creating the world his words envisioned. Du Bois was then a man of praxis and not simply an intellectual who stood apart from the fray of social struggle commenting from the safety and security of the ivory tower.

A third aspect of Du Bois that is fascinating is Du Bois's views on sex. Listen to Du Bois in his February 1924 *Crisis* review of Jean Toomer's book *Cane*—and we should remember that when *Cane* first appeared it was barely noticed and shortly went out of print. *Cane*'s status as a classic required a long gestation period, and yet, Du Bois early on understood the gender significance of this innovative work.

The world of black folk will some day arise and point to Jean Toomer as a writer who first dared to emancipate the colored world form the conventions of sex. It is quite impossible for most Americans to realize how straightlaced and conventional thought is within the Negro World, despite the very unconventional acts of the group. Yet this contradiction is true. And Jean Toomer is

---

[2] Du Bois, *Writings*, 1000.

the first of our writers to hurl his pen across the very face of our sex conventionality.[3]

But wasn't Du Bois "straightlaced and conventional" in his views on sex? There has been a misreading of Du Bois. His views on sex when examined closely suggest a serious reevaluation of Du Bois and offer us clues to reinterpret and better understand some of Du Bois's reactions and positions, specifically with respect to the publication of *Fire* by the young writers of the Harlem Renaissance and Du Bois's often ad hominem quarrels with Marcus Garvey.

Writing in his 1968 autobiography, Du Bois candidly notes:

> In the midst of my career there burst on me a new and undreamed of aspect of sex. A young man, long my disciple and student, then my co-helper and successor to part of my work, was suddenly arrested for molesting men in public places. I had before that time no conception of homosexuality. I had never understood the tragedy of an Oscar Wilde. I dismissed my co-worker forthwith, and spent heavy days regretting my act.[4]

Evaluating his own sexuality, Du Bois writes:

> Indeed the chief blame which I lay on my New England schooling was the inexcusable ignorance of sex which I had when I went south to Fisk at 17. I was precipitated into a region, with loose sex morals among black and white, while I actually did not know the physical difference between men and women. At first my fellows jeered in disbelief and then became sorry and made many offers to guide my abysmal ignorance. This built for me inexcusable and startling temptations. It began to turn one of the most beautiful of earth's experiences into a thing of temptation and horror. I fought and feared amid what should have been a climax of true living. I avoided women about whom anybody gossiped and as I tried to solve the contradiction of virginity and

---

[3] Du Bois, *Writings*, 1209.
[4] Du Bois, *Writings*, 1122.

motherhood, I was inevitably faced with the other contradiction of prostitution and adultery. In my hometown sex was deliberately excluded from talk and if possible from thought. In public school there were no sexual indulgences of which I ever heard. We talked of girls, looked at their legs, and there was rare kissing of a most unsatisfactory sort. We teased about sweethearts, but quite innocently. When I went South, my fellow students being much older and reared in a region of loose sexual customs regarded me as liar or freak when I asserted my innocence. I liked girls and sought their company, but my wildest exploits were kissing them.

Then, as teacher in the rural districts of East Tennessee, I was literally raped by the unhappy wife who was my landlady. From that time through my college course at Harvard and my study in Europe, I went through a desperately recurring fight to keep the sex instinct in control. A brief trial with prostitution in Paris affronted my sense of decency. I lived more or less regularly with a shop girl in Berlin, but was ashamed. Then when I returned home to teach, I was faced with the connivance of certain fellow teachers at adultery with their wives. I was literally frightened into marriage before I was able to support a family. I married a girl whose rare beauty and excellent household training from her dead mother attracted and held me.[5]

Here I find the clue to Du Bois's disgust with Wallace Thurman and with the journal *Fire.* Du Bois was no prude about heterosexuality, but instead was, in his early years, intolerant of homosexuality. Furthermore, Du Bois's arguments with Garvey were probably colored by the fact that Du Bois had engaged in an interracial romance and thus was surely at odds with the Garvey racial essentialist position, much in the same way forty-odd years later, a number of critics were at odds with the Black Arts Movement, their opposition fueled in part by their advocacy and practice of interracial relationships clashing inevitably with the strident rejection of White women that was a sine qua non in the Black Arts Movement.

---

[5] Du Bois, *Writings,* 1119-1120.

None of the above noted attributes of Du Bois the man are quite as radical, however, as Du Bois's stand on religion.

My religious development has been slow and uncertain. I grew up in a liberal Congregational Sunday School and listened once a week to a sermon on doing good as a reasonable duty. Theology played a minor part and our teachers had to face some searching questions. At 17 I was in a missionary college where religious orthodoxy was stressed; but I was more developed to meet it with argument, which I did. My "morals" were sound, even a bit puritanic, but when a hidebound old deacon inveighed against dancing I rebelled. By the time of graduation I was still a "believer" in orthodox religion, but had strong questions which were encouraged at Harvard. In Germany I became a freethinker and when I came to teach at an orthodox Methodist Negro school I was soon regarded with suspicion, especially when I refused to lead the students in public prayer. When I became head of a department at Atlanta, the engagement was held up because again I balked at leading in prayer, but the liberal president let me substitute the Episcopal prayer book on most occasions. Later I improvised prayers on my own. Finally I faced a crisis: I was using Crapsey's *Religion and Politics* as a Sunday School text. When Crapsey was hauled up for heresy, I refused further to teach Sunday School. When Archdeacon Henry Phillips, my last rector, died, I flatly refused again to join any church or sign any church screed. From my 30th year on I have increasingly regarded the church as an institution which defended such evils as slavery, color caste, exploitation of labor and war. I think the greatest gift of the Soviet Union to modern civilization was the dethronement of the clergy and the refusal to let religion be taught in the public schools.

Religion helped and hindered my artistic sense. I know the old English and German hymns by heart. I loved their music but ignored their silly words with studied inattention.[6]

---

[6] Du Bois, *Writings*, 1124-1125.

This short passage contains so many iconoclastic concepts that one is forced to completely reassess Du Bois's character. Clearly his scholarly stint in Germany (1892-1893) was critical to the development of Du Bois as an intellectual "free thinker." The Germany connection helps clarify what seems to be a major contradiction. In the *Souls of Black Folk*, Du Bois starts each chapter with a quotation of music. The book also contains the magnificent essay, "The Sorrow Songs." *Souls* would seem to indicate that Du Bois was an ardent Christian, but perhaps it was not Christianity that Du Bois was extolling but rather cultural theories exemplified by the German philosopher Herder who asserted that national cultures are based on folk culture. Du Bois was celebrating the cultural mores of the folk rather than focusing on the religious specifics of Christianity.

In any case, Du Bois the man was not a Christian moralist and haughty social snob. Du Bois was a complex and challenging black man who advocated and struggled for radical change on behalf of his people. Du Bois was far more than generally meets the eye when we think of this great intellectual and activist.

INDEX